Splinters in Your Eye

Also by Martin Jay

*The Dialectical Imagination: A History of the Frankfurt School
and the Institute of Social Research, 1923–1950 (1973 and 1996)*

*Marxism and Totality: The Adventures of a
Concept from Lukács to Habermas (1984)*

Adorno (1984)

*Permanent Exiles: Essays on the Intellectual
Migration from Germany to America (1985)*

Fin-de-Siècle Socialism and Other Essays (1988)

Force Fields: Between Intellectual History and Cultural Critique (1993)

*Downcast Eyes: The Denigration of Vision in
Twentieth-Century French Thought (1993)*

Cultural Semantics: Keywords of Our Time (1998)

Refractions of Violence (2003)

*La crisis de la experiencia en la era postsubjetiva,
ed. Eduardo Sabrovsky (2003)*

*Songs of Experience: Modern European and American
Variations on a Universal Theme (2004)*

The Virtues of Mendacity: On Lying in Politics (2010)

Essays from the Edge: Parerga and Paralipomena (2011)

Kracauer l'exilé (2014)

Reason after Its Eclipse: On Late Critical Theory (2016)

Splinters in Your Eye

Frankfurt School Provocations

Martin Jay

VERSO

London • New York

First published by Verso 2020
© Martin Jay 2020

All rights reserved

The moral rights of the author have been asserted

1 3 5 7 9 10 8 6 4 2

Verso
UK: 6 Meard Street, London W1F 0EG
US: 20 Jay Street, Suite 1010, Brooklyn, NY 11201
versobooks.com

Verso is the imprint of New Left Books

ISBN-13: 978-1-78873-601-5
ISBN-13: 978-1-78873-604-6 (LIBRARY)
ISBN-13: 978-1-78873-603-9 (US EBK)
ISBN-13: 978-1-78873-602-2 (UK EBK)

British Library Cataloguing in Publication Data
A catalogue record for this book is available from the British Library

Library of Congress Cataloging-in-Publication Data
A catalog record for this book is available from the Library of Congress
Library of Congres Control Number: 2020936045

Typeset in Minion Pro by Hewer Text UK Ltd, Edinburgh
Printed and bound by CPI Group (UK) Ltd, Croydon, CR0 4YY

For Sidney

Contents

Acknowledgments ix

Introduction xi

1 Ungrounded: Horkheimer and the Founding
   of the Frankfurt School 1
2 "The Hope That Earthly Horror Does Not Possess the Last
   Word": Max Horkheimer and *The Dialectical Imagination* 19
3 Max Horkheimer and *The Family of Man* 33
4 "In Psychoanalysis Nothing Is True but the
   Exaggerations": Freud and the Frankfurt School 48
5 Leo Löwenthal and the Jewish Renaissance 66
6 Adorno and Blumenberg: Nonconceptuality
   and the *Bilderverbot* 80
7 Chromophilia: *Der Blaue Reiter*, Walter Benjamin
   and the Emancipation of Color 98
8 Timbremelancholy: Walter Benjamin
   and the Fate of Philately 113
9 The Little Shopgirls Enter the Public Sphere:
   Miriam Hansen on Kracauer 124
10 Irony and Dialectics: *One-Dimensional Man* and 1968 135
11 Dialectic of Counter-Enlightenment: The Frankfurt
    School as Scapegoat of the Lunatic Fringe 151

Notes 173
Index 227

ACKNOWLEDGMENTS

When you've been grappling with the intellectual challenges and historical development of the Frankfurt School for over half a century—the
dissertation that became *The Dialectical Imagination* was begun in
1967—you incur a virtual lifetime of debts to the people and institutions that kept you going. Luckily, I have had the opportunity in previous books to acknowledge my gratitude to the legions of friends, family
members, supporters, critics and fellow devotees of Critical Theory
who made those works possible. Let me now focus only on those whose
generosity and stimulation provoked the essays collected here to come
into being.

First, I would like to thank those whose invitations to conferences,
talks or essay collections induced me to focus on the specific issues in
individual essays or who helped publish the first iterations of the results:
Sidonia Blättler, Jonathan Boyarin, Judit Bokser, Briankle Chang,
Moritz Epple, Johannes Fried, Richard Gipps, Shai Ginzburg, Peter
Gordon, Raphael Gross, Janis Gudian, Espen Hammer, Gerd Hurm,
Andreas Huyssen, Mathias Jehn, Max Pensky, Anke Reitz, Jeffrey
Rubinoff, Bernd Schwibs, Jay Winter and Shamoon Zamir. As I have so
often had a chance in the past, I would like to express my special thanks
to Robert Boyers, the indefatigable editor of *Salmagundi*, where two of
the entries first appeared as my biannual Force Fields column.

In ways both direct and indirect, I have also benefited enormously
from my ongoing contact with members of the burgeoning international community of scholars engaged with the legacy of Critical Theory.
Despite the inevitability of my failing to include many who deserve

mention, let me single out John Abromeit, Andrew Arato, Richard Bernstein, Paul Breines, Susan Buck-Morss, Seyla Benhabib, Detlev Claussen, Jean Cohen, Deborah Cook, Maeve Cooke, the late Helmut Dubiel, Andrew Feenberg, Fabian Freyenhagen, Lydia Goehr, Espen Hammer, Peter Uwe Hohendahl, Axel Honneth, Robert Hullot-Kentor, Peter-Erwin Jansen, Anton Kaes, Robert Kaufman, Douglas Kellner, Stefan Müller-Doohm, Henry Pickford, the late Moishe Postone, Anson Rabinbach, Gerhard Richter, Michael Rosen, Alfons Söllner, the late Albrecht Wellmer, Joel Whitebook, Rolf Wiggershaus, Richard Wolin, Robert Zwarg and Lambert Zuidervaart. Their fingerprints are all over the essays that follow. Let me also thank my more proximate colleagues at Berkeley, especially in the History Department and the Program in Critical Theory, who have sustained me both while I was actively teaching and now as I fade into retirement: Wendy Brown, Judith Butler, John Efron, Carla Hesse, David Hollinger, Thomas Laqueur, Anthony Long, Jonathan Sheehan, Hans Sluga and the late Paul Thomas.

I also very much appreciate the generosity of the Berkeley History Department's Sidney Hellman Ehrman Chair, which provided me the resources to support my research, and the American Academy in Berlin, where the earliest of these essays was composed. Sebastian Budgen and Cian McCourt of Verso have provided excellent editorial and contractual guidance, and the final results have benefited from the copyediting of Jennifer Harris and the indexing skills of Lois Rosson. Finally, let me try to acknowledge what always exceeds my ability to express: the gratitude I feel for the love and sustenance of my family, my daughters Shana and Rebecca, their husbands Ned and Grayson, my sister, Beth, and my grandchildren, Frances, Sammy, Ryeland and the most recent arrival, Sidney. But as always, it is to my wisest reader, most constructive critic and loving wife, Catherine Gallagher, that my debt is boundless.

INTRODUCTION

"The splinter in your eye," wrote Theodor W. Adorno, "is the best magnifying glass."[1] This provocative assertion is made in section 29, called "Dwarf Fruit," of *Minima Moralia*. It appears alongside other, now canonical aphorisms, most notably: "in psychoanalysis nothing is true except the exaggerations" and "the whole is the false." Although not immediately obvious, Adorno's vivid if implausible image plays on the celebrated admonition against judging, lest you be judged, from the Gospel of St. Matthew (7:3–4): "And why beholdest thou the mote that is in thy brother's eye, but considerest not the beam that is in thine own eye? Or how wilt thou say to thy brother, Let me cast out the mote out of thine eye; and lo, the beam is in thine own eye?" For what is normally translated from the original Aramaic as "mote" in English is rendered as "*Splitter*"[2] in German, the common German word for "splinter," which is the way E. F. N. Jephcott then retranslated it into English. Although perhaps imprecise, the word choice was fortunate. For whereas "mote" suggests a speck of dust that can seem trivial in comparison to the "beam" (or sometimes "plank") in the eye of the hypocritical judge, a "splinter" is far more irritating, producing a pain that cannot be ignored. Adorno, moreover, turned the metaphor in an unexpected direction. Not only did he adopt the perspective of the other—the brother whose eye has the "splinter" rather than his judgmental sibling with the "beam" in his—but, more importantly, he made the irritation itself into an inadvertent virtue by claiming that only through discomfort might we more clearly glimpse the truth. Indeed, only by registering the experience of suffering—one's own and, through empathy, that of others—is valid knowledge of society possible.[3] Magnification induced by pain produces the exaggerations that grant Freudian theory—and not it alone—its insights.[4]

There is, however, one important limitation that follows when one magnifies details or fragments, painful or otherwise: it inhibits our ability to view the whole with a panoptic gaze. Indeed, one of the consequences of what Adorno called our "damaged lives," where "wrong life cannot be lived rightly,"[5] is that there is no privileged vantage point from which to observe the totality and even less warrant to call what we can see "true" in a normative, emphatic sense. Nor is there a coherent meta-narrative that can read "world history" as if it were a meaningful story, whether of progress or decline.[6] All we have left are shards of a splintered totality and a kaleidoscope of disjointed temporalities. If there is a coherent "whole," it can be grasped only inferentially from its effects, in particular through the pervasive force of capitalist relations in our lives. But rather than being a whole replete with positive meaning, it is an oppressive totality that thwarts our potential to enjoy lives that might be "lived rightly" and provide a vision of a different whole that could be justly called the "true."[7] That laudable alternative can only be posited, if at all, as an absent desideratum in tension with what is the case. For, as Adorno was to put it in a discussion of Schoenberg's atonal music, "the whole, as a positive entity, cannot be antithetically extracted from an estranged and splintered reality by means of the will and power of the individual, if it is not to degenerate into deception and ideology; it must assume the form of negation."[8]

But however totalizing and pervasive capital's oppressive power might have been for Adorno and his Frankfurt School colleagues, the gap between concept and object emblemized by the epistemological value of exaggeration means that it is never so dominant as to render critique itself impossible. After all, an exaggeration that knows itself as such necessarily registers an incongruence between idea and object or word and thing, and this implies that efforts to master the contingent messiness of the world through conceptual domination—and by extension, social, economic or political domination as well—will inevitably come up short. Because there is always a remainder that stubbornly resists inclusion, always a block to total control, there is also a chance for critical theoretical distance, and some opportunity, however slim, to undermine actual oppression. The concept of a fully "one-dimensional society" producing only "one-dimensional men," famously elaborated by Herbert Marcuse, was thus itself an exaggeration allowing some room for resistance, some space for negation, to manifest itself. But what form such a critique should take—macro- or micrological in scale, immanent or transcendent in vantage point, hypotactically or paratactically presented, written esoterically or for a general public—has never been a question easily answered. Nor, of course, were the practical political implications clear that were supposed to be drawn from that critique, which ranged from the maximalist resistance of Marcuse's "great refusal" to what Jürgen Habermas called Horkheimer and Adorno's more cautious "strategy of hibernation."[9]

Because these questions remain open, it would be problematic to formulate a fully coherent and normative, let alone "orthodox" version of Critical Theory comparable to the "orthodox Marxism" Georg Lukács defined in methodological terms in *History and Class Consciousness*.[10] In fact, the very concept of orthodoxy is anathema to an approach that knows the dangers of "straightening" opinions—the Greek etymology of the word "orthodox"—into a uniform doctrine requiring uncritical fidelity. What goes under the name "Critical Theory" has always been an open-ended, internally contested field of overlapping but never fully congruent assumptions, methods and arguments. If it hangs together, it is more in terms of Wittgenstein's family resemblances than in those of a rigid system with logical consistency, impermeable boundaries and fully shared conclusions. Even in terms of styles of presentation, its adherents have embraced a wide range of strategies, ranging from impressionistic thought-images (*Denkbilder*) and condensed aphorisms to social scientific research reports and extensive philosophical treatises. Symptomatically, when Leo Löwenthal, the last surviving member of the first generation of the Frankfurt School, was pressed to define it by his biographical interviewer Helmut Dubiel, he playfully kicked the can down the road: "It is a perspective. For that reason I'm always a bit baffled when someone requests that I offer a seminar on Critical Theory—I never know how to deal with that." He then added, with his usual puckish humor, "I usually call my friend Martin Jay and ask him to define the main characteristics of the so-called Critical Theory. Now I'll ask you—after all, you wrote a book about it." To which Dubiel replied: "It's really impossible to come up with a few general characteristics and say: this is Critical Theory."[11]

Not only, *pace* Löwenthal, have I long shared Dubiel's reluctance to essentialize the tradition into easily digestible sound bites, but I am also aware that however much a historian may seek to fashion a comprehensive and unified account, narrative coherence has been no less elusive.

Even with the wisdom of hindsight, it has not been easy to craft a fully intelligible, neatly packaged history of what came to be called Critical Theory. An inadvertent brand name (like "the Frankfurt School"), it has seemed to some as little more than a euphemism for Marxism, coined only to cover its exponents' radical tracks.[12] But whatever its origins and intended function, it came to designate an ongoing, still developing series of efforts by a disparate and ever-growing cast of unruly theoreticians spanning several generations and situated in more than one location. During the earliest days of Max Horkheimer's directorship of the Institute of Social Research in Frankfurt—a position he assumed in 1930 and maintained for a quarter century, through his American exile and return to Germany—efforts were made to follow an organized, interdisciplinary research program. But the inclinations of different members and the vicissitudes of history soon drove them apart.[13] If "marginalization," "exile," "outsider" and "extra-territoriality" were the descriptive terms often adopted as honorifics by the participants themselves to define their condition, and the virtues of "non-identity" one of their highest values, it would do a certain violence to their diversity to yoke them together as obedient students in a distinct "school" with a shared curriculum. And no less problematic is the imperative, so often urged on intellectual historians, to situate them firmly in the contexts of their genesis and receptions, entirely immanent in the milieux that formed them. For in addition to deciding which of these might have been determinant and which not—an issue raised, for example, in considering the oft-mooted question of their debt to their predominantly Jewish backgrounds and experiences—their own cogent theorizing about the reductive dangers of a sociology of knowledge approach makes it difficult to subject them to its mandate.[14]

As a result, attempts to fashion a synthetic narrative—and I count my own earlier efforts among them[15]—have always had to contend with even such basic challenges as whom to include among the protagonists of the story and how to weigh their respective importance. Just to list a few of the questions that have arisen: Should Erich Fromm's role before his bitter estrangement from his colleagues in the late 1930s be emphasized or minimized?[16] Was Walter Benjamin ever really a core member or, as Adorno once said, a *l'écart de tous les courants*?[17] Can Siegfried Kracauer be considered a heterodox Critical Theorist or merely an ambivalent fellow traveler?[18] Were Franz Neumann and Otto Kirchheimer outsiders beyond the inner circle or did they constitute a subordinate current within the tradition?[19] Should the conflicting economic analyses of Institute members, most notably Henryk Grossmann and Friedrich Pollock, be given their due?[20] If it is true that "without the United States," as Detlev Claussen argues, "there would be no Critical Theory,"[21] how should we treat the roles of Benjamin and Habermas, who never migrated? Moreover, were all who were exiled in America as isolated and alienated from its cultural life as is sometimes claimed?[22] Did Marcuse's activism in the 1960s set him apart from the publicly cautious Horkheimer and Adorno, whose unwillingness to jeopardize the liberal political achievements of post-Nazi Germany was seen as a betrayal by their more radical students? Were the contributions by second-generation figures like Habermas and Albrecht Wellmer, third-generation ones like Axel Honneth or fourth-generation individuals like Rainer Forst creative revisions of the first generation's work or tacit betrayals of its abiding, if somewhat attenuated Marxist sympathies?

No less problematic in fashioning a coherent historical account are the issues of scale and focus, for, as Kracauer was fond of pointing out, there is no easy passage for the historian from micro- to macrohistory, no smooth path from densely detailed accounts of individual lives, episodes, events or texts to larger generalizations that hover above the fray.[23] Telling anecdotes, no matter how meaningful, are not always simple illustrations of larger patterns. The lives of individual figures do not always follow parallel trajectories or cohere into shared generational experiences. Nor is one level of analysis inherently closer to the truth of the past, as each captures an aspect of the heterogeneous historical universe that defies fully synthetic coherence, even with the benefit of hindsight. If we return to our guiding metaphor and consider the paradoxical effect of magnification as an obstacle to a panoptic gaze, it becomes clear why the Devil as well as God is often taken to be "in the details."[24]

Kracauer's argument was intended to apply to all historical narrations, especially ones that seek to build a cohesive general account by accumulating more proximate microhistorical stories and synthesizing the results into a single master narrative. But it is perhaps especially cogent for attempts to write the history of the particular cluster of thinkers who have come to be collectively identified with the Frankfurt School. Smoothing over their differences, homogenizing their ideas, commensurating their styles of argumentation and presentation all clearly have their costs. Although there may be a discernible common denominator underlying their work—and perhaps one even more substantial than that vague critical "perspective" of which Löwenthal spoke—it is important to remember that the numerators of their individual trajectories were never the same.

Thus, we might say, to give Adorno's words a slight twist, that their history was itself always already a "splintered reality." To amplify the power of those splinters might well require acknowledging their awkward tension with other shards of a whole that was perhaps never unbroken in the first place. Rather than pieces of a coherent puzzle, they may always defy smooth integration into a single pattern, giving new meaning to Adorno's well-known phrase, "torn halves of an integral freedom, to which, however, they do not add up."[25] Benjamin's predilection for "dialectical images" and the metaphor of a "constellation" he shared with Adorno acknowledge the value of jarring juxtapositions rather than the sublation of negations into positive mediations. For all of the Frankfurt School's respect for the legacy of Hegelian dialectics, it resisted the urge to follow his triumphalist logic of historical development, which could, even in its Marxist guise, produce what Adorno called, with reference to the late Lukács, "extorted reconciliations."[26]

Fidelity to this metaphor of splintered reality also requires taking into account the inevitably partial and changing vantage point of the historian in whose eyes the splinters may lodge, eyes that cannot avoid experiencing the discomforts they provoke, even as he or she hopes for the magnifications they may provide. For there can be no dispassionate distance, no serene objectivity granted to the commentator who is drawn to the exigent questions posed by Critical Theory, questions whose answers still elude us today. In fact, one of the beneficial results of immersion in the history of the Frankfurt School is a heightened self-reflexivity about the evolving constellation of interactions between past and present, which prevent judgments from ever becoming final and assessments definitive.

In accordance with this lesson, the exercises that follow are left in their unintegrated form, with no pretense to be a coherent narrative written by a disinterested observer hitching a high-flying ride on Hegel's owl of Minerva. The scale of their approach varies—some are more focused, others wide-ranging—and they often include ruminations of a more personal nature than is typical of academic prose, including on the author's own earlier attempts to present the Frankfurt School's legacy. Although confining themselves to figures drawn from the School's first generation, they are informed by lessons learned from subsequent ones, which have been elaborated elsewhere in more total-izing narratives.[27] And they conclude with considerations of a troubling and, alas, increasingly potent misappropriation of the legacy of Critical Theory, which has gained recent popular credence and a political signif-icance that would be laughable were its consequences not so tragic. Here eyesight has truly been blinded by beams rather that magnified by splinters, and the pain is, unfortunately, not in the service of greater insight.

1

Ungrounded: Horkheimer and the Founding of the Frankfurt School

A perennial issue in the reception of Critical Theory is the difficulty of locating secure ground for critique once the traditional Marxist reliance on either the partisan standpoint of the proletariat or the scientific nature of Marxist theory is questioned.[1] Can we establish a firm foundation—either transcendentally or immanently, in a particular history—for the normative impulse, the conviction that the current order can and should be replaced by a more just and humane alternative that distinguishes a critical from a traditional theory, as Horkheimer contended in his seminal essay of 1937? Taking seriously the parallel question of the historical founding of the Institute for Social Research, out of which the Frankfurt School developed, this chapter argues that, in both cases, there is sufficient uncertainty to warrant rethinking the apparent necessity of explicit origins, firm grounds and identifiable points d'appui in assessing the ability of an intellectual tradition to claim critical purchase for its work. Even conventional attempts to situate Critical Theory firmly in the tradition of Hegelian Marxism may falter if we take seriously the less appreciated role played by anti-Hegelian figures such as Schelling in stimulating doubts about his legacy.[2] The temporal underpinning of normativity, it turns out, may well be more an imagined future than a remembered past.

In the 1962 preface to the republication of *The Theory of the Novel*, Georg Lukács introduced an epithet that has served ever since to belittle the Frankfurt School's alleged pessimism, distance from political practice and privileged personal lives:

A considerable part of the leading German intelligentsia, including Adorno, has taken up residence in the "Grand Hotel Abyss" which I described in connection with my critique of Schopenhauer as "a beautiful hotel, equipped with every comfort, on the edge of an abyss, of nothingness, of absurdity. And the daily contemplation of the abyss between excellent meals or artistic entertainments, can only heighten the enjoyment of the subtle comforts offered."[3]

As he admitted, Lukács had used the term before, but, as it turns out, not only in reference to Schopenhauer in his 1954 *Destruction of Reason*. It had, in fact, been coined even earlier, in a piece he wrote in 1933, but never published in his lifetime, to mock soi-disant progressive intellectuals like Upton Sinclair or Thomas Mann, who refused to abandon their bourgeois lifestyles and affiliate themselves with the Communist Party.[4] This more diffuse usage did not, however, resonate publicly, and it was not really until the identification with Adorno and his colleagues that it gained any real traction. Although normally employed by leftist detractors of the Frankfurt School, the term gained enough familiarity that a sympathetic "photobiography" of the School, edited in 1990 by Willem van Reijin and Gunzelin Schmid Noerr, could be titled, without apparent irony, *Grand Hotel Abgrund*.[5]

I want to pause for a moment with this term because it raises an important question that goes beyond the easy condemnation of unaffiliated radical intellectuals for their alleged betrayal of the link between theory and practice. The German word *Abgrund* has a connotation that is absent in the English equivalent "abyss," for it suggests the loss of the foundation or ground (*Grund*) on which one might securely support critique. For a Communist militant like Lukács, the only way for an intellectual to avoid hurtling into the abyss was to stand firmly on the ground of the vanguard party of the workers' movement, subordinating himself to the dictates of its enlightened leadership. No matter how brilliant the analysis of an anticapitalist critic might be or how intense his moral indignation, it was only by joining with the forces that would change society that he could avoid impotence and be on the right side of history. The metaphor of a firm ground or foundation was also evident in the frequent use of the word "*Standpunkt*" by other Marxists of Lukács's generation like Karl Korsch, who insisted on the proletarian standpoint of historical materialism.[6] Although located in a world still riven with class divisions, it was potentially that of the universal class that would end those very divisions, and as such transcended relativism. Whether it be the consciousness of the proletariat, either actual or ascribed, an objective historical process leading to the terminal crisis of capitalism or a subtle combination of both, there was assumed to be ground on which the critical intellectual could stand, a concrete location like the French military point d'appui where forces could gather before an assault, a foundation to support a solid critique of the status quo.

In labeling the Frankfurt School "the Grand Hotel Abyss," Lukács was thus not only denigrating the supposedly comfortable existence of its members, but also their refusal to credit the necessary role of the party and class as the concrete historical ground of radical ideas. Whether or not he was right about the former—their "damaged lives" in exile, to cite the celebrated subtitle of *Minima Moralia*, suggests otherwise—his second reproach was on target. From its inception, the intellectuals who gathered around the Institut für Sozialforschung knew that critique could not be directly grounded in the praxis or consciousness of the class that Marx had assigned the historical role of incipient universal class, let alone the vanguard party that claimed to be the repository of its imputed or ascribed class consciousness.[7] They understood the limits of the claim, classically expressed in Vico's *verum factum* principle, that those who made the world were able to know what they had made better than those who were merely contemplating it.[8]

Was it possible to ground it instead in an objective "scientific" grasp of the totality of social relations to allow an unaffiliated nonpartisan theoretician to decipher not only the surface phenomena of contemporary society but also the deeper, more essential trends that foreshadowed a potential future? Could intellectuals who "floated freely," to borrow the metaphor that Karl Mannheim would make famous at the end of the decade when the Institute set up shop, have a totalizing perspective on the world below? Or is it a dangerous myth to assume anyone might have a disinterested view above the fray, especially when the very distinction between facts and values was itself being questioned? Max Horkheimer had little use, however, for Mannheim's solution, which assumed intellectuals from different classes could somehow harmonize their positions and turn them into complementary perspectives on the whole.[9] Neither rooted nor free-floating, critique was located somewhere else on a map that included utopias still to be realized.[10]

One possible alternative drew on the unconstrained will, in which the act of founding was *ex nihilo*, a gesture of assertion that drew whatever legitimacy it might have entirely from itself rather than any preceding authority, whether based in tradition, rationality or the practical activity of a privileged social group. Here the ground was temporal more than spatial, an origin more than a place.[11] It was established through what came to be called decisionist fiat, most famously defended by the Weimar and then Nazi jurist Carl Schmitt, who argued that the decision to found a legal order could not itself be rooted in a prior legality. But this alternative was frankly irrationalist. Drawing as it did on an analogy from the purely voluntarist version of God that had been promulgated in the Middle Ages by nominalists like William of Ockham, who denied the limitations on divine will placed by any notion of rational intelligibility or ideal form, it relied solely on a spontaneous act of a sovereign subject. As such, it implied a unified metasubject, prior to individual subjects, with the power to do the founding—a subject whose unconstrained will might also lead to material world domination. Consequently, Critical Theory was never tempted by it.[12]

For a while, the alternative favored by Horkheimer and his colleagues was what became known as "immanent critique"—that is, eschewing any universal or transcendent vantage point above the fray and seeking an alternative in the specific normative claims of a culture that failed to live up to them in practice. Or, in more explicitly Hegelian terms, it meant finding some critical purchase in the gap between a general concept and the specific objects subsumed under it. As a recent champion of this approach, Robert Hullot-Kentor, put it, "Immanent criticism turns the principle of identity, which otherwise serves the subordination of object to subject, into the power for the presentation of the way in which an object resists its subjective determination and finds itself lacking." To criticize without an Archimedean point beyond or outside of the target of criticism, he continues, "is the development of the idea as the object's self-dissatisfaction that at every point moves toward what is not idea; it potentiates from within the requirement of an objective transformation."[13]

But what if immanent critique acknowledges the possibility that objects are *always* in excess of the concepts that define them or, in other words, that the Hegelian presupposition of an immanent dialectical totality fails to acknowledge the nonsublatable quality of radical otherness? Interestingly, in his analysis of phenomenology in *The Metacritique of Epistemology*, Adorno himself came precisely to this conclusion. Although claiming that "dialectic's very procedure is immanent critique," he conceded:

The concept of immanence sets the limits on immanent critique. If an assertion is measured by its presuppositions, then the procedure is immanent, i.e. it obeys formal-logical rules and thought becomes a criterion of itself. But it is not decided as a necessity of thought in the analysis of the concept of being that not all being is consciousness. The inclusiveness of such an analysis is thus halted. To think non-thinking [*Nichtdenken*] is not a seamless consequence of thought. It simply suspends claims to totality on the part of thought. Immanence, however, in the sense of that equivocation of consciousness and thought, is nothing other than such totality. Dialectic negates both together.[14]

What this convoluted passage suggests is that the folding of all objects into a field of conceptual immanence is an idealist fantasy in which the nonidentical is absorbed into the identical with no remainder. Thus, immanent critique cannot be in itself fully grounded, as the totality is itself never fully self-contained and concepts are never fully able to subsume all objects under them.

In addition to the problems in the dialectical concept of total immanence, what if "the self-dissatisfaction of the object," its striving to be adequate to its concept, fails to manifest itself in a society that Herbert Marcuse could call "one-dimensional" and Adorno "totally administered"? What if the possibility of "objective transformation" is thwarted by the ideological seamlessness of a social order that actually functionalizes apparent dissatisfaction in the service of system maintenance? What if the totality that prevails is not one whose contradictions and antinomies threaten to undermine it, but rather one in which they serve to keep it going through a kind of autoimmune equilibrium? In *Minima Moralia*, Adorno acknowledged precisely this danger with reference to the decline of irony:

Irony's medium, the difference between ideology and reality, has disappeared. The former resigns itself to confirmation of reality by its mere duplication . . . There is not a crevasse in the cliff of the established order into which the ironist might hook a fingernail . . . Pitted against the deadly seriousness of total society, which has absorbed the opposing voice, the impotent objection earlier quashed by irony, there is now only the deadly seriousness of the comprehended truth.[15]

With all possible grounds for critique thus, in one way or another, insufficient, was it then perhaps simply a vain quest to seek a legitimating point d'appui? If there was no social subject position or historical agent whose praxis could be the source of critique, no purely philosophical first principles or a priori, transcendental grounds from which to launch such an analysis, and no immanent totality in which objects might become adequate to their concepts, might looking for such ground be itself part of the problem, rather than the solution?[16] In the subsequent history of the Frankfurt School, this antifoundationalist conclusion became increasingly hard to avoid, as the material basis for critique grew ever more remote and both the appeal of a philosophy of transcendent principles and the confidence in immanent critique diminished. Even the call for an "objective" or "emphatic" notion of reason, which Horkheimer still desperately undertook as late as *Eclipse of Reason* in 1947, lost its capacity to inspire much confidence, as rationality itself seemed to suffer a self-liquidation embedded from its very beginnings in the need for self-preservation against a hostile nature.[17]

And yet Critical Theory did not, as we know, give up the mission of critically analyzing the status quo in the hope of enabling a radically different and better future. Might not some explanation of its stubborn refusal to abandon that task be found not in abstract principles, or at least not in them alone, but also in the history of its own institutional foundation in the Weimar era? The remainder of this chapter explores the school's historical origins so as to interrogate its assumption of a critical vantage point on the world it inhabited. How can we characterize the literal foundation of the Frankfurt School and what kind of authority, if any, did it provide for the work that followed? Might its willingness to draw intellectual sustenance from a heteroclite variety of sources—including, as I will suggest, even the anti-Hegelian philosophy of Schelling—be illuminated by acknowledging those origins?

The details of the origins of the Institute of Social Research have, of course, been known for some time.[18] What must be emphasized is the ragged, inadvertent, adventitious quality of its beginnings. Nothing expresses this dimension of the story as explicitly as the source of its financial support, which came from the fortune of German-Jewish grain merchant Hermann Weil, who had cornered the Argentine trade in wheat in the late nineteenth century and came to play a critical role in the economic policies of Germany during World War I, when he advised the kaiser and the general staff. He shared the ambitious war aims that fueled German aggression in 1914, but, by the end of the war, had come to argue for a negotiated peace with England to avoid economic disaster. After the armistice, he turned away from politics to philanthropy, joining the many other generous bourgeois donors who had helped create a "*Stiftungsuniversität*" in Frankfurt before the war.[19] Weil's political sympathies, however, were certainly not on the left, so it is hard to gainsay Bertolt Brecht's sardonic remark about the Institute's founding in his unfinished satire of contemporary intellectuals, *The Tui Novel*: "A rich old man, the grain speculator Weil dies, disturbed by the miseries on earth. In his will he leaves a large sum for the establishment of an institute to investigate the sources of that misery, which is, of course, he himself."[20]

Brecht was, to be sure, off the mark in his precise history, but he did put his finger on the irony involved in the generosity of an unabashed capitalist supporting a venture that was anything but a defense of the system that made him rich. In the history of Marxism, of course, this is not a new story, as demonstrated by Engels's financing Marx's revolutionary writings and research through his work for the family firm of Ermen and Engels, which owned the Victoria Mill in Manchester. But it does complicate our understanding of the point d'appui from which Critical Theory launched its critique, opening it to the accusation of militants like Brecht and Lukács that its radical credentials were tainted from the start (even though the latter's own background was anything but plebian).

Hermann Weil had first attempted to create an institute, focused on labor law, at the university in 1920, but it had been unsuccessful; with the vigorous participation of his son Felix, though, the second venture came to fruition. Felix Weil, born in 1889 and raised for the first nine years of his life in considerable comfort in Buenos Aires, had come to Frankfurt to study during the war and was caught up in the revolutionary events of 1918. Because of a prior connection with Social Democrat Hugo Sinzheimer, a leading labor lawyer who served for a short while as police president of the city's workers' council, he had a brief taste of action, but, apparently, it was the reading of the SPD's [German Social Democratic Party's] 1891 Erfurt Program on the night of November 11, 1918, that converted him to socialism.[21] He joined a socialist student group at the university, among whose members was Leo Löwenthal, later a colleague at the Institute. After a year at the university in Tübingen, working under political economist Robert Wilbrandt but prevented for political reasons from getting his degree, Felix Weil returned to Frankfurt. There, with political economist Adolph Weber, he was able to complete his dissertation, "Socialization: Essay on the Conceptual Foundations and Critique of Plans for Socialization," which was published in a series on "Practical Socialism" edited by Karl Korsch, still then a left-wing member of the KPD [Communist Party of Germany].

During the early 1920s Weil was politically close to the Spartacists, although he later acknowledged that he was always a "salon Bolshevik" who was never jailed and never considered renouncing his fortune.[22] He used his position instead to support many left-wing causes, including the Malik Verlag, the theater of Erwin Piscator and the corrosive art of Georg Grosz, who in fact painted his portrait in 1926 while Weil read the proofs of a German translation of Upton Sinclair's book on the Sacco-Vanzetti case. Among his projects was the "First Marxist Work Week," which took place near the Thuringian town of Ilmenau at Whitsun in 1923. The participants, mostly from the orbit of the newly formed German Communist Party, included Korsch, Lukács, Karl August Wittfogel, Konstantin Zetkin (son of the KPD luminary Clara Zetkin), Julian and Hede Gumperz, Béla Fogarasi, Richard Sorge, Eduard Alexander, Fukumoto Kuzuo, Friedrich Pollock and four young friends from Weil's student days in Tübingen.[23] Here, papers were given on such subjects as socialist planning and the theory of imperialism, with Lukács's recently published *History and Class Consciousness* as a major source of discussion. Although the meeting was apparently a success, a second week the following year did not ensue because of Weil's founding of the more permanent institution. According to Friedrich Pollock, who was later married to one of Weil's cousins, it was conceived in conversations with a third figure, who had not been in Ilmenau, in the castle garden in the Taunus mountain town of Kronberg in 1922.

That third figure was, of course, Max Horkheimer, who, with Pollock, had been introduced to Weil by Konstantin Zetkin in the fall of 1919 in Frankfurt. Horkheimer's important role in the early years of the Institute has not always been recognized. But as his most recent biographer, John Abromeit, has noted, "Horkheimer was instrumental in the planning of the Institute from the very beginning, a fact that is often overlooked due to his lack of involvement in the Institute's affairs under its first director, Carl Grünberg. It was not a mere formality that Horkheimer was listed as one of the nine original members of the Society for Social Research, the organization formed to found the Institute."[24]

Horkheimer brought to their deliberations a growing identification with socialism without any particular party affiliation, combined with a strong commitment to academic studies, which manifested itself in a successful philosophical apprenticeship first with Edmund Husserl in Freiburg and then Hans Cornelius in Frankfurt. Although not as wealthy as Hermann Weil, Horkheimer's father, Moritz, was a successful factory owner from Stuttgart and a liberal assimilated Jew who patriotically supported the German war effort. His mother was entirely devoted to domestic pursuits, the most avid of which, by all reports, was providing her only son with unconditional love. Trained to succeed his father at the factory, the young Horkheimer was, however, motivated more by aesthetic yearnings than commercial ones. Although growing increasingly alienated from his parents' values, he never broke with them personally, even when they disapproved of his love for the "unsuitable" woman he eventually married and objected to his academic career. Through the lifelong friendship he began at the age of sixteen in 1911 with Pollock, also the son of an assimilated Jewish industrialist, Horkheimer seems to have found a microcosmic foretaste of the egalitarian community of like-minded souls for which he clearly yearned.[25] Although a sympathetic observer of the political turmoil after the war, he merely watched the events unfolding in Munich with the group around radical bohemian photographer Germaine Krull rather than participating directly in them. Nor was he swept up in the quest for religious authenticity that would inspire future Institute colleagues like Leo Löwenthal and Erich Fromm, who were for a while part of the Frankfurt Lehrhaus directed by Franz Rosenzweig.

During the Institute's first few years, when Carl Grünberg served as director and its focus was on the history of the labor movement, Horkheimer was occupied primarily with his university studies, working with mentors like Cornelius and Gestalt psychologist Adhémar Gelb. However, he resisted becoming absorbed into the world of academic careerism, which Fritz Ringer would later call the realm of German mandarins in decline.[26] As Adorno recollected about his first encounter with Horkheimer in Gelb's seminar, he was "not affected by the professional deformity of the academic, who all-too-easily confuses the occupation with scholarly things with reality."[27] In addition to his more scholarly writings, he wrote a steady stream of aphoristic ruminations that only appeared pseudonymously in 1934 under the ambiguous title *Dämmerung*, which means both "dawn" and "twilight." Wrestling with a number of issues—the relationship between theoretical and practical reason, the materialist underpinnings of philosophy, the complex interaction of theory and empirical research, the contribution psychoanalysis might make to social theory—Horkheimer came to the conclusion that only interdisciplinary work guided by a common goal might provide answers to questions that traditional scholarship and conventional politics had failed to address. When the opportunity came to replace Grünberg as Institute director following his debilitating stroke in 1928, Horkheimer was ready to launch an ambitious program whose outlines he spelled out in the inaugural address he gave in 1931 on "The Current Condition of Social Philosophy and the Task of an Institute of Social Research."[28] Two years earlier, Weil had succeeded in convincing the minister of education to transfer Grünberg's chair in political science, originally endowed by his father, to one in social philosophy. Horkheimer, author of a newly published *Habilitationschrift* titled *The Origins of the Bourgeois Philosophy of History*, was selected to fill it and assumed the directorship in January 1931.

From this very sketchy portrait of Horkheimer, whose acceptance of the directorship might be considered more properly the origin of the Frankfurt School than of the Institute of Social Research, it is clear that the institutional founding of Critical Theory was as scattered, uneven and diffuse as its theoretical point d'appui. Financially, it was dependent on the inadvertent largess of the class whose hegemony it sought to undermine. Politically, it kept its distance from the parties or movements that might provide the historical agency to realize its hopes. Academically, it was only obliquely integrated into a university system whose advocacy of scholarly neutrality and disinterested research it could not embrace. Personally, its leadership was unsettled and uncertain, at least initially. Even its name—the bland "Institute of Social Research"—covered over its deeper agenda expressed in an earlier candidate, "Institute for Marxism," which had been rejected as too provocative.[29]

Although for some unfriendly commentators, such as Brecht, these anomalies smacked of hypocrisy and self-deception, it might be more useful to see them as enacting the very uneasiness with seeking a firm theoretical ground that also eluded Critical Theory. In fact, over time, the very need for an explicit foundation from which critique might be launched lost its exigency. Instead, the search for origins as ground from which thinking might securely begin became itself an explicit target of Critical Theory. In his consideration of phenomenology, Adorno condemned the quest for an "ur" moment from which all else followed. "The concept of the absolutely first," he wrote in his book on Husserl, "must itself come under critique."[30] Whether it be the concept of Being or the priority of the Subject, philosophies that sought a first principle—*prima philosophia* or *Ursprungsphilosophien*—were guilty of privileging one moment in a totality of relations that could only be entered in medias res. Dialectics, even negative ones, understood that nothing was ever immediate and logically prior to the mediation of the whole.

The search for foundations and origins, the Frankfurt School came to argue, is not only problematic from a purely theoretical point of view; it is also politically suspect. As Adorno made clear in *Minima Moralia*, particularly in the aphorism "Gold Assay" and later in *Jargon of Authenticity*, there was a sinister link between prioritizing the assertion of origins and the fascist cult of blood and soil.[31] The search for authenticity and genuineness contains the "notion of the supremacy of the original over the derived. This notion, however, is always linked with social legitimation. All ruling strata claim to be the oldest settlers, autochthonous."[32] Here the angry voice of the exile, expelled from any connection to his original home, can be heard, but there were earlier sources for Critical Theory's distrust of foundationalist claims, both historical and philosophical.

Although the evidence for it is largely conjectural and indirect, a hitherto underappreciated stimulus to resist first philosophies and immanentist holism may paradoxically have been the idealism of Schelling, who was particularly aware of the function of an *Ungrund* or *Abgrund* in resisting totalizing rationalism.[33] For those who identify Critical Theory as a variant of Hegelian Marxism or who know the Frankfurt School's critique of Schelling only from Marcuse's *Reason and Revolution*, such a suggestion will seem implausible. In that 1941 work, Schelling was identified, along with Auguste Comte, as the exemplar of a "positive philosophy" that sought to undermine the critical impulse in Hegel's "negative philosophy." Despite their differences, Marcuse charged, "there is a common tendency in both philosophies to counter the sway of apriorism and to restore the authority of experience,"[34] which meant a rejection of metaphysical rationalism. From Marcuse's essentially Hegelian Marxist point of view, the political implications of both kinds of "positive philosophy" were affirmative, even reactionary, as evidenced by the inspiration Schelling provided to conservative theorists like Friedrich Joseph Stahl. Understood as an episodic defender of intuition against reason, nature against history and art against politics, Schelling seems an unlikely inspiration for Horkheimer and his colleagues.

But the younger Schelling, the one who collaborated with Hegel on the posthumously discovered fragment "The Oldest System-Program of

German Idealism"[35] and resisted Fichte's excessive reliance on the constitutive subject (on which he had himself once relied), was a very different story. Although he initially embraced the challenge laid down by Karl Leonhard Reinhold and Solomon Maimon to generate a meta-critical, phenomenological foundation for systematic philosophy that would surpass the limits of Kant's cautious transcendentalism, Schelling, who gave up publishing his work after 1812, came to understand how difficult squaring that circle would be.[36] As remarked by no less a commentator than Jürgen Habermas, who had written his dissertation on Schelling,[37] the philosopher's protomaterialist defense of an otherness that escaped the idealist assimilation into a relational totality resonated in unexpected places:

> In his remarkable polemic against the bias toward the affirmative, against the purification and the harmonization of the unruly and the negative, of what refuses itself, there also stirs an impulse to resist the danger of idealist apotheosis—the same impulse for the critique of ideology that extends all the way up to the pessimistic materialism of Horkheimer and to the optimistic materialism of Bloch.[38]

Horkheimer had in fact written and lectured on German Idealism in general and Schelling in particular in the 1920s, before assuming the Institute's directorship.[39] Although distancing himself from what he saw as Schelling's goal of absolute identity located in nature or symbolized in art, he applauded the philosopher's critique of Fichte's constitutive subjectivism and solipsistic reduction of nature to a mere effect of subjective creation. Toward the later antirationalist Schelling, to be sure, he remained hostile, but he acknowledged that there was something in his search for an absolute beyond a subjective constitution that comported well with a materialist critique of idealisms of any kind.

In his middle period, exemplified by the unfinished *Ages of the World*, Schelling had addressed the issue of foundations directly.[40] Although the book is an uncompleted torso, often cryptic and hard to decipher, the gravamen of its argument is that attempts to know the absolute are always aporetic, as it ceases being absolute when it is transformed into an object of knowledge. Schelling's primary animus was against the rationalist monism of philosophers like Spinoza, although his contemporaries Fichte and Hegel were also inviting targets. Without regressing to a no less problematic dualism of the kind associated with

Descartes, Schelling struggled to articulate a way to gesture toward something unknown that could not be adequately expressed.

It is not true, Schelling opined in opposition to the subjective idealism of his day, that "a deed, an unconditioned activity or action, is the First. For the absolutely First can only be that which the absolutely Last can be as well. Only an immovable, divine—indeed, we would do better to say supradivine—indifference is absolutely First: it is the beginning that is also at the same time the end." The very notion of "ground," he contended, is hard to defend coherently. The distinction between *Urgrund* and *Ungrund* is paper thin.[41] If "ground" is more than just an empty word,

> the people must themselves acknowledge that there was something before the existing God *as such* that did not itself exist because it was only the ground of existence. Now, that which is only the ground of existence cannot have an essence and qualities that are as one with what exists; and if existence is to be regarded as free, conscious, and (in the highest sense) intelligent, then what is merely the ground of its existence cannot be conscious, free, and intelligent in the same sense.[42]

There is thus an unbridgeable gap between absolute ground and empirical existence, and subject and substance cannot, *pace* Hegel and Spinoza, be seen as one, despite a sublation of their differences. Žižek glosses the implication of all this as follows: "Prior to *Grund* there can only be an abyss (*Ungrund*); that is, far from being a mere *nihil prativum*, this 'nothing' that precedes Ground stands for the 'absolute indifference' qua the abyss of pure Freedom that is not yet the predicate-property of some Subject but rather designates a pure impersonal Willing (*Wollen)* that wills nothing."[43]

Not surprisingly, Schelling's critique of rationalist metaphysics was attractive to thinkers trying to extricate themselves from an overly ambitious philosophy in which all contingency was absorbed into a relational system, and all ineffable mystery was interpreted as ultimately intelligible. In Weimar, a salient example was Franz Rosenzweig, whose abandonment of his earlier Hegelianism was abetted by his reading of Schelling's *Ages of the World*.[44] As Paul Franks and Michael Morgan put it, "For Rosenzweig, Schelling's tremendous achievement was to disclose the twin actualities of the unique individual and the actually existing Absolute that are excluded from and yet presupposed by the system of reason, the philosophy of Idealism. These gave his thinking a new foundation in the experience of the contingent, existing individual and its relation to the preconceptual, pretheoretical Absolute, the *Urgrund*, the 'dark ground.'"[45] The latter was also an abyss (*Abgrund*) prior to the system of rational relations that made up the world described by metaphysicians. There was no way to illuminate this negative space out of which creation had emerged.

The proto-existentialism in Schelling, who anticipated Sartre in denying that essence preceded existence, is not hard to discern. Nor is it surprising that later advocates of what has broadly come to be called poststructuralism, such as Slavoj Žižek, would find in Schelling a kindred spirit.[46] His warning against the excessive reach of rationalism could be interpreted as a psychoanalytic—in Žižek's case, Lacanian—defense of the resistance of the unconscious to the claims of consciousness.[47] His critique of the reflection theory of knowledge, in which subjects and objects mirror each other, anticipated the antirepresentalism of poststructuralist epistemology.[48] And his version of an absolute that cannot be objectified or made present has been seen as proto-Derridean, foreshadowing the ways in which *différance* both attacks identitarian concepts and serves as an anti-originary parasite dependent on them.[49]

But how does Schelling help us to understand the early Frankfurt School, which in so many ways drew on the power of Hegelian dialectical negation? How could a philosopher who fashioned a theory of identity at one point in his career and affirmed positivity at another be a possible source of Critical Theory's defense of nonidentity and negation? If there is a distance from Hegelian Marxism in Horkheimer's work, it is, after all, normally understood to be a product of his abiding sympathy for Schopenhauer's legacy, not Schelling's.[50] As we have seen, Lukács had first employed the epithet "Grand Hotel Abyss" with reference to Schopenhauer rather than Schelling, although the latter was also a target of his critique in *The Destruction of Reason*. And in the case of Adorno, it is the anti-Hegelian Benjamin who is often credited with alerting him to the limits of even a materialist dialectic.

Yet it is not implausible to see some Schellingian motifs, especially when it comes to the question of ground in Critical Theory, most clearly evident in Adorno's version of it. It is worth recalling that Adorno, as Susan Buck-Morss first argued, was likely to have learned of Rosenzweig's "New Thinking" in Jewish theology in the 1920s.[51] Neither he nor Horkheimer were, to be sure, ever in the Frankfurt Lehrhaus circle, unlike Löwenthal and Fromm, but he certainly knew of Rosenzweig through Benjamin and Scholem. And, although Adorno did not follow Rosenzweig in explicitly repudiating Hegel, he might well have absorbed some of his reservations about an identitarian dialectic in which all otherness was absorbed into a rational totality.[52] After his return to Germany, Adorno would, in fact, acknowledge that "in [Schelling's] approach from the standpoint of identity philosophy many themes can be found that I reached coming from completely different premises."[53] Here he was referring in particular to Schelling's *Lectures on the Method of Academic Study*, a work that Benjamin had also appreciated.[54] Habermas would in fact remark on the continuing influence of this book at the Institute even in the 1950s: "What Schelling had developed in the summer term, 1802, in his Jena lectures to serve as a method of academic studies as an idea of the German university, namely to 'construct the whole of one's science out of oneself and to present it with inner and lively visualization,' this is what Adorno practiced in this summer term in Frankfurt."[55]

There was also a substantive debt to Schelling in Adorno's suspicion of seeking firm ground for philosophical critique. In his 1931 lecture "The Idea of Natural History," he mediated history by nature and nature by history without seeking a higher level sublimation of the two terms. Although Schelling is not explicitly mentioned, one can discern his shadow in Adorno's resistance to a purely historicist model in which "second nature" is identified solely with Lukács's idea of a reification that must be overcome by the power of a collective subjective constitution of the historical world. As one commentator put it, "Arguably *Ages [of the World]* invents this history of nature which will inform Benjamin's and Adorno's reformulation of 'natural history' as history subject to nature: 'the self-cognition of the spirit as nature in disunion with itself'."[56] Indeed, the essay may even have provided a nuanced critique of Benjamin, to which it is in many ways indebted, for as Hullot-Kentor has noted: "Benjamin's study of the Baroque is a research of *origins*, which Adorno distantly criticizes."[57] The same impulse courses through *Dialectic of Enlightenment*, written in the 1940s. As Andrew Bowie puts it, "Schelling makes, throughout his career, many of the moves which are the basis of Horkheimer and Adorno's conception of a 'dialectic of enlightenment,'" in which reason deceives itself about its relationship with nature, and thereby turns into its dialectical opposite."[58] The melancholic tone suffusing much of Schelling's work also bears comparing with the "melancholy science" Adorno practiced so diligently.[59]

In his 1959 lectures on Kant's *Critique of Pure Reason*, Adorno would continue to denounce the "mania for foundations" (*Funderiungswahn*) that had led Kant and other philosophers to seek firm ground for their arguments. "This is the belief," he wrote, "that everything which exists must be derived from something else, something older or more primordial. It is a delusion built on the idealist assumption that every conceivable existent thing can be reduced to mind, or, I almost said, to Being . . . You should liberate yourselves from this 'mania for foundations' and . . . you should not always feel the need to begin at the very beginning."[60] In *Negative Dialectics,* he positively cited *Ages of the World* as an antidote to rationalist consciousness philosophy, noting that "urge, according to Schelling's insight, is the mind's preliminary form."[61] Although resisting Schelling's privileging of intuition above reason, an inclination that Hegel had found particularly disturbing, Adorno did seek a balance between noetic and dianoetic roads to the truth. As Herbert Schnädelbach once noted, Adorno was a "noetic of the non-identical. He always stressed, above all in his remarks on formal logic, that the goal of dianoetic operations was noetic."[62] Accordingly, in his *Aesthetic Theory,* his debts to Schelling—who, more than any other German idealist, granted a special privilege to the work of art as able to express, indeed to perform, nonidentity in a way that purely discursive (that is, dianoetic) philosophy cannot—have not been hard to find.[63]

In short, the Frankfurt School's willingness to live with the abyss— or, more correctly, at its edge—meant that it avoided the problematic reliance on an "expressive" concept of totality, which Hegelian Marxists like Lukács had defended.[64] It reflected their recognition that nature could not be subsumed under the rubric of history and that the world of natural objects could not be seen as the projection of a constitutive subject. It allowed them to free critical thought from its dependence on an ur-moment of legitimating empowerment prior to the imperfect present.

Their hesitation before a Hegelian rationalist immanentism that would fold prerational ground into the totality did not, to be sure, mean that they followed Schelling in the direction that Heidegger and others wanted to take him, a direction that could end by celebrating the irrational.[65] Not only Marcuse's *Reason and Revolution*, but also works like Horkheimer's *Eclipse of Reason* testify to their dogged insistence on the critical potential in rationalism. Even when Habermas could jettison the emphatic, still metaphysical concept of reason that had animated the first generation of Critical Theorists, he would warn that "whenever the one is thought of as absolute negativity, as withdrawal and absence, as resistance against propositional speech in general, the ground (*Grund*) of rationality reveals itself as an abyss (*Abgrund*) of the irrational."[66] For Habermas, the reliance on a pre-propositional, world-disclosing intuition of the absolute paradoxically led to abandoning the one version of "*Grund*" that he could support: ground as the giving of reasons. Yet by acknowledging the limits of reason in its more emphatic sense and accepting the legitimate claims of something else—aesthetic experience, mimesis, the unconscious desires of the libido, even the hopes expressed in the idiom of religion—the Frankfurt School understood that living on the edge of the abyss would not be without its benefits.

There is, in short, an unexpected congruence—perhaps better put as a symbolic affinity—between the lack of a secure foundation in the institutional history of the Frankfurt School and its openness to the theoretical lessons of an unexpected influence like Schelling. This is not to say that either can be called the true "origin" of Critical Theory's suspicion of origins, for to do so would be to undermine precisely the force of their resistance to a firm and stable *Grund* from which to support critique itself. The Institute's "founding fathers" seem to have understood that the only viable point d'appui of critique was in the imagination of a possible future rather than a recollected past, a utopian hope rather than a past moment of originary legitimation.

To clarify this point, one might perhaps compare their practice with that of the American founding fathers as interpreted by another German émigré luminary, Hannah Arendt, in *On Revolution*.[67] In this work, Arendt contrasts the attempt to begin *ex nihilo* in the French Revolution, deriving legitimacy from a Rousseauist sovereign general will, with the American Revolutionaries' tacit reliance on prior compacts, covenants and precedents. Aligning it more with the Roman Republic, which drew its authority from the earlier founding of Troy, than with the act of creation *ex nihilo* by the Hebrew God, she argued that the American Revolution did not seek a monolithic foundation, a moment of decisionist legitimation before legality. Power, she argues, "was not only prior to the Revolution, it was in a sense prior to the colonization of the continent. The Mayflower compact was drawn up on the ship and signed upon landing."[68] By placing the act of legitimation in a receding train of possible founding moments, prior even to the colonial settlement out of which the new republic was fashioned, the American experience was one in which the potential for future perfection was as much grounds for critique as any past episode of actual founding.

It is, to be sure, a long way from the Pilgrims' landing at Plymouth Rock to the founding of the Institut für Sozialforschung, and perhaps

an even longer journey between the Enlightenment hopes of the founding fathers and Schelling's obscure arguments about the irrational God
whose existence cannot be subordinated to his essence. But what these
loose comparisons help us understand is that the *Abgrund* may well be
less fatal to Critical Theory—and emancipatory practice—than one
might suspect. It alerts us to the anarchic moment—in the sense of
lacking an original ur-moment or *archē*—in Critical Theory, as well as
its surprising similarity to Heidegger's notion of a simultaneous origin
that defies a primal ground (*Gleichursprünglichkeit*).[69] It allows us to
realize that there may be many different starting points and disparate
grounds for critical reflection without searching for the one Archimedean
point on which critique must be balanced. It is perhaps symbolically
meaningful that the actual location of Weil's First Marxist Work Week
was not a luxurious grand hotel "equipped with every comfort" at the
edge of an abyss, but rather a much more modest train station hotel,
owned by a Communist named Friedrich Henne, in the small town of
Geraberg bei Arnstadt near Ilmenau in Thuringia.[70] From such humble
origins—although not from them alone—something remarkable came
into the world.

2

"The Hope That Earthly Horror Does Not Possess the Last Word": Max Horkheimer and *The Dialectical Imagination*

The title of this chapter cites a remarkable admission from the preface Horkheimer graciously provided for the first edition of my history of the Frankfurt School, which appeared shortly before his death in 1973. It acknowledges that the long-standing Marxist insistence on the scientific validity of its theories is insufficient to motivate the yearnings that fueled its critique of capitalist oppression. However, one construes the alternative—the precise word in Horkheimer's German draft was "metaphysical," which he reconsidered in vetting my translation—it raises the question once again of the implicit normative basis of Critical Theory, a question that haunts its evolving history. This chapter recounts the enabling interaction, albeit at times delicate, I had with Horkheimer while writing the dissertation that became The Dialectical Imagination. *It recalls, among other things, his unease with two possible explanations for the Frankfurt School's dogged insistence on critique: their experience as exiles and the legacy of their (for the most part) Jewish backgrounds. Neither one, he impressed upon me (with the fervent concurrence of Felix Weil, the Institute's major benefactor), should be stressed as sources of their critical distance from conventional academic and political assumptions. Although I appreciated the reasons for his resistance—and indeed, as the final chapter of this book shows, the fears he and Weil had about the dangers of foregrounding the Jewish identity of their colleagues were, alas, justified—I was unwilling to forego at least conjecturing about the contextual matrix out of which their ideas developed.*

"Today for the first time, I sat in on a conversation between Fred and Jay. Naturally I didn't say a word that we knew about the lecture;

otherwise probably a report on disagreements would have ensued. We should seek that no great story is made out of it."[1] So wrote Max Horkheimer to Theodor Adorno on March 25, 1969, from Montagnola, Switzerland, where he had lived for a decade following his retirement from the directorship of the Institute for Social Research in Frankfurt. The Fred in question was, of course, economist Friedrich Pollock, Horkheimer's lifelong friend and collaborator, who was then generously allowing a young dissertation student from Harvard's History Department to pick his brain about the Institute's history. We have no record of Adorno's response, nor is it absolutely clear what problematic lecture Horkheimer might have wanted to avoid discussing. The passage is, however, significant because it indicates that the leaders of the Frankfurt School were very much concerned about the ways in which their history might be written. By chance, it was on that very day that Adorno wrote a much less flattering letter about the would-be historian to Herbert Marcuse, which came to light many years later and led me to write a reflection on what I called, with my tongue firmly planted in my cheek, "the ungrateful dead."[2]

Unlike Adorno, Horkheimer and Pollock seem somehow to have reached the conclusion that their history was in reasonably secure hands, and so they continued to cooperate with the historian until the dissertation became a book called *The Dialectical Imagination* in 1973. In what follows, I want to return to the role Horkheimer played in its creation, drawing on some twenty letters and telegrams he sent while I was preparing it. There are no major revelations in the correspondence, but revisiting it now may help illuminate the ways in which historical protagonists try to shape the stories told about them and the challenges historians may have when writing about living figures.

It will not, of course, be a surprise to learn that people prefer to be remembered fondly by posterity, but, in this case, what stands out is the highly charged context in which this historical account was undertaken. The end of the 1960s and the early 1970s was a period of extraordinary tension for the surviving members of the Institute's inner circle, who were then trying to cope with the unanticipated turmoil unleashed at least in part by their own earlier work. The situation is accurately captured by the subtitle of Wolfgang Kraushaar's three-volume collection of documents concerning the Frankfurt School and the German student movement: "From messages in the bottle to Molotov cocktails."[3] Although one does not want to turn what may well have been contingent events into expressions of something deeper, it is worth remembering that Adorno, Pollock and Horkheimer were all to die before the turmoil ended: Adorno in 1969, Pollock in 1971 and Horkheimer in 1973. At least the first of these deaths has often been interpreted as hastened by the stress of confrontation with students.

It is thus not surprising that they were highly cautious about cooperating in the potential framing of their history in ways that might play into the hands of contemporary critics. In fact, certain aspects of their past were then serving as sources of, or at least excuses for, critiques of their present positions. Most notably, their reluctance to endorse the more explicitly radical arguments they had made in the prewar era enraged students who had been stimulated precisely by those arguments. This reluctance was most famously captured in Jürgen Habermas's oft-quoted remark that when he had been a student at the Institute in the 1950s, "Horkheimer was terribly afraid of us opening the chest in the basement that contained a complete series of the [*Zeitschrift für Sozialforschung*]."[4] It was only with considerable trepidation that he permitted the reprinting of some of them in the two-volume collection edited by Alfred Schmidt as *Kritische Theorie* in 1968.[5]

What such fear demonstrates is that beyond worrying about getting their history right, they were also anxious about the uses to which it was already being put. And to compound the anxiety, they did not share a united position on precisely what the right response should be. Although in public they maintained a united front, we now know from the revealing correspondence between Adorno and Marcuse the depth of their disagreement over the student movement and the Institute's stance toward it.[6] My research trip to Frankfurt and Montagnola overlapped with the most volatile moment in that deeply vexed history, the student occupation of the Institute in late January and Adorno's calling the police to disburse it, which embittered the relationship between Marcuse and his old colleagues. It is in fact probable that the unnamed lecture mentioned in Horkheimer's letter was the one Marcuse was to give in Frankfurt later that spring, which, much to the chagrin of the Institute's leaders, he had tied to a demand to speak with the students.

The nexus between theory and practice, always a problematic one, was thus further complicated by a triangulation with historical reconstruction. For in addition to the explicit conflict over the ways to translate critical theory into politically effective action, there was also an implicit tension over the proper way to narrativize the Institute's past. When I arrived in Europe to begin my research in January 1969, I was only dimly aware of all that was at stake. In retrospect, my dimness—and here I would include the still uncertain grasp I had of many of the issues raised by the Frankfurt School's work—was probably an advantage. As an outsider to the controversies then swirling around the Institute, neither a student nor disciple of any of the principle players, I was not identified with any one position.

I had, to be sure, already benefited from contact with several figures in the Institute's history who were still living in America, including Marcuse, Leo Löwenthal, Karl August Wittfogel and Paul Lazarsfeld. And I was in contact with Felix Weil, who wrote extensive letters to me about the Institute's early history. Although Horkheimer, Adorno and Pollock were diplomatic about their relations with all of them, it was not hard to sense certain tensions. Thus, for example, in a cordial letter sent to me on November 11, 1968, in which he assured me that Horkheimer and Pollock would be happy to meet in Montagnola, Adorno explicitly wrote that Lazarsfeld "was only connected with the Institute for a relatively short time and very loosely in America."[7] Clearly, he wanted to caution me against accepting Lazarsfeld's view of Critical Theory, which he likely assumed would be unfriendly.[8] Many years later, Habermas would speculate in a conversation that Adorno's hostile response might have been motivated by his identifying me with Löwenthal, who had provided an enormous amount of help to me in the summer of 1968. I had not realized at the time that they had had a very serious falling out, due, among other things, to disputes over Löwenthal's being owed a pension by the Institute, but perhaps Adorno's suspicion was fueled by the assumed link.[9]

In any event, when I first approached Horkheimer by letter on November 18, it generated a warm response only four days later: "You will certainly be welcome in Montagnola," he wrote. "I suggest you let me know as soon as possible when you can be here so I can see to it that we can really talk to each other and you can use the archives." He then added: "I am sure that you know that the Institute's history in the USA started with Nichlos Muray Butler's [sic] great kindness and understanding. I met him the first time a few weeks after my arrival in New York and I shall never forget what we owe to him. Needless to say that there are many things which I can tell you and even more which you may find here in our files."[10] Butler, it should be recalled, had been the autocratic president of Columbia University, a position he held for a remarkable forty-three years, and was a figure of considerable controversy. He was a prominent Republican, an early admirer of Mussolini's Italy and a genteel anti-Semite. He also won the Nobel Peace Prize in

1931 for his work with the Carnegie Endowment for Peace. In December 1933, he refused to bar a Nazi speaker from the Columbia campus on the grounds of free speech. And yet, only a few months later, he was open-minded enough to welcome the Institute, despite its leftist leanings, to Columbia, thus earning Horkheimer's undying gratitude many years later.[11]

I provided Horkheimer a schedule of my planned visit, and he responded warmly on December 11, 1968, albeit with one qualification. Adorno had informed me that the Institute's materials were in Pollock's possession, but Horkheimer said that Pollock had told him "the files concerning the Institute as such being at his disposal are very few. Most of the files in the archive contain personal correspondence which during the lifetime of the authors should not be made public. You will have mostly to rely on printed materials. Therefore, the larger part of the information you will need will be given in your conversations with Professors Adorno, Pollock and myself."[12] Those conversations began with several meetings in Frankfurt in January and February with Adorno, when I also had a chance to speak with Habermas, Alfred Schmidt and Albrecht Wellmer.

I had expected to meet Horkheimer in Montagnola in late March, but in the middle of the month, he took a trip to Frankfurt. So, in fact, our first personal contact came when he unexpectedly burst into a conversation I was having with Adorno in the director's office of the Institute. It was a remarkable moment, as suddenly I was in the presence of both authors of *Dialectic of Enlightenment*, the only time I would have that experience. In a piece I later composed following Adorno's death, I recalled that he had shown what seemed to me "deference" to his older colleague, a characterization that Gretel Adorno later disputed when I sent her a copy of the piece: "Deference is much too strong," she wrote; "consideration would be better."[13]

Whatever the adjective, it was clear to me that Horkheimer remained the senior figure in their relationship, although Adorno had long outstripped him in terms of scholarly productivity and was to exercise a much more substantial influence in subsequent years. My next contact with Horkheimer came at the end of March, when I left Frankfurt for Switzerland, staying for a month in Lugano, a short drive from the twin houses that Horkheimer and Pollock had built in the beautiful Ticino region of northern Switzerland.[14] Pollock, it turned out, was a much more voluble source of information about the Institute than Horkheimer. He allowed me to tape our conversations, something that Horkheimer and Adorno had refused to do. The latter had denied my request using the metaphor of "verbal fingerprints," which I cited in the essay I composed after his death. I later discovered, thanks to an illuminating footnote by Rolf Tiedemann to Adorno's lectures on Kant, that he had used the same expression on other occasions to prevent transcriptions of his verbal performances, which were less precise than his carefully wrought written ones.[15] As a result of Horkheimer's similar caution, the only sound of his voice I have on tape came during one of my interviews with Pollock, when a bird call is heard outside the room and Pollock says, "aha, that is Horkheimer!"

Bird calls aside, my recollection of Horkheimer during the unrecorded interviews we did have is of a very large, imposing, always impeccably dressed figure who would lean in to emphasize a point and speak in a deliberate and measured way. He was in his mid-seventies by then and seemed to me less sprightly in conversation than Adorno or Pollock. He was warm but somewhat guarded, clearly concerned to put as positive a face as possible on the Institute's history. As forewarned, I was not allowed to see any personal correspondence but was given access to very helpful scrapbooks of materials they had collected over the years.

Shortly after my time in Switzerland, I drove to Vienna and settled in for what I thought would be several months of writing. On a trip to Budapest, where I'd hoped to connect with Georg Lukács, I made the mistake of driving my little BMW 1600 through an intersection at the same time a large truck was going in the other direction. The result was that I only got to speak with Lukács on the telephone and spent several weeks in the Költõi Traumatological Clinic recovering from a cracked pelvis, and then another two in a Viennese hospital, before returning to America to complete my recovery. Pollock sent a letter on June 20 expressing his and Horkheimer's concern; they also commented generously on a review I had done of Walter Benjamin's *Illuminations*, the first publication of his work in English.[16] Of some interest is Pollock's observation, which doubtless expressed Horkheimer's opinion as well: "In the last years of his life B[enjamin] seems to have fled into the Marxist world of thought [*Gedankenwelt*] as an escape from his despair. It can never be known, had he lived longer, if he would have overcome the contradictions between his work and what he had learned from Brecht and Sternberg as Marxism."[17]

My next contact with Horkheimer followed the sudden death of Adorno on August 6, 1969, when I sent him a condolence letter. His secretary, G. E. Kluth, responded on August 14: "Your letter of August 8 did not yet reach Professor Horkheimer. Because of the sudden death of Professor Adorno he had to interrupt his vacation in the mountains. At the time being, he is in Frankfurt, where he attended yesterday his friend's funeral. I telephoned briefly with Professor Horkheimer and informed him about the contents of your letter. He asked me to convey to you his deeply felt thanks. For obvious reasons he will not be able to answer you personally in the near future. He is certain to find your understanding."[18]

It was in fact more than a year later that our correspondence resumed. In the interim, I sent drafts of my chapters to Pollock and Löwenthal for their respective thoughts and received carefully detailed and wonderfully helpful suggestions from both. At the same time, Pollock shared with me the increasingly troubling news of health problems he was suffering. I remember still being shocked to receive an official notice of his death on December 16, 1970, jointly issued by his widow, Carlota, and Horkheimer. Once again, I had the melancholy task of sending a message of condolence to Horkheimer, who replied in a moving letter on January 5, 1971:

> I thank you for your kind words of December 23. For 60 years I had lived together with Fred Pollock. He helped me so much in every respect that I don't know how my life may continue without his wonderful understanding. It is a true consolation to know that when you wrote about the Institut, you were aware of his decisive role when it was founded and during its history up to the moment when we left for good. You are perfectly right when you say, your work will be a real help for all those who wish that the most important period of the Institut will not be forgotten.[19]

I completed my dissertation late in the spring of 1971, directed by H. Stuart Hughes, who had been a friend of Franz Neumann and Marcuse from their days together in the Central European Bureau of the Office of Strategic Services.[20] I sent a copy to Horkheimer, who impatiently wrote on May 2 that it had not yet arrived, adding, "I think it is very important that I can let you have my remarks, your study should be one of the decisive sources for all those interested in the Institute's history. Should you have another copy, please send it to me by airmail."[21]

A copy did finally arrive and Horkheimer shared it with Matthias Becker, who had begun writing his biography, which, alas, Becker never finished because of his untimely death in 1974 at the age of forty-one. We corresponded over the course of my research and writing, and he was enormously helpful. Becker had been able to win Horkheimer's trust to the extent that he permitted him to tape their conversations, which were only discovered in 2008.[22] On June 8, Horkheimer wrote to introduce him and included his first letter to me:

> Here is a letter from Dr. Becker of Bremen who will be Professor at Bremen University when it starts functioning. He is a highly intelligent young philosopher and I had given him the first chapter of your impor-tant thesis. His remarks seem precise to me, and it is indeed a pity that the three of us can't have a common discussion. In a recently published book of my late friend Adorno, he quoted a sentence of a review: "God dwells in the detail." This certainly goes for descriptions like the history of the Institute.[23]

The letter from Becker accompanying Horkheimer's contained several useful suggestions for changes, which were gratefully incorporated in my book, as were others he offered in three subsequent letters in 1971.[24] In addition to suggestions for minor alterations in details, Becker's letters also hint at a certain tension between Horkheimer and Felix Weil over some aspects of the Institute's founding and early history. How to handle Weil, whose generosity had initially funded the Institute, was a perennial challenge for its leadership over the years. Becker requested that I not share with Weil all of the suggestions he had made in order to "avoid being burdened with an unforeseeable correspondence."[25] Weil, who was then teaching real estate law to American GIs at the army base in Ramstein, Germany, was in fact, an indefatigable letter writer, but, from my historian's point of view, this was a great blessing. He responded quickly and with great eagerness to my questions and to drafts of my chapters.

Two issues in particular most exercised him and were also of concern to Horkheimer, with whom he frequently telephoned as my project devel-oped. Both were of some importance. The first concerned the role that the Jewish background of most of the Institute's members might have played in their development. This is, of course, an enormously complex and sensitive matter that has received frequent treatment in the Frankfurt School literature.[26] Much depends on which figures are stressed, which periods in their lives, the definition of what it means to be Jewish—reli-gious, ethnic, cultural—as well as the intangible issue of influence itself.

In light of crude anti-Semitic denigrations of Critical Theory as an expression of something sinister to be deplored in the legacy of Judaism—a denigration that, alas, continues to this day[27]—it is fully understandable that both Horkheimer and Weil wanted to avoid being reduced to whatever version of Jewishness might be held responsible for their ideas. Like Freud, who was famously anxious to avoid the same reproach, they were very wary of such a simplistic reduction. Even though Löwenthal and Fromm had gone through periods of serious religious commitment during their association with the Frankfurt Lehrhaus, and Benjamin, abetted by his friendship with Gershom Scholem, had drawn on theological motifs in his work, the Institute in the 1920s had maintained a strongly materialist—that is, essentially Marxist—orientation.

There was, however, a subtle difference in the acknowledgment of the residual importance of their Jewish origins between Horkheimer and Weil. Although conceding that the Institute had always been especially sensitive to the dangers of anti-Semitism, Weil was adamant that he and his colleagues had long since left any trace of a meaningful Jewish heritage, understood in religious or other terms. To suggest that something else still mattered, he argued, was to fall into the trap of accepting racist definitions of Jewish identity. Horkheimer, for his part, had come to acknowledge in contrast at least a certain link between Critical Theory's refusal to picture utopia and the Jewish prohibition on picturing God, the famous *Bilderverbot*. When he had returned to Germany after the war, he increasingly identified as a Jew, so much so that a headline of an interview with him in the *Allgemeine Wochenzeitung der Juden in Deutschland* in 1952 was titled "The Jewish Rector and his German University."[28]

When I pointed this out to Weil, he replied impatiently:

> You refer to Horkheimer's stressing his Jewishness as Rektor of the university. You seem not to know that then he even, on the high holidays, attended synagogue services (but not of the orthodox kind, just the reform-liberal one). But, as he told me, he did this not as a late Believer, but as an ostentatious act of a political nature . . . anyway you cannot project back into the 20s what the old Horkheimer of the 60s said or is now saying (including the "other" and the *Bilderverbot*, where I can't follow him at all).[29]

The issue was also raised in Horkheimer's letter to me of July 10, 1971, in which he wondered what I had meant by the "ethnic origins" of the members of the School. Whatever response I made—my own letters were not preserved—seemed to placate him, as on July 23, he responded:

> Many thanks for your letter of July 15 and especially for what you said about the positive relations between the Critical Theory and the Bilderverbot. I myself frequently pointed to this connection. What a pity that we cannot talk personally about the significance of the materialistic as well as the theological elements in the development of the Frankfurter Schule.[30]

I ultimately veered closer to Horkheimer than Weil in my account, but I also remained convinced that, however much fuel it might give to anti-Semitic critics of Critical Theory, it was impossible to ignore the volatile and rapidly evolving situation of German Jews in the Weimar era in making sense of the Frankfurt School's origins and perhaps its intellectual investments as well. I felt some vindication when I read in Leo Löwenthal's autobiographical interviews with Helmut Dubiel the following admission: "However much I once tried to convince Martin Jay that there were no Jewish motifs among us at the Institute, now, years later and after mature consideration, I must admit to a certain influence of Jewish traditions, which were codeterminative."[31]

On the other sensitive issue that arose, Weil and Horkheimer were firmly united. The dissertation had lacked a snappy title, so when I looked for one for the book, I returned to the essay I had written for *Midstream* in 1969 after Adorno's death, which had been called "The Permanent Exile of Theodor Adorno." Although Marcuse and Löwenthal were in favor, both Weil and Horkheimer had grave misgivings about calling the book *Permanent Exiles*. When I floated it as a possibility, Horkheimer responded in January 1972, that it "seems to me problematic, as it doesn't apply to a number of our members, Theodor W. Adorno, Fred Pollock and myself. Leo Löwenthal and Herbert Marcuse made America their home."[32] When I wrote back explaining that I had meant it metaphorically to suggest the even before their actual emigration, Institute members had been anxious to avoid co-optation and after the war, Critical Theory had maintained its distance from any real "homecoming," Horkheimer was not placated. On March 5, he sent an urgent telegram that read "title still seems misleading to me," backed up by a letter sent the same day, which is worth extensively quoting:

The idea that during "the period from 1923 to 1950" the Institute's members had been obsessed by "the fear of co-optation and integration" is certainly not precise. As long as [Carl] Grünberg was the director this surely was not the case, and after I had been appointed up to our emigration several of us definitely were non-conformists in some ways but no "Exiles." During our stay in America most of us were exiles with regard to fascist Germany, but certainly not with regard to democratic states like the USA and postwar Germany. Otherwise our relations to conservative people like President Butler would have never been what they were, nor would Franz Neumann have spent so much time in West-Berlin to help organizing [sic] the university, nor had I returned to Frankfurt to do about the same there and in addition to rebuild the Institute with American and German public funds.[33]

Weil was no less distressed by the initial idea for a title, which he and Horkheimer had discussed by phone, and let me know more explicitly why it was not only imprecise, but also, in his eyes, dangerous:

Here is why I consider this title fundamentally wrong and damaging: especially because of the reinforcement of misunderstanding you give by your insistence on saying, or broadly hinting at, the influence the so-called joint ethnic origins of our group is supposed to have had on our way of thinking, the "Exiles" title will lend retroactively to justify all the attacks our enemies launched against the Institute and the Frankfurt School, to wit, that we as rootless outsiders had no business or justification to instill "*undeutsche Gedanken*" [un-German thoughts] = subversive feelings into German students.[34]

Clearly, I had unintentionally entered a minefield by assuming that the status of "permanent exile" would be more a badge of honor than a source of reproach, but I could now better understand the source of their anxiety. There were—and continue to be—criticisms from the nationalist right of the allegedly baleful influence of returning émigrés on postwar German culture.[35] Whereas I thought, perhaps naively, that slanders against "rootless cosmopolitans" were things of the past, Horkheimer and Weil still felt their sting and were determined not to let my book give ammunition to their purveyors. Ironically, such charges anticipated a comparable critique of the emigres' influence on American culture later leveled by xenophobic cultural conservatives like Allan Bloom.[36]

Hoping to dissuade me, Horkheimer and Weil offered a few alternatives, ranging from the pedestrian "The Early Stages of Critical Theory" to the melodramatic "Rebels with a Cause." Finally, I hit on the title that the book ultimately bore, which I derived consciously from two earlier works—C. Wright Mills's *The Sociological Imagination* and Lionel Trilling's *The Liberal Imagination*—and unconsciously from a passage in Norman O. Brown's *Life against Death*, which I had read a number of years earlier.[37] Later, someone casually mentioned to me that source, and I had a chance to publicly credit Brown in the preface to a later book, a collection of my essays on the intellectual migration from Germany to America, which I titled *Permanent Exiles*.[38] In any event, both Horkheimer and Weil were pleased with the new choice, and as I ultimately got to use both titles, I was also happy with the outcome.

Much of our wrangling over the title played out against the backdrop of one final episode in the story of Horkheimer's role in the book: the writing of the preface he graciously provided. Despite my concern that having such a preface might leave the impression that the book was somehow a "court history," I thought it worth mulling over the possibility shortly after the dissertation was completed. Horkheimer replied cautiously in a letter of July 23, 1971, asking if I would be satisfied with a two-page preface without an imminent deadline. A succession of illnesses was making it hard for him to concentrate on his work, but my positive answer had encouraged him to try. On August 31, 1971, at the end of a letter that dealt primarily with details of Paul Tillich's role in the Institute's early years and some uncertainty over the existence of a Psychoanalytic Institute in Frankfurt before the migration, he added, "I hope my little preface, which I intend to write at a time when I am not overburdened as during these weeks, will not disappoint you too much."[39]

On December 12, 1971, I received a letter from Matthias Becker with Horkheimer's promised preface. "During his serious illness of the past weeks," Becker wrote, "he was greatly concerned to make the deadline he had promised. We are a bit late, but I think that you will be very satisfied with his introductory words."[40] Needless to say I was not only grateful, but also deeply moved by the gesture. I translated the text and sent it to Montagnola for any emendations Horkheimer might want to make. With a few minor changes, the preface appeared when the book was finally published in the spring of 1973. Perhaps the most meaningful change appeared in the second thoughts he had about the moving sentence from which I have taken the title of this chapter. In German, it reads, "Die Sehnsucht danach, dass die Gruel auf Erden nicht die letzte Gültigkeit besässen, ist freilich ein metaphysischer Wunsch." Looking at my translation, Horkheimer changed "metaphysical" to "non-scientific," but he left standing the formulation "the hope that earthly horror does not possess the last word."[41]

These were not themselves the last words I received from Horkheimer. In addition to the dispute over the title, he responded generously to an essay I published in 1972 called "The Frankfurt School in Exile" and wrote of his impatience for the publication of the book, which he hoped would coincide with the imminent English translation of *Dialectic of Enlightenment*. Finally, on March 10, 1973, he informed me that two copies of the book had arrived and that he found them "beautiful and [was] happy with them." The last words of that final letter, after he requested I send him the reviews, were simply ones of friendship: "How are you? Are you well in Berkeley; will you be coming any time soon back to Europe?"[42]

Four months later, on July 7, 1973, Horkheimer died in a hospital in Nuremberg at the age of seventy-eight and was buried in the Jewish cemetery in Bern, Switzerland. Shortly after his death, I was sent a copy of a photograph, one of the last taken of him, in which he was dressed impeccably, as always, in a three-piece suit, and reading a copy of *The Dialectical Imagination*. There can be few more moving images for a historian than one that shows the hero of your narrative, nearing the end of life and apparently finding some solace in your attempt to make sense of it. During the period I knew Max Horkheimer, he lost his closest friends, Adorno and Pollock, as well as his much-beloved wife, Maidon, who died in October of 1969. He was in many ways a diminished figure, beset by illness and wary of the ways in which his legacy was being read by critics on both ends of the political spectrum.

I was enormously fortunate to have had an opportunity to be the first to provide a general history of that legacy and even more fortunate to win Horkheimer's trust in so doing. Although it was always clear that he was invested in my telling it in a way that redounded to his credit, I never felt coerced into bending the evidence to paint a rosier picture than the documents afforded. I can fully appreciate the anxieties he— and Felix Weil—felt about reducing their thought to an expression of some ill-defined Jewish spirit or even the experience of Weimar Jewry, although I would also still hope that a nonreductive analysis of that dimension of their story can prove illuminating. As for the dispute over my proposed title, the outcome was favorable for everyone. The alternative rightly emphasized their thought rather than their lives, and I ultimately got to use *Permanent Exiles* for a collection about a more disparate group of émigrés who did not share a common intellectual position.

What is perhaps most moving is the fact that, more than four decades after Horkheimer's death and the publication of *The Dialectical Imagination,* the message bottles thrown into the sea by the Frankfurt School continue to wash up on unexpected shores, to be opened by new generations of readers who find in them inspiration for the development of a twenty-first-century critical theory. Whether metaphysical or non-scientific, the wish that such a theory may help us to diminish the cruelties of a world still a long way from the utopia yearned for by the Frankfurt School remains very much alive today.

3

Max Horkheimer and *The Family of Man*

Horkheimer's increasing ambivalence about the militantly radical nature of prewar Critical Theory manifested, among other ways, in his reluctance to be called a "permanent exile." "During our stay in America," he insisted, "most us were exiles with regard to fascist Germany, but certainly not with regard to democratic states like the USA and postwar Germany." He very clearly demonstrated his revised estimation of the value of what Marxists had traditionally denigrated as "bourgeois democracy" in 1958, when he introduced Edward Steichen's traveling exhibition of photographs called The Family of Man *to a Frankfurt audience. Horkheimer was determined to promote to the German public the liberal democratic values he had come to appreciate, if with nuanced qualification, during his years in America. Tellingly, the philosophical touchstone of his analysis was Kant rather than Marx, and he defended cosmopolitan humanism against the prioritization of cultural, class or national difference. More precisely, he saw in the concrete images of the exhibition—and here there was no trace of the* Bilderverbot *he so often invoked in other contexts—a happy mediation of difference and universalism.*

Not surprisingly, Horkheimer's 1958 introduction provided welcome ammunition for current art historians seeking to reverse the long-standing dismissal of Steichen's exhibition by a wide range of critics—from Roland Barthes, Jacques Barzun and Susan Sontag to the editors of October *magazine—all of whom damned it as "photographic ideology." But when read in the context of another essay Horkheimer wrote a year earlier, "The Concept of Man," which was far less sanguine about abstract humanism or the crisis of the modern family, his defense seems more of a tactical maneuver than a reflection of a wholesale retreat from his earlier position. Or, perhaps better put, the unresolved tension between the two pieces may be said to reflect the Frankfurt School's postwar struggle to adapt to new circumstances in which the Marxist intransigence of their earlier years was tempered by a recognition that democratic ideals and universalist humanist values were more than mere window dressing for class domination.*[1]

> If only I knew a better term than humanity, that poor, provincial term
> of a half-educated European. But I don't.
> > Max Horkheimer, "Humanity," (1957–8)[2]

With no special fanfare or extended justification, the distinguished authors of the ambitious overview of twentieth-century art, *Art since 1900*, all stalwarts of the influential journal *October*, refer disparagingly to Edward Steichen's "blockbuster exhibition of postwar photographic ideology, 'The Family of Man' at the Museum of Modern Art in 1955."[3] The context for this casual dismissal is an argument about the transfiguration of prewar avant-garde and social documentary photography into a vehicle for consumer capitalist advertising and fashion in the so-called New York School, which rose to prominence in the postwar era. Having absorbed the critiques of Steichen's show leveled by Roland Barthes, Susan Sontag, Alan Sekula, John Berger, Abigail Solomon-Godeau and a host of lesser commentators, the book's authors echo their scorn for *The Family of Man* as an ideological exercise in sentimental humanism in the service of Cold War propaganda and the middle-brow visual culture typified by *Life* magazine.[4]

Given the now widespread disdain for the triumphalist American culture of the 1950s, their offhand characterization of the show is not surprising. But it has its cost, as the authors of *Art since 1900* were oblivious to a burgeoning resistance to the conventional wisdom that sought to restore at least some of the once-glittering reputation enjoyed by the exhibition when it was first seen by millions around the world in the 1950s. Eric Sandeen's 1995 *Picturing an Exhibition* began the advancement of a more nuanced, forgiving, even positive estimation of the political intentions, aesthetic achievements and popular impact of *The Family of Man*, and this momentum carried into later essays by Blake Stimson, Fred Turner, Sarah E. James, Gerd Hurm and others.[5] In this revisionist effort, unexpected ammunition has been supplied by the recent rediscovery of a forgotten text by the Frankfurt School's leading figure, Max Horkheimer, that accompanied the show when it opened in that German city in 1958.[6]

What are the implications of Horkheimer's delayed insertion in the debate? Can remembering his intervention help counter the still power- ful grip of the negative characterization of the exhibition as little more than an exercise in "photographic ideology"? Does his enthusiasm for the exhibition in the specific context of a postwar Germany struggling to move beyond its recent Nazi past and deal with its divided present translate into a more general legitimation of its cultural import and political effect, which can be useful today? Or does the more general attitude of the Frankfurt School toward humanism—which Horkheimer expressed in an essay called "The Concept of Man" just a year before his introduction to the exhibition—suggest a less comfortable fit between his position and that of those seeking to rescue entirely *The Family of Man* from the charge of photographic ideology?[7]

The occasion for Horkheimer's talk—the exhibition's opening on October 25, 1958, at Frankfurt's Amerika-Haus, an institution funded by the American government—was hardly auspicious for the full display of his critical skills. Having recently returned to Germany to reestablish the *Institut für Sozialforschung*, with support enabled by his mutual trust with the enlightened US high commissioner for Germany, John H. McCloy, Horkheimer understood his public mission as a reeducator of Germans, especially youth, in the demo- cratic values he had learned in exile.[8] Although in private he main- tained many of the darkly pessimistic sentiments and intransigent radicalism he and Theodor W. Adorno had expressed in *Dialectic of Enlightenment*—a work, it should be noted, that remained out of print and absent from public discussion until pirated editions began to be circulated in the 1960s—in public, he was determined to play a constructive role in weaning Germany from the pathologies that had led to the Third Reich.[9] In the context of the Cold War, where Horkheimer increasingly came to discern similarities between Stalinism and Nazism, it was clear that he had no hesitation about siding with the West, despite its many defects.[10] Horkheimer in fact sought to retain his naturalized American citizenship even as he returned to Europe to live out the remainder of his life. For all his dismay with the culture industry he had witnessed firsthand in exile, he did not hesitate to consider himself an ambassador of the liberal democratic values, however imperfect their actual implementation, he had also absorbed during his sojourn in America.

Horkheimer began his introduction to the exhibition by stressing what he saw as its implicit philosophical point d'appui, which he argued tied together American and European, most notably German idealist, thought. Here, though, his touchstone was not Hegel, and certainly not Marx, but rather Immanuel Kant, who shared with American philosophers like Ralph Waldo Emerson and John Dewey a strong belief that the individual human being should be treated only as an end and never as a means. If there were a difference between the two traditions, it lay in the additional American assumption, derived from the immigration of people from many different backgrounds, "that there are close ties of kinship between all members of the human race, that there is a brotherhood of mankind."[11] This was a lesson that only an elite of educated Europeans had learned, because of the poison of national enmities.

To make his point, Horkheimer cited the hopeful words of Francis Lieber, whom he identified simply as "a German professor who emigrated to America in the last century"[12] to the effect that nationalism might someday be replaced by a single global community. "The Family of Man," he then argued, "illustrates this way of thinking; indeed it is representative of all the forces that are now counteracting the severe cultural shocks and regressive movements that have occurred in Europe in recent years. In this context it is eminently constructive."[13] Once again turning to Kant to spin out his argument, he evoked the philosopher's celebrated essay of 1784, "Idea for a Universal History with a Cosmopolitan Purpose,"[14] claiming it provided a model not of the world as it was, but as it might be: "Humanity for Kant was not an entity, a living instance of which had to be found, indeed, not even a form with a content, but a posit that, in connection with other philosophical ideas, underlies much of the historical work of individuals and peoples."[15] An "idea," we should understand, meant in Kant's special vocabulary a purely theoretical concept to which no corresponding object could be given in sense experience and for which no synthetic a priori judgment, no cognitive claim, might therefore apply. By invoking it, Horkheimer was making clear what he saw as the regulative, counterfactual, even utopian quality of the notion of a unified humankind. As had Kant, he hoped that it might serve as a telos of human practice rather than a description of what was destined to occur.

However, because it spoke in the vaguest terms about humanity, Horkheimer went on, Kant's model was far too abstract. Steichen's exhibition happily provided a corrective to Kant's abstract notion, and it did so by drawing on photography's power to represent concrete differences rather than generic identities, the real motley variety of the world rather than a single model of human essence. But, because of the way in which the exhibition had been organized, he said, it transcended the irreconcilability or incommensurability of those differences. On the level of everyday life, it seemed to suggest, people in all cultures faced the same challenges and sought the same solutions. Without intention, the curators "were obeying, possibly without being fully aware of it, an inner logic of the whole, of the way these pictures interact and address one another, which gives them in their entirety a meaningfulness that is difficult to ignore."[16] By showing similarities and the interrelatedness of apparent opposites, the exhibition "tells us that individual human beings within a group and one community of people in relation to another should support each other rather than torment each other and work together to the best of their ability to bring about a world constitution based on reason with which everyone can be satisfied." Thus, the philosophical and visual ideals are ultimately the same, even though the abstract idea of what Kant would have called "perpetual peace" could not actually be shown as such.

That admirable desideratum was anticipated instead through the way in which the exhibition enabled emotional identification with people of different backgrounds. Mimetic empathy was a path, Horkheimer observed, to the love that binds people together. In that effort, photographs—in fact, images in general—were needed to supplement the abstractions of theoretical concepts:

> Even Plato's Eros force, uplifting the spirit to eternal ideas, needed the knowledge of ephemeral things in order to achieve infinite knowledge, which, for him, is the meaning of all human existence. That is why thought needs the image, that is why the image can lead us to people and things, that is why the image has the valuable and not infrequently also dangerous power that thought alone cannot exert.[17]

Unlike cinema, photographs allow you to linger with details, discover the unexpected, and disclose the unfamiliar. "Indeed, this is what the exhibition has in common with real artists: it provides us with a new way of looking at things that we will never forget, of however little practical use it may be."[18]

Horkheimer finished his introduction to the exhibition by returning to the question of identification. He noted that there was an important exception to the mimetic empathy aroused by Steichen's selection of photographs that appears in those depicting what he called, once again following Kant, "radical evil."[19] Because the exhibition thwarts such identification in at least two cases—he does not specify the images or spell out exactly how they do so—it "insists on the consciousness of the freedom and the responsibility of the individual. It sides with human beings yet at the same time does not absolve them of guilt. It inspires tolerance of weakness, but not of barbarism."[20]

With these remarks, Horkheimer was clearly identifying with those who shared the exhibition's goals and ratified its methods for achieving them. But for a student of his *oeuvre,* much in this introduction will seem very surprising. Unlike other critics of a scientistic version of Marxism, such as his erstwhile colleague Erich Fromm, he had always resisted the lure of a humanist alternative suggested in Marx's 1844 Paris manuscripts.[21] His evocation of Kant rather than Hegel or Marx, endorsing what Michel Foucault came to call Kant's "empirico-transcendental doublet" of the individual and humanity,[22] was in tension with what are normally taken to be the primary philosophical inspirations for Frankfurt School Critical Theory. Nor do we find any indication of his life-long fascination with Schopenhauer, whose illusionless pessimism he could still call in 1961 "the philosophic thought that is a match for reality."[23]

Perhaps because of its Kantian perspective, the introduction underplays the persistent power of intermediate identifications, whether with class, gender, nation, religion, or status group, which resist, for good or for ill, abstract homogenization on the level of the whole or the isolated singular. Rather than uncritically celebrating the American cult of individuality, as he seems to in his paean to the exhibition, Horkheimer had long harbored doubts about its darker side. In *Dialectic of Enlightenment,* he and Adorno had bitterly remarked that

> the decay of individuality today not only teaches us to regard that category as historical but also raises doubts concerning its positive nature . . .
> In the autonomy and uniqueness of the individual, the resistance to the blind, regressive power of the irrational whole was crystallized. But that resistance was made possible only by the blindness and irrationality of the autonomous and unique individual.[24]

In the chapter entitled "The Rise and Decline of the Individual" in his 1947 *Eclipse of Reason,* Horkheimer bemoaned the survival of the ideology of individual self-preservation at a time when there no longer seemed a coherent self to preserve. "The dwindling away of individual thinking and resistance, as it is brought about by the economic and cultural mechanisms of modern industrialism, will render evolution towards the humane increasingly difficult."[25]

But nothing of these bleak assessments of the weaknesses of the bourgeois humanist notion of the individual remained in his introduction to *The Family of Man*. Additionally, Horkheimer glossed over one of Kant's most fateful moves from "The Idea for a Universal History with a Cosmopolitan Purpose," which would have been inconvenient to foreground in this context: the philosopher's unsentimental justification of social conflict or what he called "asocial sociability" as the hidden mechanism of progress toward the goal of a cosmopolitan order of federated states. Instead of stressing the functional value of social strife, even violence, as had Kant, Horkheimer short-circuited the indirect process by which the ultimate pacification of social existence might be achieved. Unlike Hegel, who stressed the role of dialectical negation expressing the "cunning of reason," and Marx with his valorization of the class struggle, he moved quickly from the still imperfect present to a more utopian world constitution based on reason.

But perhaps most unexpected of all is Horkheimer's valorization of the power of images, photographic or otherwise, to give concrete meaning to the abstract yearnings expressed in philosophical language.[26] After his return from exile, Horkheimer came increasingly to identify with his Jewish roots, often invoking the taboo on graven images, the *Bilderverbot*, in Exodus 20:1–7 as a still potent reason for Critical Theory's distrust of positive utopian fantasies.[27] Adorno would also frequently cite the same source in his characterizations of a doggedly negative dialectic, refusing all higher affirmative sublations.[28] They likewise invoked the *Bilderverbot* in the other direction, as explanation for their distrust of attempts to give realistic aesthetic form to the experience of the Holocaust.[29] Although often extolling the virtues of mimetic similarity rather than conceptual subsumption as a way to avoid the domination of otherness, they were deeply suspicious of the ways in which it could slide into denigrating mimicry, a pattern they had witnessed firsthand in the Nazi mockery of Jews.[30] In his introduction, however, mimesis is firmly on the side of empathetic identification alone.

The anomalous character of this text in Horkheimer's thinking in this era is even more apparent if we compare it with another essay written at virtually the same time, his 1957 "The Concept of Man."[31] Impatient with the incessant pious chatter about the "crisis of man" in the postwar era—a phenomenon trenchantly probed by the American intellectual historian Mark Greif in his recent *The Age of the Crisis of Man*[32]—Horkheimer argued that "the word 'man' no longer expresses the power of the subject who can resist the status quo, however heavily it may weigh upon him. Quite differently than in the context of critical philosophy, to speak of man today is to engage in the endless quest for an image of man that will provide orientation and guidance."[33] The abstract appeal to "man," whether anthropological or existential, is a deception designed to distract attention from the contradictory social realities that still smolder beneath an alienated totality that remains irrational to the core.

Rather than upholding the virtue of empathetic identification with individuals, "The Concept of Man" repeats the bleak characterization of the fate of individuality in the modern world that Horkheimer had lamented in earlier works written in the shadow of the Holocaust, such as *Dialectic of Enlightenment* or *Eclipse of Reason*: "The factors in the contemporary situation—population growth, a technology that is becoming fully automated, the centralization of economic and there-fore political power, the increased rationality of the individual as a result of his work in industry—are inflicting upon life a degree of organization and manipulation that leaves the individual only enough spontaneity to launch himself onto the path prescribed for him."[34] Any appeal to personal "authenticity" is thus ideological, an "empty well from which those who cannot achieve their own private life, their own decisions and inner power, fill up their dreams."[35]

Significantly, Horkheimer bemoaned the ineffectiveness of the contemporary nuclear family in resisting these tendencies, an argu-ment that drew on the empirical work the Institute had done on the crisis of the bourgeois family in the 1930s.[36] Because children were becoming ever more directly socialized by society, particularly by the seductions of consumerism, they could not develop the interior strength needed to reject its conformist blandishments. The family was no longer a "haven in a heartless world," defended by a nurturing mother, where an experience of childhood happiness might serve as a spur to critical reflection about its denial in later life.[37] Instead, the family's integrity had been eroded, so that it now functioned only as a porous shield against the penetration of commodification and the modern media. Ironically, the seemingly progressive entry of women into the labor force, Horkheimer worried, had had its costs: "The principle of equality is penetrating even into the family, and the contrast between private and social spheres is being blunted. The emancipation of woman means that she must be the equal of her husband: each partner in the marriage (the very word 'partner' is significant) is evaluated even within the home according to criteria that prevail in society at large."[38] Such equality was a sinister expression of the exchange principle in bourgeois society in which everything qualitatively different was rendered quantitatively fungible.

Mentioning the erosion of the traditional family lamented by Horkheimer in "The Concept of Man" raises the larger question of the symbolic function of the family in Steichen's exhibition, which operated on two levels: the repetition of parallel images of happy nuclear families in different cultures and the metaphor in the title implying that humanity as such should be seen as one giant family. Many critics of *The Family of Man* excoriated it precisely for its tacit affirmation of the patriarchal, heteronormative nuclear family of the 1950s as a model of the family tout court. From our perspective today, at a time when families come in so many different varieties and the appeal to "family values" has turned into a coded way to decry those developments from a conservative perspective, it is easy to mock the homogenizing effect of the images in the exhibition.

Defenders of the exhibition, however, have contended that a tacit distinction was at work behind the depiction of the ideal family, which ironically mirrored criticisms made by Horkheimer's own colleagues at the time in their classic study *The Authoritarian Personality*.[39] Mindful of the ways in which fascism had been welcomed by personalities trained to obey tyrannical fathers rather than absorb maternal love, the authors of *The Authoritarian Personality* had argued that such families produce a child who "can apparently never quite establish his personal and masculine identity; he thus has to look for it in a collective system where there is opportunity both for submission to the powerful and for retaliation upon the powerless."[40] Unprejudiced "democratic" characters, in contrast, "received more love and therefore have basically more security in their relationships to their parents. Disagreements with, and resentment against, the parents are openly worked out, resulting in a much greater degree of independence from them. This independence is carried over into the subject's attitude toward social institutions and authorities in general."[41] It was this version of the family, so champions of the exhibition have argued, that Steichen tacitly hoped to foster.

Although Horkheimer too favored this version of the family, he feared in "The Concept of Man" and elsewhere that it was in danger of disappearing even in ostensibly democratic countries such as the United States. This anxiety was not, however, apparent in his introduction to the exhibition. Instead, he contented himself with vague assurances that the images exhorted people to "support each other rather than torment each other and work together to the best of their ability to bring about a world constitution based on reason with which everyone can be satisfied. And that this constitution is possible." This was clearly not the occasion, he must have reasoned, for sour pronouncements about ubiquitous threats to the type of nonauthoritarian family he thought necessary to realize that utopia.

What about the exhibition's more general evocation of "man" as a kind of extended family? In his introduction, Horkheimer turned to the American "melting pot" experience as the source, to cite his words once again, of the healthy "awareness that there are close ties of kinship between all members of the human race, that there is a brotherhood of mankind." Unlike Roland Barthes, with his bitter question, "But why not ask the parents of Emmett Till, the young Negro assassinated by the Whites what *they* think of *The Great Family of Man*?,"[42] he did not pause to ponder how pervasive that awareness actually might be in the racially divided America of his day. Instead, he optimistically asserted that through the magic of empathetic visual identification, the viewer, and here he is talking to the citizens of Frankfurt, "can even see himself in the native in the jungle."[43] Whether or not the reverse was just as likely to be true is not a question he felt compelled to pose. Nor did he voice any concern about the gender implications of evoking universal "brotherhood" as the model of familial solidarity or think twice before invoking the stereotype of non-Westerners as "natives in jungles."

In response to these absences, recent defenders of the exhibition's intentions have pointed to Steichen's acknowledgment that the title had, in fact, been suggested by his brother-in-law, poet Carl Sandburg, who had traced it to various speeches by no less an admirable figure than Abraham Lincoln.[44] The distinguished pedigree of the phrase, they contend, points to its implications not only for racial equality but also for women's suffrage, which Lincoln had explicitly championed. So, by tacitly endorsing the rhetoric of the human family and not foregrounding his anxiety over the crisis of actual families, Horkheimer, the inference might be drawn, was actually supporting the inclusivist agenda pursued by Steichen.

There is, however, another pedigree for the metaphor, which Horkheimer himself had in fact noted elsewhere with alarm. In his study of "Authoritarianism and the Family Today," which appeared in 1949, he had noted that the Nazis had employed the rhetoric of the nation as a collective family, which had meant not only the suppression of class and other social differences but also the creation of dangerous pseudo-biological kinship distinctions that served to stigmatize alleged outsiders as racially inferior. Extending the boundaries of the putative family to the species was admittedly designed to avoid such in/out group distinctions, but it tacitly perpetuated them when it came to the domination of other animals, who were treated as not part of the family of man. Horkheimer, indebted as he was to Schopenhauer, was, in fact, an earlier critic of the instrumental treatment of animals.[45] But none of this anxiety about the ambiguous implications of humanism and the family metaphor was evident in his introduction to the exhibition.

Nor did Horkheimer ponder the limits of understanding more general human relations in familial terms. Not only have patriarchal analogies been easily abused in antidemocratic defenses of monarchy— for example, Robert Filmer's *Patriarcha*, famously the target of John Locke's ire—but paternalist rule in general was in tension with the right of an allegedly "immature" subaltern to full autonomy. Spousal violence and child abuse were, after all, lamentably widespread practices, rarely protested until recently.[46] The metaphor of brotherhood as idealized human interaction, even when extended to mean siblings in general, was also vulnerable to the charge that it forgot the ability of brothers, at least since Cain's assault on Abel, to become rivals, indeed deadly ones. If humankind were really a family, might it not just as well be a dysfunctional one? Think, for example, of the house of Atreus—or even the family of Antigone, that epitome of sibling love, who was, it must be remembered, the daughter/sister of Oedipus, not exactly a model of filial piety.

More fundamentally, the extension of kinship to embrace the entire species, while plausible on some attenuated genetic level, ignores the powerful distinctions between endogenous and exogenous groupings that underlay the incest taboo so fundamental to human civilization. Politics, it might be said, is the art of learning to live with exogenous others, who may be marriage material, but until the knot is tied, are anything but kin, loving or otherwise. At best they may be recognizable neighbors in a tightly knit community, but they are more often anonymous strangers within the borders of a more capacious and impersonal society or a fortiori aliens outside its borders. If politics means anything, it means dealing impersonally with rivals and adversaries, as well as friends, both genuine and of convenience, who are not in any meaningful sense bound to us by the affective ties of family. A political community, as we know, is more imagined than real, the inclusivity of its members premised on the exclusion of those outside its boundaries. We may owe temporary hospitality to strangers should they come to our shores seeking succor—Kant thought it was the one binding law of a cosmopolitan world order[47]—but not permanent domicile in the way we might to family members. Toleration of otherness and respect for what makes us all human does not mean absorbing the stranger into our family, no matter how extended we might construe it. Moral duty does not rest on ties of affection and indeed might at times contradict them, and it is impossible to build a healthy polity on emotional grounds alone. Indeed, as Hannah Arendt once remarked, "Love, by its very nature, is unworldly, and it is for this very reason rather than its rarity that it is not only apolitical but antipolitical, perhaps the most powerful of all antipolitical human forces."[48]

All of these considerations were absent from Horkheimer's introduction and did not surface to derail his enthusiasm for the familial metaphor underlying Steichen's exhibition. But before we dismiss him too quickly as yet another Cold War apologist for "photographic ideology," it would be wise to pause with his self-evident motivation, which helps explain the difference between his response and that of Roland Barthes to the exhibition. In a Germany still struggling to move beyond the insidious ideology of racial hierarchy and ethnic exclusion that had brought such a ruinous outcome, it was necessary to swallow whatever qualms one might have about the potential costs of overly abstract humanist universalism and the implications of extending the metaphor of a family from the nation or race to the species. At a time when Martin Heidegger's elevation of Being over humanity as the central focus of philosophy posed a danger to the hope of making a clean break with the Nazi past, it was important to remind Germans that Kant still remained relevant and that his thought might be compatible with liberal American intellectual traditions as well. Against the existentialist insistence that essentialism was an outmoded philosophical concept that transformed one contingent set of conditions into a dubious universality of reductive sameness, it was healthy to remember the critical work that the concept of essence

might do when it is transformed from an eternal truth into a normative potential to be realized historically.[49]

In contrast, Roland Barthes could draw on the very different lessons
a Frenchman might have learned from the negative effects of an overly
abstract humanism, which had lost its appreciation of the value of
cultural difference and historical variation in its zeal to carry out its
alleged "civilizing mission." These lessons, as Stefanos Geroulanos has
recently shown, were shared as early as the 1930s by many in France
who had developed antifoundational negative anthropologies as a
result.[50] Although there had long been religious condemnations of
humanism, the innovation of these thinkers was their explicit atheism,
which resisted the assumption that all men were the same because they
were allegedly created in God's image. Barthes, it should be noted, made
precisely this connection in attacking the putative unity underlying
depictions of difference in images chosen by Steichen: "This means
postulating a human essence, and here is God re-introduced into our
Exhibition: the diversity of men proclaims his power, his richness; the
unity of gestures demonstrates his will."[51] From the perspective of an
atheistic historicism, in which any positive philosophical anthropology
was a "myth" grounded in the secularization of religious universalism,
the exhibition could only be ideological, and Horkheimer's defense of it
a mystifying exercise in false consciousness.

From Barthes's perspective, it is thus easy to see why the exhibition
might warrant dismissal as ideological—as indeed it also might, as
noted, from that adopted in many of Horkheimer's other writings. But
before we then conclude that this dismissal is the last word and reject
the recent attempts at rebuttal, we need to put a little pressure on the
vexed concept of ideology itself. When casually used, "ideology" is a
term of opprobrium, suggesting false consciousness and mystification, either deliberate or not, and is implicitly opposed to the nobler
ideals of truth, scientific knowledge or at least critique. It is understood to reflect either the interests of a group that employs it for its
own partial ends, masking and/or justifying its power, or the unconscious reaction to collective psychological stress that generates ideology as a dubious way of relieving that stress (for example, through
scapegoating). As such, it acts as a distorting mirror or refracting filter
through which reality is prevented from revealing itself in its unmediated and naked form.

But in addition to the explicitly negative connotation of the word
that draws on a positive alternative more often implied than forcefully

defended, there is a more complex, dialectical alternative that acknowledges the latent critical function of ideology as well. Take, for example, the classic example of Marx's characterization of religion as the opiate of the masses. The paragraph in his "Contribution to the Critique of Hegel's *Philosophy of Right*: An Introduction," where this famous formulation appears, begins with the acknowledgment that "religious suffering is at the same time an expression of real suffering and a protest against real suffering. Religion is the sigh of the oppressed creature, the sentiment of a heartless world, and the soul of soulless conditions." Marx then says that critique, which was the methodological basis of historical materialism, "has plucked the imaginary flowers from the chain, not in order that man shall bear the chain without caprice or consolation but so that he shall cast off the chain and pluck the living flower."[52]

It is worth recalling these familiar lines to remind us that critiques of ideology may well depend on acknowledging the discontent, albeit in mediated and distorted form, generated by intolerable and unjust conditions, and the desire to relieve those conditions, that is harbored in even the most insidiously consolatory ideological formations. Returning to our main concern, it lets us recognize that we need not reduce our response to a culturally complex phenomenon like *The Family of Man* to either a simple-minded dismissal or a defensive celebration. In other words, even if its detractors had a point in decrying its inadvertent ideological function, the exhibition can also be credited with possessing a critical potential—the "protest against real suffering" that Marx saw in religion—that also demands recognition.

Thus, even if Barthes is right to see a religious source of the humanist faith in a shared human essence, it is possible to acknowledge that origin not merely to unmask and debunk it, but rather to recognize that critical protest against an unjust status quo often appears, as Marx himself conceded, in the garb of religion.[53] If we take Horkheimer's interpretation of the exhibition as less a celebration of the present than a challenge to make a different and better future, his endorsement of an essential human condition as normative rather than descriptive, and his adoption of perpetual peace as the telos of history in a Kantian counterfactual, regulative ideal with practical intent, we can discern the utopian impulse lurking beneath the surface of what may appear as unabashed Cold War ideology. Even if Horkheimer's introduction should be situated in the larger context of his work, which provides ample ammunition for those who lament *The Family of Man*'s complicity with a problematic status quo, we can still honor his intention to read the exhibition against that grain and inspire a still volatile post–Nazi Germany to work through the unresolved issues of its recent past. Insofar as many of these issues still, alas, remain exigent in the twenty-first century, new sets of eyes can still profit from the experience of viewing Steichen's "blockbuster exhibition of postwar photographic ideology."

4

"In Psychoanalysis Nothing Is True but the Exaggerations": Freud and the Frankfurt School

In his classic essay "The Legend of Hitler's Childhood," émigré psychoanalyst Erik H. Erikson stressed the role played by psychological projection in the anti-Semitic denigration of Jews. He then added, "While projections are hostile and fearful distortions, however, they are commonly not without a kernel of profound meaning. True, the projector who sees a mote in his brother's eye overlooks the beam in his own, and the degree of distortion and the frightfulness of his reaction remains his responsibility. Yet there usually is something in the neighbor's eye which lends itself to specific magnification."[1] Having already published his essay in 1950, a year before Adorno's Minima Moralia, Erikson could not have known of his fellow émigré's evocation of the same biblical passage for somewhat different purposes. But it is striking that both would be drawn to it as a way to stress the importance of projection, at once cognitive and psychological, as a source of both the distortion and illumination—or, more precisely, magnification—of reality. Both were also convinced that familial dynamics and childhood development were crucial in the formation of adult political inclinations, although Erikson was somewhat less pessimistic about the crisis of the traditional bourgeois family. Unlike other émigré analysts of totalitarianism in general and fascism in particular—Hannah Arendt and Carl Joachim Friedrich come immediately to mind—Erikson and members of the Frankfurt School understood the necessity of applying psychoanalytic insights to make some sense of the seemingly inexplicable appeal of nightmare politics in the twentieth century.

Erikson, to be sure, is normally grouped with either the ego psychologists or neo-Freudian revisionists who were disdained as social *conformists by the Frankfurt School. Despite his having been born in 1902 in Frankfurt, only a year before Adorno, and emigrating from Nazi Germany in 1933, first to Denmark and then America, Erikson seems to have had little sustained contact with members of the Frankfurt School. An essay he wrote in 1942 entitled "Hitler's Imagery and German Youth" was, to be sure, cited approvingly several times in* The Authoritarian Personality,[2] *and he was included in the celebrated lecture series in 1956 at the reconstituted Institute in Frankfurt, which brought Freud back to Germany after the war. But rather than discern ominous signs in America of the continuation of fascism by other means, he celebrated its culture during the Cold War (despite ultimately criticizing the war in Vietnam) and had little interest in the marriage of Marx and Freud. He was, moreover, a practicing clinician who had been trained by Anna Freud and worked throughout much of his career with children.*

It was precisely a disdain for the therapeutic function of Freud's theories that distinguished Marcuse and Adorno from Erikson and most other émigré psychoanalysts. Nor did Marcuse and Adorno champion the smooth integration of the psychological level of analysis with the social, which set them apart not only from Erikson but also from their erstwhile colleague Erich Fromm. But what perhaps most of all distinguished Critical Theory's use of Freud from that of Erikson, Fromm and virtually all other defenders of his legacy was its proponents' insistence on the biological moment in Freud's work, including his much maligned instinct theory. Against the grain of those who saw it as a warrant for pessimism about the rigidity of human nature, they argued it could also inspire very different thoughts in a political imaginary that led not to dystopian fascism, but dreamt instead of utopian redemption.

> Inherent in psychoanalysis is the protest against reality. Equilibrium on the basis of inner freedom. *Non conformism.*
>
> Max Horkheimer[3]

When Herbert Marcuse, one of the leading figures of the Frankfurt School, was asked by a skeptical questioner how Marx and Freud could be unified in one coherent theory, he defiantly replied: "I think they can easily be married, and it may well be a happy marriage. I think these are two interpretations of two different levels of the same whole, of the same totality."[4] Leo Löwenthal, another founding member of the School, would likewise recall that "the systematic interest that must have spawned this fascination with psychoanalysis for me and many of my intellectual fellow travelers was very likely the idea of 'marrying' histor-ical materialism with psychoanalysis."[5] The metaphor of marriage was often, in fact, employed to characterize the bold integration of Marx and Freud in the Critical Theory developed at the Institute of Social Research, out of which the Frankfurt School emerged.[6] It suggests more than just a conceptual integration, but also one charged with affect, expressing an emotional bond between two loving partners joined together harmoniously and capable of producing heirs inheriting the best traits of each.

But whether it was a true and enduring marriage—let alone a happy, harmonious and productive one—is a question that needs to be reopened. For it is still not clear that two such seemingly different tradi-tions—one stressing socioeconomic relations, confident in scientific rationality and radically political; the other individualist in focus, dwell-ing on unconscious irrational desires and cautiously therapeutic—can ever find the theoretical and practical equivalent of connubial bliss. Among the Marxist skeptics was Walter Benjamin, himself loosely associated with the Institute of Social Research in the 1930s, who denounced "capitalism as a religion" and argued that psychoanalysis "belongs to the hegemony of the priests of this cult. Its conception is capitalist through and through."[7] Other, later commentators also invested more in Marx than Freud have concluded with Fredric Jameson that "we have all probably overstressed the 'Freudo-Marxism' of the Frankfurt School, which is finally realized only in Marcuse."[8] For, if a marriage did take place, he went on, it was profoundly unequal, because the Frankfurt School applied Freud's categories as "a kind of supple-mentary social psychology ... but never as any centrally organizing concept."[9] Defenders of Erich Fromm, who, ironically, was largely responsible for the Frankfurt School's initial attempt to combine the two before his break with the Institute in 1939, likewise came to praise him as a champion of Marxist humanism who recognized the ahistori-cal, biologistic limitations of psychoanalysis.[10]

Purist exponents of Freud, for their part, stressed Marxism's funda-mental indifference to psychological questions and its radical historici-zation of human nature (which they trace back to the founder himself), and thus the sterility of the forced marriage.[11] In the words of Philip Rieff, "Marx followed Hegel in his anti-psychological orientation. Capitalism elicits personality types; personality types do not first elicit capitalism."[12] Later pro-Freudian skeptics have pointed to theorists like Jacques Lacan, whose "return to Freud," according to one recent account, "reflected the waning of the New Left and the end of its hopes for a Marx/Freud synthesis."[13]

Such a counterintuitive synthesis, call it marriage or not, was, of course, envisaged well before the Frankfurt School emerged as a distinct intellectual formation. Intimations of it can be traced as far back as Leon Trotsky in Soviet Russia, before it was explicitly proscribed when Stalin came to power and Pavlovian behaviorist conditioning became the reigning orthodoxy. One can find even more determined advocates in interwar Central Europe, such as Siegfried Bernfeld and Wilhelm Reich, and among the surrealists in France.[14] What came to be called "the Freudian Left" included even non–explicitly political figures such as Géza Róheim and underground radicals such as Otto Fenichel.[15] But the abiding interest in Freud shared by most theorists associated with the Frankfurt School—and one would have to include second- and third-generation members such as Jürgen Habermas and Axel Honneth[16]—makes Critical Theory an illuminating test case for the fruitful combination of the two traditions.

In what follows, I focus on four motivations that overlapped but emerged to prominence at different moments in the Frankfurt School's history and which compelled the first generation of members to serve as marriage broker between Marx and Freud. The first incentive for the matchmaking, apparent even before Max Horkheimer took over official directorship of the Institute in 1930, was the hope that psychoanalysis might help answer the exigent question generated by the failure of orthodox Marxist theory to generate revolutionary practice: why did the working class fail to assume the leading role assigned to it by historical materialism in the overthrow of capitalism? The second reason was the complementary insight it might offer into the unexpected success of a political movement, fascism, that traditional Marxism had not foreseen and that stubbornly survived after World War II in what might be called the "fascism with a human face" of an "administered society" comprised of "one-dimensional men." The third motivation, evident especially in Marcuse's mature thought, grew less from the dystopian anxiety driving the first two than paradoxically from a stubbornly residual utopianism. It drew on an imaginative reading of Freudian theory to envisage a civilization very different from the one whose discontents Freud himself accepted with resignation as inevitable in any conceivable alternative. And, finally, the Frankfurt School, in particular Horkheimer and Adorno, looked to psychoanalysis as a resource in the philosophical struggle to defend a plausible materialism against idealism or "consciousness philoso-phy" and its denigration of somatic pleasure and indifference to the sufferings and needs of the creaturely self.

Before, however, exploring each of these motivations and their consequences, we have to clarify one important premise of the Frankfurt School's approach concerning the relationship between psychoanalytic theory and therapeutic practice. Three of the early members of the *Institut für Sozialforschung* had in fact themselves undergone psycho-analytic treatment: Erich Fromm, Leo Löwenthal and Max Horkheimer. The first two had been involved in the early 1920s with a therapeutic community that had Jewish religious ties and was organized by Frieda Reichmann, who was for a while Fromm's wife.[17] Fromm went on to become an analyst himself, training with Karl Landauer, a leading figure in the German psychoanalytic movement. In 1927, Horkheimer was analyzed by Landauer, albeit only for a year and apparently with little concrete effect beyond the loss of anxiety about lecturing without notes.[18] But, because of his enthusiasm for the intellectual content of Freud's theories, Horkheimer encouraged the creation of the Frankfurt Psychoanalytic Institute in 1929, led by Landauer and Heinrich Meng, even inviting it to take up quarters in the Institute of Social Research's newly constructed building. Fromm and Frieda Fromm-Reichmann were among its most prominent collaborators, and other members of the Institute of Social Research often joined in their discussions. Löwenthal recalls that "the mere fact that a psychoanalytical institute was allowed to use rooms on a university campus was then almost a sensation,"[19] and also proudly recalls his role in helping Freud get the city of Frankfurt's Goethe Prize in 1930.

Communications with Freud himself followed in which he praised the Institute for bringing his ideas into a university setting for the first time.[20] In a letter written by Horkheimer in March 1932 in which he sought Freud's advice about a substitute for Fromm, who was then temporarily sidelined with tuberculosis, at the Institute's branch in Geneva, the importance of psychoanalysis to the interdisciplinary project of the Institute was emphasized: "I am convinced that without the use of psychoanalytic knowledge [*Kenntnisse*] our project will not be fruitfully realized, and I believe and hope I am allowed to say that such a participation in social scientific research will not be without value for the development of psychoanalysis itself."[21]

What is perhaps most revealing about this letter is Horkheimer's stress on the cognitive payoff of psychoanalysis rather than the therapeutic. During his student days in Frankfurt, he cultivated an enthusiasm for Gestalt research into the holistic workings of the mind, which helped him overcome the hostility to psychology typical of most philosophers of the era but did not lead him toward anything like the efforts made by contemporaries like Reich, with his Sex-Pol clinics to alleviate the suffering of sexual alienation.[22] Although assuring Freud that he had been personally analyzed by Landauer, he gave no indication that the Institute would emulate the model of Reichmann's religious/therapeutic community or even Landauer's Institute, whose leaders were active analysts, but instead would rigorously separate theory from practice. In one of the aphorisms in his pseudonymously published collection *Dawn and Decline*, Horkheimer had already expressed his distrust for the ideal of "inner health" as an antidote to "objective suffering" and asked scornfully if the revolutionary can "determine at any given moment how healthy, neurotic, at one or at odds with himself he may be? These bourgeois categories reflect their own world and not the struggle which proposes to unhinge it."[23] Although here the distinction was between political activism and therapeutic practice, when the former grew less likely, radical theoretical speculation informing interdisciplinary social science replaced it as therapy's antonym.[24]

Significantly, the same attitude came to characterize the Frankfurt School's approach to two other traditions that had vigorously sought to unite theory and practice: religion and socialism. Despite the frequent introduction of theological ideas into critical theory, they were never tied to the observation of religious practices.[25] A similar pattern can be seen in their complicated attitude toward the unity of radical theory and revolutionary political practice, the shibboleth of Marxism ever since the eleventh *Thesis on Feuerbach*. Horkheimer himself distinguished a genuinely "critical" theory from a "traditional" one explicitly in terms of the former's insistence that social emancipation rather than disinterested contemplation was its goal.[26] But the failure of the working class to be the vehicle of that transformation meant that the gap between theory and practice yawned wider, and the Frankfurt School increasingly resisted well-intentioned but vain efforts to bridge it.

The selective and evolving incorporation of psychoanalysis into the Frankfurt School's theoretical arsenal was likewise marked by a coolness to therapy, which became especially clear after its members' emigration to America, where ego psychology and "neo-Freudian revisionism" could be condemned for enabling conformist adaptation to the status quo in the service of a dubious individual "cure."[27] As a result, there seems to have been little if any ongoing reflection on the psycho-logical dynamics within the Frankfurt School itself—for example, the intensity of the friendship between Horkheimer and Friedrich Pollock, the rivalry for Horkheimer's favor between Adorno and Löwenthal, and the unconscious motives in the break between Fromm and his colleagues—or much effort spent in a self-examination of tacit gender and heteronormative biases in much of their work and the organization of their research program.[28] The validity of Freudian theory, like its theological and historical materialist counterparts, was not to be tested pragmatically, but should be understood as what Horkheimer called in a programmatic essay in the inaugural issue of the Institute's *Zeitschrift für Sozialforschung* "an indispensable auxiliary science for history."[29]

In that essay, "Psychology and History," Horkheimer acknowledged that historical context was more important than allegedly permanent traits of human nature, and he challenged the liberal emphasis on the eternal priority of the individual over the social. But he was no less insistent that historical materialism had erred in reducing individuals to mere functions of their economic class and in minimizing the role of irrational desires rather than rational interests in motivating human action. Insofar as the economic substructure of society influenced the ideological superstructure—and this did not imply a straightforward "reflection" of one by the other—the mediation of psychological forces, operating on the individual and not collective level, was crucial. "That human beings sustain economic relations which their powers and needs have made obsolete, instead of replacing them with a higher and more rational form of organization," Horkheimer argued, "is only possible because the action of numerically significant social strata is determined not by knowledge but by a drive structure that leads to false conscious-ness." Rather than assuming a simplistic model of rational self-interest of the type favored by, say, utilitarianism, radical social theory should "penetrate to these deeper psychic factors by means of which the econ-omy conditions human beings; it must become largely the psychology of the unconscious."[30] People's relevant drives were not merely to assure self-preservation and achieve sexual pleasure, but also "to employ their aggressive powers, to gain recognition and affirmation as persons, to find security in a collectivity,"[31] which Freud has shown need to be distinguished from hunger in their plasticity and capacity to be satisfied indirectly.

In the same inaugural issue of the *Zeitschrift*, Erich Fromm expressed the Institute's position in a manifesto titled "The Method and Function of an Analytic Social Psychology."[32] Approving the ambition of psycho-analysis to be listed among the natural sciences, he concurred with its belief in biological instincts. Indeed, he went so far as to claim that "man's instinctual apparatus is one of the 'natural' conditions that forms part of the substructure of the social process."[33] By the instincts, it should be understood, Fromm meant Freud's early dichotomy of sexual pleasure and self-preservation, not Eros and Thanatos, developed in *Beyond the Pleasure Principle* in 1920. Fromm stressed that the first of these, sexual pleasure, was more malleable than the second, which meant it had to be understood in terms of the life history in which it was realized. Rejecting the idea of a mass or societal soul, psychoanalysis thus rightly focuses on individual development, but—and this was the source of its compatibility with Marxism—it understands that process in social and historical rather than purely personal terms. The key mediation between childhood development and the larger social world was, so Fromm argued, the family, which is itself heavily influenced in turn by class. Against the normalization of the bourgeois, patriarchal family, which had led Freud erroneously to universalize the Oedipus complex, an analytic social psychology of the type advocated by Fromm acknowledged the malleability of both psychological and social conditions and thus the existence of different libidinal structures in different circumstances. It also recognized the crucial role of psychological factors in the fostering of false consciousness or "the formation of ideologies as a type of 'production process,' as another form of the 'metabolism' between man and nature. The distinctive aspect here is that 'nature' is also within man, not just outside him."[34]

As the Institute's sole trained analyst who had a doctorate in sociology, Fromm was entrusted not only with the task of theoretically integrating Marx and Freud, but also with addressing concrete empirical questions illuminated by their complementary insights.[35] In 1929 with the aid of Hilde Weiss, he designed an ambitious research questionnaire that sought to gauge the readiness of the working class to assume the revolutionary role assigned to it by Marxist theory.[36] Although its completion was interrupted by the Institute's forced migration from Germany and publication initially thwarted for reasons that remain in dispute, it anticipated several later projects, including the *Studies on Authority and Family* in the 1930s and the five-volume postwar *Studies in Prejudice*, the most influential of which was *The Authoritarian Personality*.[37] Positing a spectrum of "personality types"—Fromm would later call them "social characters"—ranging from the "revolutionary" to the "authoritarian," the survey revealed a troubling discrepancy between conscious political allegiance and underlying psychological inclination: "without doubt, the most important *result* is the small proportion of left-wingers who were in agreement in both thought and feeling with the socialist line. In critical times the courage, readiness for sacrifice and spontaneity needed to rouse the less active and to overcome the enemy, could only be expected from a rather small group of 15%."[38] Although there were some 25 percent who were ambivalent, an even more alarming finding was that some 20 percent of those supporting workers' parties were "authoritarian."

It was, in fact, the dawning realization that growing authoritarianism, found on both ends of the political spectrum, required a psychologically informed analysis of contemporary society and politics that provided the second motivation for the integration of psychoanalysis into Critical Theory. Leftist theoreticians of all stripes, many writing in post-1933 exile, were compelled by events to account for the unanticipated rise of fascism and the dismaying Stalinization of the Soviet experiment.[39] Freud's analysis of the etiologies and symptoms of various individual psychopathologies seemed to some applicable to social phenomena as well. Reich's *Mass Psychology of Fascism* (1933) was a pioneering attempt, stressing the importance of the family and the repression of adolescent sexuality, although it lacked any empirical research to support its conclusions. Drawing on extensive empirical studies, the Institute's *Studies on Authority and Family*, a sprawling collective effort that was never fully completed, also drew on psychoanalytic categories to explain the dangers of the "sadomasochistic character" rampant among lower-middle-class supporters of fascism.

Fromm's later single-authored text, *Escape from Freedom* (1941), grew in certain respects out of this analysis, but it also reflected his growing disenchantment with Freud and estrangement from the other Institute members, leading to his bitter separation from the Institute in 1939. Tacitly repudiating his own earlier position, he attacked orthodox psychoanalysis as excessively biologistic and pansexualist, as well as overly invested in childhood development and the putative universality of the Oedipus complex. In its place, he praised the more socially inclined perspectives of Karen Horney and Harry Stack Sullivan, who focused on interpersonal relations in the present.[40] "Contrary to Freud's viewpoint," he explained, "the analysis offered in this book is based on the assumption that the key problem of psychology is that of the specific kind of relatedness of the individual towards the world and not that of the satisfaction or frustration of this or that instinctual need *per se*; furthermore, on the assumption that the relationship between man and society was not a static one."[41] Relief from the discontents of this specific society would come not through realizing the desires of the libido, let alone an instinctual drive toward self-destruction, but rather through the ability of man to "unite himself with the world in the spontaneity of love and productive work" which would avoid the search for "security by such ties with the world as destroy his freedom and the integrity of his individual self."[42]

Fromm's alienation from Horkheimer's circle only became widely known in the 1950s, when he engaged in a vigorous public polemic with Herbert Marcuse, whose *Eros and Civilization* we will examine shortly.[43] But the estrangement was well under way by 1938, when Adorno left Europe and joined the Institute's ranks in New York, an event that has often been seen as initiating a paradigm shift in the development of Critical Theory. Adorno's respect for Fromm had, in fact, always been tempered, although he could still approach him as late as November 1937 with an unrealized proposal to write an essay for the *Zeitschrift* on "the feminine character."[44] Fromm himself had shown a recent interest in the matriarchal theories of Johann Jakob Bachofen and Robert Briffault, but Adorno's interest lay elsewhere. He denounced the "pre-Marxist, Feuerbachian" celebration of "wholesome sensuousness" he saw in Reich and rejected the romanticization of completely uninhibited women as an antidote to patriarchal repression. Instead, he contended that women were maimed even more than men by capitalism because of their susceptibility as consumers to commodity fetishism. "More and more I am convinced," he wrote Fromm, "that the actual coincidence of Marxist theory and psychoanalysis lies not only in analogies of superstructure and base with ego and id, etc., but rather in the connection between the fetish character of the commodities and the fetishized character of human beings."[45] As early as 1935, in fact, in a letter to Benjamin in which he outlined his views on Freud, Adorno had asserted that "in opposition to Fromm and, in particular, to Reich, I defended the position that the true 'mediation' between society and psychology was to be found not in the family, but rather in the commodity and fetish character itself, that the phenomenon of fetishism is the authentic correlate of reification."[46]

Adorno had not participated in the Institute's research program on family and authority, and although the mediation of the family was to be included as one factor in the analysis of *The Authoritarian Personality*,

it was not in the section he composed.[47] Adorno's stress on the importance of fetishism instead, both in economic and psychological terms,
was also evident in his analysis of what he and Horkheimer came to call
"the culture industry."[48] Thus, for example, in his important essay "On
the Fetish Character of Music and the Regression of Listening" of 1938,
it played a key theoretical role, alongside other such psychoanalytic
categories as masochism, neurosis and regression.[49] He could, however,
still insist that "the concept of musical fetishism cannot be psychologically derived. That 'values' are consumed and draw feelings to themselves, without their specific qualities being reached by the consciousness of the consumer, is a later expression of their commodity character.
For all contemporary musical life is dominated by the commodity form;
the last pre-capitalist residues have been eliminated."[50] Marx, in other
words, still trumped Freud, especially now that the mediating role of
the patriarchal family had been diminished with the erosion of paternal
authority.

But when it came to explaining the rise of the particular fascist
pathology that had developed in capitalist society, Adorno recognized
the value of psychoanalysis. In an essay of 1951, drawing on *Studies in
Prejudice* as well as his own empirical work on fascist propagandists in
the 1930s,[51] he made clear his debt to Freud's *Group Psychology and the
Analysis of the Ego*: "It is not an overstatement if we say that Freud,
though he was hardly interested in the political phase of the problem,
clearly foresaw the rise and nature of fascist mass movements in purely
psychological categories."[52] Adopting Gustave Le Bon's influential
theory of the crowd without the Frenchman's contempt for it, Freud had
understood the libidinal ties that bind the masses together into a kind
of "brother horde" and that explain more than any primitive herd
instinct how individuals regress to members of a mass when they identify with an idealized leader, generally an "oral type" who uses language
to appear magically as both unique and everyman. The apparent contradiction between the two, Adorno claimed, could be explained by Freud's
theory of narcissism, in which the "little man" both submits to authority
and identifies himself with it. Hostility to an "out-group" was also a
mark of the excessive self-love characteristic of narcissism.[53]

Lest, however, he be thought to advocate an essentially psychological
explanation of fascism, a misunderstanding that often dogged *The
Authoritarian Personality*, Adorno insisted that "fascism as such is *not* a
psychological issue," for "any attempt to understand its roots and its
historical role in psychological terms still remains on the level of

ideologies such as on 'irrational forces' promoted by fascism itself . . .
Psychological dispositions do not actually cause fascism; rather, fascism
defines a psychological area which can be successfully exploited by
forces which promote it for entirely nonpsychological reasons of self-
interest."[54] In fact, one of the great ironies of drawing on psychoanalysis
to explain mass behavior in the age of fascism is that it was originally
developed at a time when the individual self was still relatively strong
and coherent enough to be the focus of therapy, whereas now such a self
has been almost entirely hollowed out, leaving "postpsychological,
de-individualized social atoms, which form the fascist collectivities."[55]
It was for this reason that Adorno could later cite with approval
Löwenthal's pithy insight that mass culture is "psychoanalysis in
reverse," because it cynically uses the tools designed to make sense of
psychic conflict "in order to ensnare the consumer as completely as
possible and in order to engage him psychodynamically in the service
of premeditated effects."[56]

Adorno's skepticism about the survival of individuals with enough
ego strength to resist the lure of fascism, even in the America in which
he found refuge, was evident in the sour remarks about psychoanalysis
in *Minima Moralia*, which also appeared in 1951. Ironically, whereas
Fromm had distanced himself from the biologistic, ahistorical premises
he saw in orthodox psychoanalysis, Adorno attacked Freud for losing
nerve in his refusal to embrace their deeper emancipatory implications.
Rejecting the revisionist advocacy of therapeutic empathy and warmth
against Freud's alleged coldness, he argued that the real problem lay
elsewhere: Freud had "tracked down conscious actions materialistically
to their unconscious instinctual basis, but at the same time concurred
with the bourgeois contempt of instinct which is itself a product of
precisely the rationalizations that he dismantled."[57] Too starkly contrasting reason with pleasure, the ego with the id, Freud had succumbed to
the very repressive ideology his theory at its deepest level had challenged: "reason for him is a mere superstructure, not—as official philosophy maintains—on account of his psychologism, which has penetrated
deeply enough into the historical moment of truth, but rather because
he rejects the end, remote to meaning, impervious to reason, which
alone could prove the means, reason, to be reasonable: pleasure."[58]

When, in the phrase that has become one of his most cited aphorisms, Adorno argued that "in psychoanalysis nothing is true except the
exaggerations,"[59] he seems to have been pointing to Freud's late metapsychology, with its controversial dualism of Eros and Thanatos. In the

case of the former, Adorno's claim is explicit: "he alone who could situate utopia in blind somatic pleasure, which, satisfying the ultimate intention, is intentionless, has a stable and valid idea of truth."[60] The shallow happiness psychoanalysis seeks to recover through its therapeutic "cure" of neuroses is instead merely "a further encroachment of institutionally planned behavior-patterns on the ever-diminishing sphere of experience."[61] Peddling the "bottomless fraud of mere inwardness" rather than acknowledging the crippling constraints of society, it abets adaptation and accommodation rather than real change. Its theory of art as sublimation is, likewise, complicit with the status quo: "Artists do not sublimate. That they neither satisfy nor repress their desires, but transform them into socially desirable achievements, is a psychoanalytic illusion . . . rather, artists display violent instincts, free-floating and yet colliding with reality, marked by neurosis . . . their lot is rather a hysterically excessive lack of inhibition over every conceivable fear; narcissism taken to its paranoiac limit. To anything sublimated they oppose idiosyncrasies."[62]

For Adorno, Eros and Thanatos each had a utopian implication, albeit the latter's was far less direct. Although Adorno did not spell it out in *Minima Moralia*, an undeveloped hint of what it might mean was expressed in his critique of the vitalist *Lebensphilosophie* (Philosophy of Life), with its cult of an abstraction called "life." Health and sickness, life and death, Adorno argued, are inevitably intertwined, and rejecting sickness and decay for the sake of life, hypostasized as a good in itself, can have inadvertently disastrous consequences. For, ironically, Adorno claimed, "Only death is an image of undistorted life."[63]

The counterintuitive import of this cryptic formula was teased out a few years later by Herbert Marcuse in *Eros and Civilization* (1955), which was the most explicit use of Freud for utopian purposes in the Frankfurt School canon. Marcuse's encounter with Freud came later than that of his colleagues, and while contributing an intellectual history of the concept of authority, he had played no role in the Institute's empirical work on authority and the family in the 1930s.[64] But anticipations of his interest in the costs of sexual repression and its role in the perpetuation of capitalism can be found in his philosophical writings of that era.[65] Like Adorno, he was pessimistic about the residual role of the patriarchal, bourgeois family as a haven from the heartless world in which modern men and women now lived. He was no less suspicious of the possibility of individual therapeutic cures in a society that had eroded any meaningful version of individuality and could only be rescued through radical wholesale transformation. And he was as dismayed as Adorno by what he saw as the undialectical, one-dimensionally culturalist (or sociologistic) and inherently conformist bromides of Fromm and the neo-Freudian revisionists, insisting instead on the enduring importance of biology.[66]

In fact, a few months before the publication of *Eros and Civilization*, a spirited debate between Fromm and Marcuse appeared in *Dissent*, recently created as a major forum for New York intellectuals, in which the full extent of the break between the Institute and their former colleague was made public for the first time.[67] Since their parting in 1939, Fromm had increasingly identified himself with the humanist Marxism contained in Marx's 1844 manuscripts,[68] de-emphasized Freud's drive theory and the Oedipus complex, and focused on the alienation rooted in capitalism and amenable to political change. Despite his own continuing adherence to Marxism, Marcuse insisted that Fromm had actually spiritualized values that could not be realized without a radical transformation of instinctual life itself, which was a much more fundamental challenge than restoring healthy interpersonal relations through what he mocked as "the Power of Positive Thinking."[69] Despite later attempts by his defenders to rebut Marcuse's charges, Fromm's reputation never recovered from this attack, which helped elevate his opponent to one of the major theoretical inspirations of the nascent New Left.

Marcuse's bold reinterpretation of Freud's metapsychological instinct theory—in which he challenged both the resignation of *Civilization and Its Discontents* and the despair of Horkheimer and Adorno's *Dialectic of Enlightenment*—blew on the utopian embers still smoldering in *Minima Moralia*, albeit without explicitly signaling his debts.[70] Reading Freud against himself, he defended the desire at the heart of the Oedipus complex as more than a yearning for a specific libidinal object, let alone the interpersonal connection praised by Fromm, but rather as "the eternal infantile desire for the archetype of freedom: freedom from want . . . Its natural object is, not simply the mother *qua* mother, but the mother *qua* woman—female principle of gratification."[71] Contesting the wisdom of repressing that desire in the name of the reality principle, spiritualized sublimation and the triumph of the ego over the id, he argued that it could actually be satisfied in a different civilization based on the ending of the "surplus repression"—with its echo of Marx's "surplus value"—that was ideologically justified by the "performance principle" driving capitalist production. Another, more utopian reality, one based on technologically enabled material abundance and the ending of scarcity (*Ananke*),[72] might help overcome the fateful designation of only certain zones of the body as erogenous, which had allowed the rest to toil without pleasure in the service of productivity. Such an overcoming would restore the undifferentiated sensuousness of primary narcissism—what Freud had called, albeit without understanding its liberating potential, "polymorphous perversity." The tyranny of genital sexuality would be ended with the revival of a more diffuse eroticization of the entire body. Here, the model was less Marx than Charles Fourier, who "comes closer than any other utopian socialist to elucidating the dependence of freedom on non-repressive sublimation."[73]

If such a utopian reading of Eros were not enough, Marcuse went even further in reimagining the desire behind Thanatos, which Freud and most of his followers had lamented as leading to destruction, both directed inwardly and out at the world, and thus inimical to the affirmation of life characterizing the opposing instinct. Instead, he drew out the implications of Adorno's cryptic remark from *Minima Moralia* cited above: "Only death is an image of undistorted life." Freud, he argued, had not pitted death against life as a simple binary, but rather understood them as dialectically related: "The objective of the death instinct is not destruction *per se* but the elimination of the need for destruction."[74] That is, the yearning of the death instinct is for the *jouissance* of a pacified existence, following what Marcuse called "the nirvana principle," beyond a life of stress and unfulfilled yearning. "If the instinct's basic objective is not the termination of life but of pain—the absence of tension—then paradoxically, in terms of the instinct, the conflict between life and death is more reduced the closer life approximates the state of gratification. Pleasure principle and Nirvana principle then converge."[75]

In so arguing, Marcuse revealed his abiding debt to the Hegel whose rationalist dialectics he had vigorously endorsed in *Reason and Revolution*, a dialectics that drew on the power of negative thinking in the ultimate service of a grand reconciliation, sublating reason and happiness, spirit and soma, individual and society, and culture and nature. Although he was to warn against "repressive modes of desublimation" in *One-Dimensional Man*, operating "as the by-product of the social controls of technological reality, which extend liberty while intensifying domination,"[76] they were understood as deviations from an emancipatory liberation of the instincts, which would involve a new reality principle beyond the one crippling contemporary society. There was a "logos of gratification," he contended, that could challenge the reigning "logos of domination." Marcuse's willing endorsement of the metaphor of a happy marriage between Marx and Freud can be understood in the same utopian spirit, which literally "fleshed out" Marx's abstract notion of human freedom after the revolution.[77]

The marriage, however, might also be understood in a far less harmonious way, as Freud could be read more in terms of Adorno's negative dialectics than the Hegelian totalizing alternative reimagined by Marcuse. If Marcuse can be said to have eclipsed Fromm in the 1960s, Adorno can be said to have done the same to Marcuse in the twenty-first century, and one reason was Adorno's less optimistic reading of Freud.[78] Adorno had, in fact, been interested in the philosophical implications of psychoanalysis as early as the 1920s, when he composed a *Habilitationsschrift* under the direction of neo-Kantian Hans Cornelius on "The Concept of the Unconscious in the Transcendental Theory of Mind,"[79] which praised Freud's cognitive disenchantment of the unconscious in the ultimate service of autonomy. In his more mature consideration of the philosophical implications of psychoanalysis, however, he struck a very different note. *Negative Dialectics*, published in 1966, included a "metacritique" of Kant's *Critique of Practical Reason* in which Adorno challenged the sway of consciousness philosophy based on the primacy of Kant's moral self or ego psychology's rational actor. Instead, he argued that "the dawning sense of freedom feeds upon the memory of the archaic impulse not yet steered by any solid I . . . Without an anamnesis of the untamed impulse that precedes the ego—an impulse later banished to the zone of unfree bondage to nature—it would be impossible to derive the idea of freedom, although that idea in turn ends up reinforcing the ego."[80] However much freedom is connected to the ability of an autonomous subject to act according to a rational will, it contains a trace of its preconscious, somatic desires, or, to repeat the formula from *Minima Moralia*, one should "situate utopia in blind somatic pleasure." Freud's materialist insistence on the claims of bodily pleasure meant that a purely rationalist philosophy based on consciousness alone or a rigorist moralism could not be truly emancipatory.[81] The attempt of idealist philosophy to banish psychologism had failed to understand the ways in which mind and body, culture and nature, were inevitably intertwined, although not identical.[82] The domination of external nature, Freud helped us to understand, was accompanied by a no less fateful domination of internal nature.

In addition to doubting the possibility of a full reconciliation of reason and desire, as well as Eros and Thanatos, in a utopian future, Adorno also continued to oppose the seamless integration of the social and the psychological, the harmonious unity that had motivated Fromm's notion of a "social character." Because of the erosion of the bourgeois family, there were no longer coherent, integrated subjects or unified personalities capable of being understood in holistic ways (even if this warning was temporarily suspended in *The Authoritarian Personality*). In addition, the attempt to mediate between the psychological and social levels of the totality through such a concept, Adorno argued, underestimated the value of maintaining the tension between them, as well as the comparable tension between the biological and the cultural, which could not be smoothed over without sacrificing one to the other. In a still antagonistic world without any immediate hope of reconciliation, the original hope of the Institute's interdisciplinary program—evident in the contributions of Horkheimer and Fromm to the initial issue of the *Zeitschrift*—was no longer viable:

> The separation of sociology and psychology is both correct and false. False because it encourages the specialists to relinquish the attempt to know the totality which even the separation of the two demand; and correct insofar as it registers more intransigently the split that has actually taken place in reality than does the premature unification at the level of theory.[83]

Ironically, the methodological tension between levels of analysis demanded by a fractured world could also be understood as prefiguring a potentially emancipatory outcome. Because the drives could not be entirely mastered by the prevailing social order, and id never fully become ego (let alone superego), there was always some hope for resistance to a world that might seem fully "administered" or "one-dimensional." Such resistance should not be understood, however, as serving the goal of an ultimately unified totality in which dialectical antitheses were harmoniously sublated, but rather a benign constellation of forces that would maintain difference without domination, and nonidentity without hierarchy. Because of Freud's acute sensitivity to the conflicts within the psyche and between it and the social/cultural world, psychoanalysis remained a valuable ally in the effort to promulgate a philosophy in which nonidentity could be understood as more than an obstacle to be overcome through a triumphalist process of dialectical mediation.

It was perhaps for this reason that even those members of the Frankfurt School who were unconvinced by the intransigently optimistic assumptions of *Eros and Civilization* continued to try to salvage the marriage of Freud and Marx in which they had so avidly invested their hopes before their exile. Although acknowledged as an open marriage, which welcomed ideas from other thinkers and traditions, it survived rough patches of mutual wariness to become an abiding feature of their common project. One of their first endeavors while reconstituting the Institute after the war was, in fact, a major conference, a series of seminars and a book of essays designed to reintroduce Freud to the German public on the occasion of his centenary in 1956.[84] In addition to restoring a tradition banished by the Nazis and highlighting the contributions of contemporary analysts such as Erik Erikson and Alexander Mitscherlich, these efforts were designed, as Horkheimer made clear in his introductory remarks, to revive a defensible notion of the Enlightenment, one in which, despite everything, the ideal of the autonomous individual might still mean something.[85] As he wrote to Löwenthal shortly before the conference took place:

> Such an event in Germany means that the backbone of enlightened cultural forces is being strengthened; because young people no longer know anything at all about these things but should experience them; because jurists, in view of the revision of the penal code, and because ministries and pedagogues, in view of the new laws governing the education of teachers, should be reminded of these things; because psychiatry in large part is a scandal. I am well aware of the risks associated with the whole undertaking, but it's one of those things that just about justify my being here.[86]

Through his assertion, Horkheimer demonstrated how much he maintained his youthful belief that Freud's work on the unconscious was not a capitulation to irrationalism, but rather an antidote to precisely that danger.[87] In so doing, he expressed the stubborn faith of the Frankfurt School as a whole that not only had there been a baleful "*dialectic of enlightenment*" in which emancipatory reason, reduced to instrumental rationality, had lost its way, but that also a "*dialectical* enlightenment," drawing on the lessons of psychoanalysis, might still somehow help us find it again.

5

Leo Löwenthal and the Jewish Renaissance

The unsublatable dialectic between particular and universal, pitting cultural difference against species-wide sameness, has rarely been as ferociously played out as in the struggle by German Jews to find a way to negotiate their hybrid identities. A considerable literature has been devoted to exploring its implications in the development of the first generation of Critical Theorists, culminating for the moment in Jack Jacobs's insightful survey of 2015, The Frankfurt School, Jewish Lives, and Anti-Semitism.[1] *Perhaps with the exception of Erich Fromm, Löwenthal was the member of the Frankfurt School whose positive identification with Jewish religious life was most intense, at least for a significant period of his youth. Unlike Walter Benjamin, whose integration of esoteric theological motifs into his work had no echo in efforts to become an observant Jew, Löwenthal was a full-fledged participant in the so-called "Jewish renaissance" of the early Weimar era. Repudiating the wan assimilationism of his liberal parents, he sought to harness the occluded energies of the orthodox tradition for radical purposes. Ultimately, his commitment waned and he returned to the more universalist values he had once scorned, albeit more Marxist than bourgeois in coloration. But, as he came to acknowledge, his passage through Jewish orthodoxy profoundly affected his later worldview. Although the apocalyptic messianism of his early religious infatuation passed, he never fully lost the utopian yearnings that were channeled into Critical Theory's "non-scientific wish" for a just and free world.[2]*

On January 24, 1922, twenty-one-year-old Leo Löwenthal,[3] then recovering from a bout of tuberculosis at the Black Forest spa of

Menzenschwand, received some shattering news from his friend Siegfried Kracauer in Frankfurt. That morning Rabbi Nehemiah Anton Nobel (1871–1922)[4] had suddenly and unexpectedly died at the age of only fifty-one. At that moment, Löwenthal, temporarily estranged from his father, was being supported at the spa by Rabbi Nobel.[5] "I know," Kracauer wrote,

> how profoundly sad you will be, how much you have lost with him, and extend to you my hand in deepest friendship. I was also indescribably shaken by the sudden death of this man, because I had honored and loved him, even if I knew him only from afar . . . he was entirely spirit—what others had taught, he *was*. I loved his *essence*, his wonderfully mild and unassuming goodness, which surrounded him like an atmosphere, yes, even radiated out from him to all—both deserved and undeserved. In an era of extreme skepticism and disbelief, he was to me the revelation of a genuine religious personality . . . was he one of the thirty *Zaddikim* who live in every generation?[6]

The powerful impact of Nobel's death was felt by others in the close-knit community of his young admirers, among them Franz Rosenzweig, who wrote to Martin Buber the following day:

> You will already have read in the newspaper of the terrible blow that has struck us here. Part of the basis of my life has been snatched from underfoot. We never know our future, but we can nevertheless see before us the beginning of the road that leads into the future. At least we call them fortunate who can see this beginning of the road before them. And until yesterday morning, I would have called myself thus.

Alluding to a "dark and seemingly hopeless conversation" he had had with Buber only shortly before Nobel's death, Rosenzweig pleaded, "stay with us, stay in this world for me!"[7]

As evidenced by this level of heartfelt anguish, Nobel was clearly no ordinary rabbi. He was the charismatic leader of an extraordinarily gifted group of young German Jewish intellectuals who were to make their mark in the Weimar Republic and gain even more fame during their exile in America and Palestine after 1933. He boasted the cultural *Bildung* of a German mandarin—his death came just after he gave the second of three planned lectures on Goethe—and the rigorous training of a professional philosopher who had written a dissertation on

Schopenhauer's theory of beauty in Bonn before going to Marburg to study with Hermann Cohen.[8] But he was also a spellbinding speaker who astounded audiences with his oratorical power. Writing to a friend after High Holy Day services in 1921, Rosenzweig groped for words to describe how moved he had been:

> Nobel's sermons were incredibly magnificent . . . it's impossible to describe . . . I have nothing to compare it with. Only the very greatest can be measured alongside of it. I, too, might have the ideas, after all, and many men have the rhetoric, but something else is involved here, a final quality, a rapture of the whole man, so that one wouldn't be surprised if he took wing in the end and disappeared. Nothing would be too audacious for him to risk saying at such moments, and there's nothing that would not be true coming from such a mouth.

After reminding his correspondent of his characteristic skepticism about all that Nobel represented—conservative Judaism, Zionism, mysticism, idealism—Rosenzweig nonetheless concluded:

> He prays the way one thinks of people praying only thousands of years ago when the great prayers originated; he speaks to the people as one thinks only the prophets should have been allowed to speak. It's really the Spirit as "cloudburst."[9]

For those in his thrall, Nobel was clearly a life-changing experience and his premature departure was truly traumatic. Löwenthal had found in him a permissive and nurturing father figure, to whom he could turn to legitimate his rebellion against his secular, assimilated, liberal father, a doctor with no patience for the more observant practices embraced, at least for a while, by his son.[10] In an essay he contributed to *Der jüdische Student*, Löwenthal wrote, "This death hit me with the force and unexpectedness of a great cosmic event, no, like the fall of an entire cosmos. Later this initial feeling revealed itself to me—as the thought of a space won back from wordless pain—as a key to understanding transience [*das Dahingegangene*]."[11] A half century later, he could still vividly recall the rabbi's impact, if now with a touch of ironic distance. Nobel, he told interviewer Helmut Dubiel, was

> a curious mixture of mystical religiosity, philosophical rigor, and quite likely also a more or less repressed homosexual love for young men. It

really was kind of a "cult community." He was a fascinating speaker. People flocked to hear his sermons. He kept his house open to all, and people would come and go as they pleased. Of course that was a godsend, especially in the chaotic years after World War I.[12]

Nobel's appeal, it is clear in retrospect, was enhanced not only by his remarkable personal magnetism and silver tongue, but also by the ability of his followers to see in him what they needed in a turbulent period of rapid and frightening change. He was an adherent of Orthodox Judaism, having studied rabbinics with German Orthodoxy's leading figure, Ezriel Hildesheimer, in Berlin, and a critic of the overly assimilationist Reform or liberal alternative that had attracted many adherents in the Wilhelmine period.[13] Yet he was also uneasy with the Orthodox establishment of his day, personally tolerant of all variants of Judaism, and able to maintain close friendships with more liberal figures like Leo Baeck.[14] A fervent defender of the German war effort and supporter of Hermann Cohen's optimistic claim that German culture and Judaism were fully compatible—he even designed the inscription in Hebrew and German for Cohen's tombstone in Berlin's Weissensee Cemetery—Nobel nonetheless identified with the Zionist project of a Jewish homeland. In 1904, in fact, he had been elected vice president of the Orthodox Zionist organization known as Mizrachi, which sought to counter religious hostility to the establishment of a Jewish state before the coming of the messiah.[15]

A strong believer in the importance of strictly observing Jewish law, Nobel was anything but an embodiment of the "dry legalism" alleged by many gentile critics from Kant on who accused Judaism of lacking devotional intensity and experiential immediacy. Instead, he was open to the recovery of mystical currents in Jewish thought, which were so tempting for many in the interwar era.[16] It was thus possible for figures like Buber, still not entirely past the romantic *Erlebnismystik* (experience mysticism) of his early years, and Rosenzweig, whose "new thinking" spurned the idealist rationalism of Cohen, to find him an inspiration.[17] Despite Buber's initial qualms about Nobel's defense of Orthodoxy, he joined Rosenzweig and thirteen other young admirers in presenting a *Festschrift* in 1921 to Rabbi Nobel to mark his fiftieth birthday.[18] It was a worthy monument to a figure who made a singular contribution to what became known as the Weimar "Jewish renaissance."[19]

The distinguished roster of contributors to Nobel's *Festschrift* included Buber, Kracauer, Ernst Simon, Rudolf Hallo, Richard Koch,

Eduard Strauss, Eugen Mayer, Max Michael, Joseph Prager, Bruno Strauss, Robert Weiss and Leo Löwenthal. Löwenthal's contribution had originally been prepared for a seminar at the University of Heidelberg in 1920, directed by no less a figure than Karl Jaspers, who was then known more as a psychologist than a philosopher. Contemptuous of what he saw as Jaspers's "scientistic positivism," Löwenthal audaciously directed his fire at the chapter on the demonic in Jaspers's recently published book, *The Psychology of Worldviews*, which he saw as "the devil incarnate." Preferring Goethe's understanding of the demonic as a link between the poet's genius and the divine, he disdained the reductionism he saw in Jaspers's account.[20] As he recalled years later, "At that time, I was in a mystical, radical, syncretic mood, a mixture of revolutionary radicalism, Jewish messianism, infatuation with an ontologically conceived phenomenology, acquaintance with psychoanalysis ... All of this was blended together to form a very missionary-messianic Bloch-like rapturous philosophy."[21] As might be expected, Ernst Bloch, whose recently published *Spirit of Utopia* had been a major influence on the young Löwenthal, later admired the essay, but Jaspers was less tolerant, indeed, as Löwenthal remembered it, "furious, even aggressive and insulting. He showed no pedagogical understanding for this young student who had just let these ideas pour out. After Jaspers's outburst, I stood up, bowed to my fellow students, and left the seminar room, slamming the door."[22]

Despite Rosenzweig and Kracauer's qualms, "The Demonic: Draft of a Negative Philosophy of Religion" appeared in the *Festschrift* for Nobel.[23] It is clearly the work of a talented, ambitious and overwrought young man, written in a florid style, syncretic in its adoption of arguments from many different sources and typical of the early expressionist years of the Weimar Republic. Even Edvard Munch's *The Scream* makes an appearance as an example of the "deep psychological secret of modern agony."[24] Like many other young Jews who were increasingly ambivalent about the mandarin ideology of *Bildung*, which had captivated assimilating German Jews for generations, Löwenthal looked for more radical solutions to the ills of modernity wherever he could find them.[25] In the words of Michael Löwy, who included Löwenthal in his admiring history of "Jewish libertarian thought in Central Europe," "The Demonic" "sketched the foundations of a negative theology which drew upon Marx, Lukács, and Bloch to argue that we are living in a world without God and without redemption, a cold world handed over to despair, a space between paradise and the Messiah which seeks God without finding him."[26] Citing Kierkegaard and Bloch, who argue that the demonic must ultimately be overcome, the work concludes: "At the end lies the ruin of all demonology, for the bright messianic light signifies the principled negation and destruction of all that is tenebrous. And the useful role of the demonic as that which interrogates without remainder is over in a final, all-comprehensive 'unio mystica' which finds its peace in God the Lord."[27] Many years later, Löwenthal himself would look back on the essay with the skepticism of maturity, calling it sarcastically "an almost unreadable 'master work'" and admitting "I barely understand a word of it now."[28] The exasperated Jaspers, it turns out, may have been right all along.

After the work's inclusion in Nobel's *Festschrift*, Kracauer wrote a delicately phrased, ambivalent letter, in which he acknowledged the personal depths out of which Löwenthal had composed the essay, admitting that he himself lacked the religious passion, "philosophical eros" and metaphysical urgency that he saw in the piece (and the work of other writers like Lukács). But he also criticized Löwenthal's undisciplined tone, which smacked too much of Bloch's histrionics.[29] Recalling a remark of Scheler's about Bloch, that his thought was "a running amok to God" (*Amoklauf zu Gott*), Kracauer said that characterization fit the piece as well. Reacting to Löwenthal's world-negating theological stance, he told his young friend: "Frankly, I *don't believe in the messianic time* (the 'fulfilled time' of Lukács means something different). I don't believe in *this* God, and when only *this* desperado attitude is religious, then am I an entirely unreligious man and will remain so."[30]

Although there remain echoes of his apocalyptic inclinations in the dissertation he wrote on the Catholic mystic Franz von Baader in 1923,[31] Löwenthal seems to have been sobered by his friend's critique, whose sentiments Kracauer more or less repeated even more vehemently a few years later in a letter following a reading of Rosenzweig's *Star of Redemption*.[32] Kracauer's disdain for what he saw as religious *Schwärmerei [rapturous effusion]* anticipated the more public 1926 break with other members of the Nobel circle that he announced in a spirited attack in the *Frankfurter Zeitung* on the initial volume of the translation of the Hebrew Bible by Buber and Rosenzweig.[33] But whereas Kracauer rarely again returned to Jewish themes—and when he did so, as in his 1937 biography of Jacques Offenbach, it was in banal terms that dismayed friends like Adorno and Benjamin[34]—Löwenthal continued to be actively involved in Jewish culture for the better part of the decade.

Serving on the Advisory Board for Jewish Refugees (*Beratungstelle für Ostjüdische Flüchtlinge*) and frequently lecturing to audiences at Jewish adult education centers, Löwenthal also wrote for community newspapers such as the *Bayerische Israelitische Gemeindezeitung*, along with Hannah Arendt and Gershom Scholem, and was coeditor with Ernst Simon of the *Jüdische Wochenzeitung*. But he grew progressively disaffected by the latter's unreflective support of Jewish settlements on Arab land in Palestine.³⁵ His allegiance to Zionism had in fact always been ambivalent. Although he joined a Zionist movement while a student in Heidelberg, he had reassured his parents in 1920: "I am not— perhaps still not—a Zionist. I am a searcher [*Suchender*], a problematic man. I will never be satisfied with a formula."³⁶ Yet he found other ways to affirm his Jewish identity. For example, Löwenthal remained an active member of the psychoanalytic circle around Frieda Reichmann, to whom he had been introduced by his wife Golde and introduced in turn to Erich Fromm, Reichmann's future husband. She was an observant Jew and a Zionist whose practice was sometimes called "Torahpeutic." Her sanatorium in Heidelberg, Löwenthal remembered, "was a kind of Jewish-psychoanalytic boarding school and hotel. An almost cultlike atmosphere prevailed there. Everyone, including me, was psychoanalyzed by Frieda Reichmann. The sanatorium adhered to Jewish religious laws; the meals were kosher, and religious holidays were observed. The Judeo-religious atmosphere intermingled with the interest in psychoanalysis." And then, notably, he added, "Somehow, in my recollection I sometimes link this syncretic coupling of the Jewish and the psychoanalytic traditions with our later 'marriage' of Marxist theory and psychoanalysis at the Institute, which was to play such a great role in my intellectual life."³⁷

Before, however, turning to the meaning of that parallel, it is necessary to attend to another aspect of Löwenthal's continued involvement with Jewish issues in the 1920s: the series of lectures he composed on a number of eminent German Jewish thinkers and intended to turn into a book called *Judaism and Jewishness in Recent German Philosophy*.³⁸ As early as 1922, in an essay he wrote jointly with Ernst Simon, Erich Fromm, Fritz Goethin and Erich Michaelis, he had bemoaned the anti-intellectual celebration of Hasidism espoused by naive followers of Martin Buber, who knew nothing of the deeper intellectual resources in the German Jewish tradition itself.³⁹ In a series of talks given at the Frankfurt Lehrhaus and other Jewish venues in western Germany, Löwenthal explored the contributions of a number of major European intellectuals with Jewish backgrounds, from Maimonides, Moses Mendelssohn, Salomon Maimon and Heinrich Heine to Karl Marx, Ferdinand Lassalle, Hermann Cohen and Sigmund Freud.[40] Löwenthal was careful to include figures who were both identified and not identified with specifically Jewish themes, figures from western Germany alongside those who had eastern origins (understood more in terms of their biographical struggles than the former), and those struggling with emancipation into bourgeois society as well as those struggling to escape from it.

The first thing that strikes the contemporary reader of these talks is the depth of Löwenthal's mastery of the work and lives of a very wide range of difficult thinkers. These do not seem the tentative exercises of a beginner still in his mid-twenties, but rather the reflections of someone who has been immersed in the material over a long career. Deftly interweaving intellectual and personal elements into the stories he tells, Löwenthal explores the challenges facing Jews moving from traditional identities into the modern world, bourgeois, secular, and assimilated, but without leaving behind the still-potent legacy of their religious heritage. He probes the attempts from Maimonides to Cohen to reconcile Judaism and rationality, the dialectic in Judaism between obedience to the law and vital experience, and the tension between national assertion and universal ideals.

Perhaps Löwenthal's most vivid portrait is of Heine, whose study begins with a blunt question: "Why did Heine become a Christian?" Tacitly resonating with the reason for Heine's disillusionment, he argues that the poet was deeply alienated from the watered-down Reform Judaism in the Germany of his day, which had left behind its creative period in the time of Mendelssohn and turned into a veiled version of Christianity, the pseudo-faith of what he called the "Sunday Jews."[41] Rather than returning to an earlier version of Judaism, which Heine mistakenly identified with dogmatic fanaticism and wan legalism, he chose baptism, but not only, as his famous explanation had it, as an entry ticket to European culture. By adopting Christianity, Heine, as Löwenthal described him, was really struggling to realize the redemptive mission of Judaism, understood in universal terms. "Heine had submitted to Christianity in order to be able to destroy it in a messianic rage ... To Heine European culture means the Europe of the French Revolution, it means the possibility of a joyful, free and full life ... it is a horrible historical irony that this specifically Jewish side of Heine, this love for a worthy life of free persons, is what drove him out of Judaism."[42]

Judaism, especially in its prophetic tradition, was thus the source of a more universal impulse that survived Heine's self-exile from a version of it that failed to realize its most ambitious goals.

Something similar informed Löwenthal's reading of Marx. The disturbing expression of anti-Semitism in Marx's notorious essay "On the Jewish Question," whose odiousness Löwenthal does not try to deny, is attributed to Marx's "profound ignorance of Jewish cultural values." But he then adds, "There remains in spite of it all, the twofold nature of his claim—on the one hand, the protest against the fact that Judaism can be the symbol of capitalism; on the other, the Jewish-universalist manner in which the protest is carried out."[43] Likewise, in the final essay of the series, which focused on Sigmund Freud a few weeks after he received Frankfurt's Goethe Prize—an honor Löwenthal had done much to assure—he squeezed out of Freud's Jewish background a very general lesson: "If we want to speak of Freud's relation to Judaism . . . we must direct our attention to those qualities he displays in the whole of life . . . Help and reconstruction for individuals and for society as a whole—that is the star that illumines Freud's life and work."[44]

By the time of that final essay in the series, Löwenthal's overtly Jewish commitments had palpably waned. Perhaps he had absorbed some of Kracauer's sourness about the enthusiasms of his youth; perhaps he was reflecting the general turn in Weimar culture against the apocalyptic messianism of the early expressionist years; perhaps he was over his rebellion against his parents and their values. Whatever the cause, he had already joined the third of the outsider intellectual communities—the first two being Nobel's circle and the psychoanalytic group around Fromm-Reichmann—that would become a more permanent resting place for his contrarian and utopian strivings: the Institute for Social Research. He had been introduced to Max Horkheimer by his school-time friend Felix Weil, whose wealthy father's generosity had financed the Institute's founding in 1924. Horkheimer had himself never been in the thrall of Rabbi Nobel, remembering many years later that "I must say emphatically that I did not belong to that circle, I did not know the Rabbi, I had never seen him . . . I didn't belong already for the reason that this Rabbi was the complete opposite of liberal Judaism, he represented conservative Judaism."[45] Adorno, three years younger than Löwenthal and also a protégé of Kracauer, had even less use for Nobel and his circle, although he may have found some indirect inspiration in Rosenzweig's ideas as conveyed by Benjamin and Scholem.[46] Only half-Jewish in origin—his mother had a Catholic background—and raised by a fully assimilated father who displayed a "somewhat ostentatious aversion to everything that was consciously Jewish,"[47] Adorno neither was drawn to the *Ostjuden* nor had much respect for their champions like Martin Buber. Nor did he ever consider, let alone try to realize, a return to Orthodox practice as a rebuke to his parents (in fact, he never really rebelled against his parents at all).[48] Löwenthal and Fromm, he dismissively remarked to Horkheimer, were "professional Jews."[49] As his influence in the Institute grew and Fromm's diminished, the palpable residues of Jewish themes were attenuated.

Assessments of the Frankfurt School's debts to Jewish sources, while often reluctantly acknowledged, have been attempted a number of times.[50] While it is clear that anti-Semitism became a focal point of the School's work, especially in the wake of the Holocaust, they often tended to subsume specifically Jewish themes and issues under larger rubrics.[51] The most egregious example of this approach was Horkheimer's 1939 essay "The Jews and Europe," which occasioned a violent condemnation by Scholem in the last letter he ever sent to Benjamin before the latter's suicide.[52] Despite its title, the essay virtually ignored Jewish issues and concentrated on the relationship between fascism and capitalism.

Löwenthal was, however, a partial exception to this rule. He seems, for example, to have remained convinced that Heine's Jewish identity was central to his cosmopolitan redemptive project. In 1947, he published a translation of his Weimar essay in *Commentary*, the major organ of the liberal Jewish intelligentsia in America, then edited by Elliot Cohen.[53] In his account of the Institute's American years, Thomas Wheatland focuses on the role of this essay in cementing relations between Horkheimer's circle and the New York intellectuals of that era. It was, he writes, "a powerfully crafted example of the kind of Jewish exploration that Cohen and the rest of the editorial board of *Commentary* were encouraging. The figure of Heinrich Heine functioned for Löwenthal as a symbol for the problems faced by the entire New York Intellectual community and by many German-Jewish exiles as well."[54] Rather than being a way station to full conversion or assimilation and the loss of any residual Jewish identification, Heine's journey ended with his disillusionment with Christianity and was best understood as a cautionary tale. "Thus, through Heine," Wheatland concludes, "was Löwenthal able to discover a distinctly Jewish identity consistent with Critical Theory and the prewar political impulses that gathered the Horkheimer circle together . . . In the wake of the war, Heine stood as a symbol—perhaps all Jewish exiles could return home."[55]

But when other members of the School turned their attention to figures like Heine after the Holocaust, they did not adopt Löwenthal's earlier focus on his Jewish roots. Thus, for example, Adorno's powerful talk for the Heine centenary in 1956, "Heine the Wound," refers to Judaism only obliquely and not as a legacy worth preserving.[56] Heine's romantic lyric poetry, he argues, was ultimately a failure, because it could not really attain the fluency it sought in the German language.[57] As such, it was an expression of the failure of Jewish emancipation, which now has become emblematic of a more general human condition of homelessness. "There is no longer any homeland other than a world in which no one would be cast out any more, the world of a genuinely emancipated humanity. The wound that is Heine will heal only in a society that has achieved reconciliation."[58] Here the conclusion drawn by Adorno was diametrically opposed to the more optimistic lesson that, if Wheatland is right, was implied in Löwenthal's piece.

In Jürgen Habermas's 1986 essay "Heinrich Heine and the Role of the Intellectual in Germany," even less attention is paid to his Jewish background, as Heine is portrayed as a critical Enlightenment "intellectual"—a word with negative connotations in Germany—who was marginalized by the mandarin *Geistigen* who dominated German letters until after World War II.[59] It is Heine the hedonist, the democrat, the politically engaged thinker who nonetheless defended artistic autonomy, rather than Heine the self-questioning Jew, who is at the center of Habermas's analysis. Although noting in passing that "the hatred that battered Heine as a Jew and an intellectual all his life made him well aware of the double-edged nature"[60] of German nationalism, Habermas ignored any positive legacy that Heine might have taken from the Jewish tradition.

Admittedly, Löwenthal himself, for a long time after the publication of his essay in *Commentary*, was inclined to do the same. Perhaps because the ethnic identities of the Institute's members had so often been evoked by its enemies, he and his colleagues were reticent to give them ammunition for the slurs.[61] Although sharing the Frankfurt School's frequent identification of the Jewish taboo on picturing God with their own reluctance to spell out what utopia might look like, he distanced himself from what he dismissively called the later Horkheimer's adoption of "concrete religious symbolism."[62] Only in interviews he gave near the end of his life did he acknowledge that he had underestimated the importance of Jewish motifs in his work and those of his colleagues at the Institute.[63] "I do believe," he conceded, "that a Jewish element, if you want to call it that, was alive in most of us, consciously or unconsciously, in the sense of 'it is yet to come,' that is, of hope, of the unspeakable, which cannot be named but only sensed, which can only be negatively determined. And that I want to acknowledge even today, for it does unite in a certain way, the hope, now seriously compromised, for a life of dignity for every person with the thought that that will probably not happen and that a tragic element is bound irrevocably to our life."[64]

But if one can say that Löwenthal's Jewish impulses—and those of Fromm, Benjamin and, in a more attenuated way, most of his other Institute colleagues—found their way into Critical Theory, what about his contribution to the Weimar Jewish renaissance itself? In many ways his participation was typical of his generation, rebelling against parental authority and conventional mandarin academic life, looking for a new community of belief, often led by a charismatic leader.[65] Although some of the other young Jews who came of age during or after World War I and were swept up in the apocalyptic mood of those years remained more or less in its thrall, Löwenthal moved quickly on. His Zionism, such as it was, was already a thing of the past by his twenty-fifth birthday, and he never contemplated migration to Palestine. Nor did his writing retain any marks of the expressionist rapture that had entranced Bloch—and appalled Kracauer—in his early essay "The Demonic." The inspiration for his personal attempt to live an Orthodox life did not long survive the death of Rabbi Nobel, and by his mid-twenties he had cast his lot with the materialists around Horkheimer at the Institute.[66]

In retrospect, Löwenthal's trajectory looks as if it moved him past the Jewish renaissance and back into another version of the universalist assimilationism, albeit no longer of the liberal variety, that he had spurned in his father's generation. But if we take a more capacious view of the ways in which Jewish life renewed itself during that era, we might discern another conclusion. To reach it, we must return to Löwenthal and Rosenzweig's expressions of sorrow upon Rabbi Nobel's sudden death, as both demonstrated the profound loss they felt. Significantly, however, only a short while after the Rabbi's death, Rosenzweig presented a far more nuanced picture to his friend Joseph Prager:

You evidently don't know how I stood with Nobel. More particularly, you are unaware of the negative side of our relationship. I respected only the Talmudic Jew, not the humanist, only the poet, not the scholar, only the prophet, not the philosopher. I rejected the qualities I did reject because, in the form in which he had them, they were deeply un-Jewish. At least this is what I always felt. All my veneration and love never blinded me to this toying with Christian and pagan ideas. True, it couldn't do me any harm, since I am armored against this kind of temptation as perhaps no Jew in *galut* [exile] has been before me. But in the effect he had on others I was always aware of the poison mixed with the medicine . . . had I met him sooner, say ten years ago, he might *possibly* have driven me away from Judaism, more likely he would have completely ruined me.[67]

And then he added, with a touch of arrogance, "What I have learned from Nobel is that the soul of a *great* Jew can accommodate many things. There is danger only for the little souls."[68]

From Rosenzweig's perspective, Löwenthal's later development away from his Jewish commitments would seem to corroborate this fear. Nobel's inspiration in his case did allow for an openness to the broader currents of German thought, if still intermingled with residues of the Jewish. But whether or not this trajectory can be taken as evidence of a "little soul" is something else. Rosenzweig may have had a very exclusivist notion of what constituted unpolluted Jewish purity, but we need not follow his lead. As David Biale has recently shown in his masterful study of the tradition of Jewish secular thought, there has been a robust alternative to normative definitions of "authentic" Jewish identity, whether understood religiously or culturally.[69] Rather than niggling over the proper credentials for inclusion in a club of the righteous, it has opened its doors to a wide range of people whose debts to and identifications with the rich legacy of Jewish experience and textual reflections on it are not homogeneous. Ironically, even those figures like Löwenthal who did not tarry with the religious identities they once fashioned in rebellion against their assimilated parents must be accounted fullfledged participants in that narrative.

At the end of his study of the Weimar Jewish renaissance, Michael Brenner turns to the towering figure of Hebrew novelist and Nobel Prize laureate Shmuel Yosef Agnon. "In contrast to most German-Jewish authors," he writes, "Agnon abstained from both stigmatizing German-Jews as assimilated 'non-Jewish Jews' and idealizing 'authentic' East European Jews . . . Agnon demonstrated his respect for the multifaceted achievements of German Jews."[70] The young Leo Löwenthal would not have agreed with this verdict, but as he matured and left behind—or more correctly, tempered—the apocalyptic intransigence and messianic yearnings of his early years, he would surely have come to recognize its wisdom. Indeed, only through his remarkable capacity to absorb impulses from many different sources, no matter their religious or cultural pedigree, did Löwenthal develop into the genuine Renaissance man that those of us privileged to have known him remember so well.

6

Adorno and Blumenberg: Nonconceptuality and the *Bilderverbot*

Although in their more utopian moments, the members of the Frankfurt School could draw on Freud's instinct theory to adumbrate the "other" of the current "administered world," they adamantly refused to spell out what it might look like in specific terms. Marx and his followers had often resisted the temptation to describe the future "realm of freedom" from the vantage point of the current "realm of necessity," but Horkheimer and his colleagues drew on an added incentive, which they identified with the traditional Jewish Bilderverbot or forbidding of graven images. A comparable prohibition, they argued, should stifle attempts to provide detailed, realistic depictions of the dystopian horror that came to be called the Holocaust. When Adorno famously cautioned against writing poetry "after Auschwitz," he may have been advocating less a ban on poetry per se than on the naive restoration of sentimental lyric poetry, but whatever his precise target, he was warning against the limitations of representational or expressive language.[1]

Visual ascesis, however, had an even more general implication. Although what he called the "nonconceptual" was a necessary antidote to the domination of concepts tied by Adorno to the predominance of subjects over objects in the "dialectic of enlightenment," visual perception was not its most valid expression. Instead, the nonconceptual proper name that harkens back, as Benjamin had contended, to the Adamic "true" names assigned in the Garden of Eden, provides a more promising alternative, which also manifests in music's ability to communicate without signification through the absolute unity of object and sign.

To appreciate Adorno's nuanced alternative to images as the "other" of dominating concepts in his "negative dialectics," this chapter compares

*his defense of "nonconceptuality" with that of the distinguished German
Jewish historian of ideas and philosopher, Hans Blumenberg. It argues
that whereas the latter defended rhetoric, metaphor and myth as cultural
expedients designed to ward off the inherent meaninglessness of the
world, Adorno—drawing on his reading of Freud—once again insisted
on the importance of instincts as a reservoir of resistance to extreme
cultural constructivism, a block to the power of the constitutive subject.
They represented the internal "other" that an overly constructivist philosophy attempted to suppress in the name of subjective domination, which
manifested itself in the attempt of concepts to master the objects under
their sway. As such, instincts could be understood as part of an emancipatory constellation that included nonconceptual names along with
concepts that could also function as more than just instruments of subjective domination.*[2]

In 1967, only one year after Theodor W. Adorno published *Negative
Dialectics*, a seminar was devoted to it at the University of Bochum. The
class was led by philosopher Hans Blumenberg (1920–96), who had
himself just published his first major work, *The Legitimacy of the Modern
Age*.[3] We have no record of the seminar discussions, nor did Blumenberg
ever write a sustained evaluation of Adorno's book. But much in it was
likely to have pleased him, as it echoed many arguments he himself had
recently advanced. In particular, *Negative Dialectics* mounted a sustained
and nuanced defense of "nonconceptuality" (*Unbegrifflichkeit*),[4] which
bore a remarkable resemblance to the critique of the privileged role of
concepts that Blumenberg had previously leveled in service of a new
philosophical discipline he called "metaphorology."[5] Adorno never
publicly expressed any awareness of these similarities, nor did he live
long enough to respond to Blumenberg's later *Work on Myth*, which, in
many ways, was in conversation with *Dialectic of Enlightenment*.
Although he did contact Blumenberg in September 1967 to convey his
positive first impressions of *The Legitimacy of the Modern Age*, he seems
to have been entirely ignorant of Blumenberg's earlier work on metaphor as an alternative to concepts.[6]

For his part, Blumenberg signaled a certain solidarity with Adorno
by employing the term "nonconceptuality" in his mid-1970s lectures,
published posthumously in 2007 as *Theorie der Unbegrifflichkeit*.[7] His
first in-print acknowledgement came in 1979, when Blumenberg
appended an essay entitled "Prospect for a Theory of Nonconceptuality"
to his little book *Shipwreck with Spectator*, the title of which referred to

one of the many paradigmatic metaphors whose histories he was to trace with astounding erudition over his long career.[8] Although their political investments were very different and Blumenberg, unlike Adorno, did not play a role in the public debate over the legacy of Nazism, on this one issue they shared a common enthusiasm.

Blumenberg had in fact already begun exploring nonconceptuality avant la lettre in 1957, in his path-breaking essay on "Light as a Metaphor for Truth: At the Preliminary Stage of Concept Formation."[9] As his subtitle reveals, however, he had then believed that metaphors should be primarily considered inchoate anticipations of concepts. "In constantly having to confront the unconceptualized and preconceptualized," he wrote, "philosophy encounters the means of articulation found in this nonconceptualizing and preconceptualizing, adopts them, and develops them further in separation from their origin." But he then added: "The notion that the philosophical logos has 'overcome' prephilosophical mythos has narrowed our view of the scope of philosophical terminology; besides concepts in the strict sense, which are measured off by definition and fulfilled intuition [Anschauung], there is a broad range of mythical transformations, bordering on metaphysical conjectures, which find expression in a metaphorics with diverse forms."[10] We can discern here not only a plea for attending to the non- and preconceptual sources of philosophical concepts in their own right, but also an anticipation of Blumenberg's later interest in the abiding importance of myth, which he came to include with metaphor as a nonconceptual alternative to the hegemony of logos and conceptualization.[11]

These prefigurations of his later position further manifested in 1960, when Blumenberg was asked to contribute to the emerging field of "conceptual history" (Begriffsgeschichte) then being developed by Erich Rothacker, Otto Brunner and Reinhart Koselleck. Although he accepted the invitation, the result was a slyly subversive text entitled Paradigms for a Metaphorology, published in 1960 both in the Archiv für Begriffsgeschichte and as a separate book.[12] In it, Blumenberg challenged the still powerful assumption, which he identified with the Cartesian stress on clarity and distinctness, that philosophical concepts should be demarcated by definitions that overcame their polysemic play and effaced their sedimented history. Blumenberg argued instead that Nietzsche had been right in The Genealogy of Morals to point out that "only that which has no history is definable."[13] In echoing this position, Blumenberg was, to be sure, embracing the newly formulated program of conceptual history, which also stressed the value of tracing a concept's development over time with no teleological favoritism showed to its current usage or archaic privileging of its alleged origin.

But—and this is where the subversion took place—unlike Rothacker, Brunner, Koselleck and their colleagues, he then explicitly rejected the idea, operative in his earlier essay on light as a metaphor for truth, that all metaphors were merely primitive elements left over in the transition from mythos to logos. From Edmund Husserl—or, more precisely, the later Husserl who had authored *The Crisis of European Sciences and Transcendental Phenomenology*—Blumenberg had learned that the discursive world of concepts is rooted in a still vibrant, prereflective "lifeworld," the realm of everyday experience, in which the roles of rhetoric in general and metaphor in particular are key. But, rather than trying to transcend these origins in the name of cultural progress and conceptual clarification, it was important, he came to believe, to acknowledge that some lifeworld metaphors remained "*foundational elements* of philosophical language, 'translations' that resist being converted back into authenticity and logicality."[14] As such, they can be called "absolute" metaphors, which, although vulnerable to historical change, nonetheless "prove resistant to terminological claims and cannot be dissolved into conceptuality."[15]

There is much in Blumenberg's defense of metaphoric nonconceptuality that will be familiar to readers of Adorno. In the opening entry in his 1958 *Notes to Literature*, "The Essay as Form," he also endorsed Nietzsche's critique of Descartes: "Just as the essay rejects primordial givens, so it rejects definition of its concepts" and "gently challenges the ideal of *clara et distincta perceptio* and indubitable certainty."[16] His 1963 essay, "Skoteinos, or How to Read Hegel," once again criticized the Cartesian fetish of clarity and distinctness, noting, albeit without citing Blumenberg, its origins in religious notions of divine light.[17] In *Jargon of Authenticity*, which appeared in the following year, Adorno expatiated on the dangers of adhering to a dubious model of authenticity in language, philosophical or otherwise, which foreclosed the ambiguous play of terms that were in healthy excess of their mandated definitions or alleged original meanings.[18] And, most significant of all, in *Negative Dialectics*, he advanced a complicated argument against the potential tyranny of concepts and the importance of valuing what was irreducible to their domination, a tyranny against which he and Max Horkheimer had already warned in the early sections of *Dialectic of Enlightenment*.

In what follows, I want to examine the overlap between Blumenberg's and Adorno's appreciations of nonconceptuality as a counterweight—although never a fully self-sufficient alternative—to the traditional philosophical preference for rigorous conceptualization. Although showing the ways in which their positions overlapped—in, for example, their embrace of the nonsublatable dialectic of concepts and their negations—I will also argue that they diverged in important ways. To anticipate my conclusion, they differed most over the relative roles that subjects and objects play in generating the nonconceptual "other" of concepts. There is, it turns out, a nonidentity in their understanding of the alternatives to conceptual hegemony and in the tasks they assign to them. By playing one against the other, we may reach a more nuanced understanding of the stakes involved in their respective projects.

It might seem prudent to begin such a comparison by defining the relevant terms and clarifying what each of our protagonists meant both by *a concept* and by *nonconceptuality*. But once we start to do so, we are confronted immediately with a dilemma that both Blumenberg and Adorno themselves fully appreciated. In *Negative Dialectics*, Adorno acknowledged it head on in considering the implications of providing an alternative positive ontology to the one he disdained in other thinkers such as Hegel and Heidegger:

> In criticizing ontology we do not aim at another ontology, not even one of being nonontological. If that were our purpose we would be merely positing another downright "first"—not absolute identity, this time, not the concept, not Being, but nonidentity, facticity, entity. We would be hypostasizing the concept of nonconceptuality and thus acting counter to its meaning.[19]

Although "nonconceptuality," Adorno conceded, might not be able to avoid being turned into a weak "concept," we should at least resist a nondialectical assertion of it as a strong one, thus effacing and neutralizing its internal tensions, historical variations and critical potential. It must be employed instead like an apophatic term in negative theology, which can only indirectly gesture toward what it cannot positively express.

Blumenberg was no less sensitive than Adorno to the dangers in the hypostasizing reconceptualization of the nonconceptual, the turning of what was irreducibly singular into merely an example of an abstract generality and nothing more. Although he was perhaps not fully successful—how, after all, can we see metaphor and myth as instances of "nonconceptuality" unless we acknowledge at least some generalizing abstraction in that term?—he performatively sought to undermine it, especially when he came to developing his argument about the role of metaphor. "It is remarkable," Anselm Haverkamp writes, "that *Metaphorology* does not contain even the slightest hint of a definition of the term metaphor itself, and retrospectively it can only be doubly striking that Blumenberg makes no attempt . . . to deduce a definition of metaphor in terms of its conceptual history, almost as if metaphor— possibly it alone—had no history."[20] That is, not only does he try to deny "metaphor" the status of an ahistorical concept in the manner of traditional philosophy, but he also denies it the status of one even in the antidefinitional, historical terms of *Begriffsgeschichte*. Thus, in his programmatic introduction of metaphorology in the aforementioned 1960 contribution to the *Archiv der Begriffsgeschichte*, he was careful to present only a series of exemplary "paradigms" of his proposed approach. Among them were the figures of "mighty truth," "naked truth" and "probability" (in German, *Wahrscheinlichkeit*, which contained *Schein*, implying both a shining forth and a deceptive semblance). In the spirit of what Kant had called reflective rather than determinant judgments in *Critique of Judgment*, he sought to avoid positing a general rule and subsuming examples under it as mere illustrations. Instead, he contended that nonconceptuality must be evoked ostensively—by pointing at instances—or demonstrated performatively rather than categorically defined. For there was no fully external observer position from which the scholar of nonconceptuality could examine it, as it were, from the outside or above, employing a meta-language itself entirely free of metaphoric indeterminacy and play.[21] Although not as insistent on the aporetic tensions of an implicitly metaphysical "ology" of metaphor as, say, Jacques Derrida was to be in his seminal 1971 essay, "White Mythology: Metaphor in the Text of Philosophy," Blumenberg, like Adorno, appreciated the performative contradiction entailed by conceptualizing the nonconceptual.[22] He understood that metaphors abetted what Husserl had called "resistance to harmony" because, as inherently transpositional figures—metaphor comes from the Greek for "carrying over"—they introduce a heterogeneous element into the differentia homogenized by concepts.[23]

But, it should quickly be added, both Blumenberg and Adorno also merged in resisting the temptation, call it either radical nominalist or romantic, to valorize nonconceptuality as a straightforward and self-sufficient antidote to the domination of concepts tout court. They acknowledged instead the necessity of conceptualization as a valuable tool in the human struggle to make sense of and survive in a world that provided no intrinsic signposts. In Blumenberg's case, this necessity was given an explicitly anthropological foundation, which he largely derived from Arnold Gehlen's notion of humans as "*Mängelwesen*" (creatures of deficiency).[24] From Gehlen, he learned that, despite the poverty of our instincts, our fecund cultural imagination allows "world-open" humans to compensate as best they can for the relative lack of the biological preprogramming that allows other animals to orient themselves automatically in the world. Rather than a fixed human nature, there is only a human condition that requires the ad hoc development of technologies, cultural and otherwise, to cope with the challenges faced since hominids left behind the unreflective patterns of instinctual behavior. Often drawing on delay and indirection, they allow us to stave off the dire challenges of an unforgiving environment.

To meet those challenges, both concepts and nonconcepts—most notably among the latter, metaphor and myth[25]—have consoled humankind for the opaque contingency of a world bereft of inherent meaning, as well as provided practical guidance to survive its dangers. What Blumenberg called the resistance of "absolute reality" to full mastery or comprehensibility could only be met with such temporary expedients, some pragmatically more successful than others, but none providing permanent solutions. Myths offer a limited sense of security and purpose by personifying forces of nature and narrativizing events whose underlying causes were occluded. Metaphors lessen anxiety by guiding us through the unfamiliar and distant via a healthy detour through the familiar and proximate.[26] And concepts make sense of the seemingly inscrutable particularities of the here and now through broader spatial and temporal categories that permit some predictive control over a future that is not entirely random and haphazard. But even if they can temporarily compensate us for our vulnerabilities in an unforgiving world, none of these expedients brings us really closer to a truthful understanding of reality. If one answer falters, another fills the space left behind, but there is no unidirectional progress from mythos to logos or metaphor to concepts. "Demythicization," Blumenberg insisted, "is in large measure nothing more than remetaphorization."[27]

Another way to formulate Blumenberg's position is to say that he was critical of both ontological universalism—in, for example, the conceptual realism of Scholastic philosophy—and the ontological particularism of its nominalist critics, which culminated in the modern positivist fetish of individual facts and entities. Against the competing impulses to synthesize and analyze, he defended the value of relationality, which maintained the difference of particulars while also avoiding the isolation of what was not identical. "Analogy," he claimed "is the realism of metaphor." In fact, metaphors and concepts are alike in their ability to represent what is not present, to introduce a productive gap between what the senses register and what language can say. "The *animal symbolicum* masters the reality that is originally lethal for him by letting it be represented; he looks away from what is uncanny or uncomfortable for him and towards what is familiar."[28] Not only is this tactic evident in the rhetorical realm, where metaphor plays a key role, but it is also in the practical one, where ritualized sacrifice draws on the power of representational substitution.[29]

Not surprisingly, Blumenberg was allergic to efforts, most notably those of Heidegger, to undo entirely the distinction between conceptuality and nonconceptuality by recovering an equiprimordial unity prior to the split. His engagement with Heidegger began with his unpublished *Habilitationschrift*, *Die ontologische Distanz*, in 1950 and continued throughout his life.[30] In *Work on Myth*, Blumenberg analyzed Heidegger's dispute with Ernst Cassirer at Davos, resisting the widespread conclusion that Cassirer had lost.[31] The latter's functionalist interpretation of myth, even if in the service of a questionable progressivist belief in the victory of *logos* over *mythos*, was superior to attempts to rescue myth as a repository of the eternal wisdom of the species. Moreover, insofar as Heidegger's insistence on the priority of Being over human beings meant a denigration of philosophical anthropology and its implications for nonconceptuality, Blumenberg remained wary of it. Already in *Paradigms for a Metaphorology*, he noted ironically that "the perfection and comprehensiveness with which one can deal with 'Being' is quite unattainable in this field."[32] In "Prospect for a Theory of Nonconceptuality," he expanded his critique, noting that Heidegger's ruminations on the "meaning of Being" failed to credit the logic of substitution that always informed metaphoric displacement.[33] In a 1987 essay, he playfully enlisted Alfred Hitchcock's celebrated notion of a "MacGuffin"—a gimmick in a movie that claims to possess meaning but is utterly bereft of it, which thus generates unfulfillable curiosity— as a surrogate for Heidegger's Being itself. In so doing, he ironically metaphorized precisely the numinous word Heidegger had claimed pointed to something beyond both concepts and metaphors.[34]

Blumenberg's argument can be spun out still further on its own, but I want to compare it now to that in Adorno's *Negative Dialectics*, where the unsublatable dialectic of concepts and nonconceptuality was also a major concern. Perhaps the first point to make is that Adorno was even more relentless than Blumenberg in his condemnation of Heidegger's bid to return to an equiprimordial moment prior to the distinction. The dangerous mission of Heidegger's archaicism, he charged, is to "heal the concept 'Being' of the wound of its conceptuality, of the split between thought and its concept . . . In this ontology, Being must be defined by itself alone because it is held to be neither comprehensible in concepts— in other words, neither 'transmitted'—nor immediately demonstrable after the model of sensory ascertainment. In lieu of any critical authority for Being we get a reiteration of the mere name."[35] The result is to isolate Heidegger's thought from any possible critique: "that Being is neither a fact nor a concept exempts it from any criticism."[36]

Second, while both Adorno and Blumenberg resisted Heidegger's attempt to overcome the inevitable tension between conceptuality and nonconceptuality and suture the wounds of Being, they nonetheless shared his concern that concepts can easily devolve into rigid and static categories abstractly homogenizing the differences they claim to subsume. Correctly applied, dialectics should serve as a protest against the reification of concepts. "The concept in itself, previous to any content, hypostatizes its own form against the content. With that, however, it is already hypostatizing the identity principle."[37] Even Hegel had mistakenly sought to sublate harmoniously what a negative dialectics kept apart. Although right in noting that particular entities are always mediated by the whole and cannot, *pace* nominalists and positivists, be grasped in their isolation, he failed, Adorno charged, to valorize the resistance of those entities to being smoothly absorbed by those mediations: "The triumphant finding that immediacy is wholly indirect rides roughshod over indirectness and blithely ends up with the totality of the concept, which nothing conceptual can stop any more. It ends up with the absolute rule of the subject."[38]

Finally, both Blumenberg and Adorno were suspicious of what is often considered the most obvious alternative to the potential domination of the concept: direct perceptual experience. Along with subpersonal representational states and the behavior of other animals and preconceptual infants, perception has emerged as the favorite exemplar of nonconceptuality for analytic philosophers.[39] Perceptual experience, they argue, cannot be adequately expressed in the propositional terms that are a necessary element of conceptual thought. Unlike concepts, perception can experience states of affairs that are contradictory (such as Escher staircases) or are irreducible to discrete units (such as distances that are experienced without precise measurement), or are more fine-grained than propositional or generic concepts can accommodate (for example, the infinite gradations of colors). They are also developmentally prior in children to the concepts that are acquired with language.

Although agreeing on the limits of propositional thought, Blumenberg and Adorno were nonetheless uneasy with calling perceptual experience the primary "other" of conceptuality.[40] This unease manifested in their refusal to elevate one perceptual experience in particular, which was traditionally understood to come through the noblest of the senses, vision. Before I turn to the differences separating them, I want to linger for a while with their reluctance to identify visual perception as the quintessential vehicle of nonconceptuality. Whatever the actual influence of their half-Jewish backgrounds, which may have been more of a post facto justification than actual cause, both appreciated the abiding power of the so-called religious *Bilderverbot*, the iconoclastic prohibition first enunciated in the Second Commandment as recorded in Exodus 20:4: "Thou shalt not make unto thyself any graven image." The secular philosophical implications of this prohibition have, of course, been widely recognized, ever since Kant invoked it in his exploration of the idea of the sublime.[41] Its role in modern interpretations of the Mosaic legacy by figures as diverse as Freud and Schoenberg has also been the object of endless discussion, as has its ethical import in the work of postmodernists like Jean-François Lyotard.[42] But both Blumenberg and Adorno made special use of it in explaining their ideas about the role of nonconceptuality.

In "Prospect for a Theory of Nonconceptuality," Blumenberg argued that concepts often generalize from what is experienced sensually. In contrast, symbols and especially metaphors move away from what is directly experienced to something absent. "What is decisive," Blumenberg insisted, "is that this elementary organ of the relation to the world makes possible a turning away from perception and visualization, a free control over what is present. The symbol's operability is what distinguishes it from representation [*Vorstellung*] and from depiction [*Abbildung*]."[43] What Derrida would call "the metaphysics of presence"—the term is not used by Blumenberg, but it is apposite—is thus avoided by the introduction of metaphoric heterogeneity, which resists the lure of perceptual or intuitive immediacy.

An even more explicit observance of the *Bilderverbot* is apparent in Adorno's negative dialectics. In the literature on the Frankfurt School in general, it has often been associated with two related taboos: one aimed at imagining future utopia in worked out form; the other at attempts to represent what is unrepresentable, most notably the Holocaust. The first paralleled the comparable Jewish taboo on directly pronouncing God's name, an example of that previously mentioned apophatic theology, which can only gesture to what it cannot positively know or express.[44] It reinforced a more pragmatic reluctance to provide a blueprint, to borrow the familiar Marxist opposition, of the future realm of freedom from the limited vantage point of the current realm of necessity. Although Adorno maintained his own adherence to the utopian impulse in Critical Theory, he insisted, as he put it in a dialogue with Ernst Bloch, that "one may not cast a picture of utopia in a positive manner . . . What is meant here is the prohibition of casting a picture of utopia actually for the sake of utopia, and that has a deep connection to the commandment, 'Thou shalt not make a graven image!' "[45]

Reversing the valence of its target, the *Bilderverbot* also informed Adorno's celebrated warning against writing poetry after Auschwitz, where the inadequacies of representation are now applied to what is demonic rather than divine, dystopian rather than utopian. It has often been noted, to be sure, that in *Negative Dialectics*, he nuanced his position somewhat by conceding that "perennial suffering has as much right to expression as a tortured man has to scream; hence it may have been wrong to say that after Auschwitz you could no longer write poems."[46] But he did not suspend his skepticism concerning the positive visual representation of that suffering.

Of particular importance for the question of nonconceptuality, however, was an additional reason for honoring the taboo that Adorno introduced in *Negative Dialectics*. In a critique of the simplistic reflection theory of orthodox dialectical materialism, exemplified by Lenin's diatribe against the alleged solipsism and subjective idealism of Ernst Mach and Richard Avenarius in his *Materialism and Empirio-Criticism*, Adorno denied that passive visual imitation was the way to reveal the object whose predominance he hoped to restore. As Gerhard Richter has noted in connection with *Aesthetic Theory*, "What he wishes for in the work of art as well as in philosophy is in fact a different kind of mimesis: a mimesis of what does not yet exist."[47] Rather than treating images in the mind as second-order representations of external reality, as had Lenin, "the materialist longing to grasp the thing aims at the opposite: it is only in the absence of images that the full object could be conceived. Such absence concurs with the theological ban on images."[48]

Honoring the ban, Adorno suggested, meant the materialist embrace of a frankly theological yearning: "Its great desire would be the resurrection of the flesh, a desire utterly foreign to idealism, the realm of the absolute spirit."[49] The literal realization of this yearning after death was less important than what it symbolically signified: the restoration of the rights of the corporeal against the ideal, the suffering, desiring body against the subjective consciousness of the mind or spirit. "The somatic moment as the not purely cognitive part of cognition is irreducible," Adorno wrote, "and thus the subjective claim collapses at the very point where radical empiricism had conserved it."[50] In this sense, nonconceptuality implied not merely acknowledging the preponderance of the object outside of the constitutive subject, but also valorizing the object within the subject, the soma in the psyche. It was, moreover, the embodied subject understood individually, which idealist philosophies of *Geist* as well as dialectical materialist theories of collective metasubjectivity had wrongly ignored or even denigrated. It honored, in other words, the animal in the *animal rationale*, whose instinctual demands Freud had helped us to appreciate. But significantly, it did so without depending on the uniqueness of the individual human face, which had been Emmanuel Levinas's favored instance of nonconceptuality, because it too privileged visual experience.[51]

It is this condensed and cryptic argument that allows us now to turn in conclusion to the salient differences between Adorno's and Blumenberg's positions. For, despite the similarities in their critique of Heidegger's equiprimordial notion of Being, their shared warning against the potential domination of subsumptive concepts, and their common reluctance to identify nonconceptuality with perception in general and visual images in particular, their ultimate understanding of nonconceptuality was not the same. Unlike Blumenberg, Adorno was suspicious of the ultimate privileging of the constitutive subject that he discerned in the assumption that concepts, metaphors, myths and the like were only cultural strategies to deal with the opacity of an unknowable "absolute reality."

His reluctance to grant such privilege to constitutive subjectivity did not mean, however, that Adorno was suspicious of concepts tout court. It is important to realize that in addition to his stress on the preponderance of the nonconceptual object, both in the world and in the subject, he also took more seriously than Blumenberg the claims of concepts over metaphors. In fact, there are indications that he still respected, as Blumenberg explicitly did not, the Hegelian legacy of what might be called ontological conceptual realism, which contends that concepts are more than just conventional linguistic expedients foisted on a contingent world in order to help us cope with its threatening meaninglessness. "The concept of nonconceptuality cannot stay with itself, with epistemology," he wrote, "epistemology obliges philosophy to be substantive."[52] It may well be that because of his residual Hegelian belief in the ontological reality of the concept, he could conclude *Negative Dialectics* by acknowledging "there is solidarity between such thinking and metaphysics at the time of its fall."[53] In a letter to Gershom Scholem on March 14, 1967, he in fact proudly admitted that "the intention to save metaphysics is actually the central point of *Negative Dialectics*."[54] In contrast, the final sentence of *Paradigms for a Metaphorology* reads: "Metaphysics has often revealed itself to us to be metaphorics taken at its word; the demise of metaphysics calls metaphorics back to its place."[55]

Essentially, Blumenberg believed that one should begin with the nonconceptuality of the prereflective lifeworld, with its often metaphoric language, and then move on to concepts, without, as we have noted, valorizing the transition as inherently progressive or denying the persistence of absolute metaphors that resisted any transition at all. Adorno, indebted as he was to Hegel, argued instead that "because entity is not immediate, because it is only through the concept, we should begin with the concept, not with the mere datum."[56] This means taking seriously the ontological status of concepts, not merely their epistemological function as subjectively created expedients making sense of an opaque world.[57] Placing too much of an emphasis on the cultural inventiveness of humans as "creatures of deficiencies" in fact is what leads to an exaggerated role for the constitutive, self-asserting subject, understood transcendentally or historically. It leads to the exaggerated critique of reification typical of Lukács's humanist Marxism, which was more idealist than materialist in inspiration.[58] In addition to the ontological status of natural kinds, objective genera that are more than just human conventions, history, he argued, often functions as if it were what Hegel would have called "second nature": some concepts, such as the commodity form or the exchange principle, have reflected institutional reifications that exist objectively in the real social world, even while others, such as "industrial society," do not.[59]

In addition to its descriptive validity, conceptual realism had a critical potential, a normative force that would be lost if it were jettisoned in favor of an undialectical celebration of pure nonconceptuality. Even the identitarian exchange principle, Adorno argued, can be rescued as a norm to be realized in a transformed reality:

> To define identity as the correspondence of the thing-in-itself to its concept is *hubris*; but the ideal of identity must not simply be discarded. Living in the rebuke that the thing is not identical with the concept is the concept's longing to become identical with the thing. This is how the sense of nonidentity contains identity. The supposition of identity is indeed the ideological element of pure thought, all the way down to formal logic; but hidden in it is also the truth moment of ideology, the pledge that there should be no contradiction, no antagonism.[60]

If, in some future utopia, that pledge would be honored and the "longing" of the concept to become identical with its nonconceptual instantiations were fulfilled, it would not, however, mean a hierarchical domination of the latter by the former. Instead, the relationship would be one of mutual respect akin to the mimesis of objects by subjects—a mimesis, however, in which similarity rather than absolute equivalence would be the rule.[61] The longing for identity would only be realized in a healthy sense if some nonidentity were preserved and the subsumptive logic of traditional conceptual realism were thwarted. There is ultimately no metaconcept under which specific concepts might be subsumed, but rather the arrangement Benjamin identified with a dialectical image: "The concepts enter into a constellation. The constellation illuminates the specific side of the object, the side which to a classifying procedure is either a matter of indifference or a burden."[62]

But it was through Adorno's insistence on the legitimate demands of the nonconceptual object, as we have noted, that he most clearly differed from Blumenberg. Here what have been called his Kantian rather than Hegelian sympathies came to the fore, at least to the extent that he warned against reducing the unmediated object to nothing but an expression of subjective constitution.[63] Whereas Blumenberg focused on metaphor and myth as rhetorical alternatives to concepts—that is, on purely linguistic or cultural expedients—designed to deal with the incomprehensibility of "absolute reality," Adorno understood nonconceptuality in terms of the material and corporeal limits to cultural constructivism of any kind. Although he too valued the ability of language to go beyond the homogenizing abstractions of discursive concepts, especially as expressed in works of art, and defended rhetoric against its philosophical detractors, he never singled out metaphor as a privileged medium.[64] Instead, without any debt to Kant, he preferred—albeit with some reservations—Benjamin's Adamic theory of proper names that communicated nothing but themselves, somehow unifying signifier and signified.[65] He thus valued music above the other arts because "what is at stake is not meaning, but gestures . . . As language, music tends towards pure naming, the absolute unity of object and sign, which in its immediacy is lost to all human knowledge."[66]

Blumenberg, in contrast, was impatient with the belief that names could serve as an effective antidote to the definitional imperatives of conceptualization. In his collection of aphorisms, *Care Crosses the River*, he recalled the Adamic power to name in the Garden of Eden with explicit suspicion:

> Whoever can call things by their names doesn't need to comprehend them. The strength of names has thereby remained greater in magic than in every type of comprehending. The tyranny of names is grounded in names having maintained an air of magic: to promise contact with what hasn't been comprehended.[67]

There was, in other words, nothing in Blumenberg of what I have called elsewhere the "magical nominalist" impulse in Adorno's negative dialectics.[68]

That impulse was clearly behind Adorno's yearning, to cite the evocative title of Robert Hullot-Kentor's collection of trenchant essays on him, to reach "things beyond resemblance."[69] At its best, art moved toward this unattainable limit through a refusal of meaning or, as he put it in *Aesthetic Theory*: "The true language of art is mute, and its muteness takes priority over poetry's significative element, which in music too is not altogether lacking."[70] Although not utterly absent, the significative or metaphoric moment in music should not be allowed to block out its more fundamental search for an acoustic equivalent to the unity of object and sign, that utopia of noncommunicative immediacy for which Benjamin had yearned in his ruminations on Adamic language.

There may well have been an unresolved tension in Adorno's work between what we have been calling its Hegelian conceptual realist moment and its Benjaminian magical nominalist moment; however, this is not the place to decide if the tension was productive or disabling. What is important to register is that both impulses can be understood as opposing Blumenberg's identification of nonconceptuality with the cultural expedients contrived to fend off the incomprehensibility of a hostile environment. For if Adorno declined to privilege metaphor, with its comforting transposition of threatening distance into familiar proximity and infinite deferral of utopian unity, he was even less disposed to consider myth a viable nonconceptual alternative to conceptual domination. "Dialectics," he insisted, "is a protest against mythology"[71] because of the latter's tacit acceptance of the status quo. Rather than adopting Blumenberg's defense of myth as an enduring alternative to the domination of concepts, he argued that both can serve the same function in canceling out the claims of the dominated object, which, as we have stressed, included the vulnerable bodies of people: "The smallest trace of senseless suffering in the empirical world belies all the identitarian philosophy that would talk us out of that suffering: 'While there is a beggar, there is a myth,' as Benjamin put it. This is why the philosophy of identity is the mythological form of thought."[72]

Thus, although he shared Blumenberg's general defense of rhetoric against the reduction of philosophy to science, Adorno nonetheless could argue that "in dialectics, contrary to popular opinion, the rhetorical element is on the side of content," not the constitutive subject.[73] As we have noted, for Adorno, even the subject had within him or her a residue of nonidentical otherness, a block to the constitutive power of the transcendental subject, epistemological or practical, bequeathed to idealism by Kant in his attempt to banish psychology from an account of the mind.[74] Thus, whereas Blumenberg argued that there is no substratum within man, no entirely inner experience that isn't already a function of metaphorical "self-externality,"[75] Adorno remained, as we have seen, enough of a Freudian to accept the ineradicable presence of instinctively motivated drives in even the most culturally mediated of psyches. One could, in other words, exaggerate the "poverty of instincts" in the human condition, leading to the one-dimensional conclusion that we have incorporated culture and subjective constitution all the way down. So, it is not surprising to find in *Negative Dialectics* Adorno explicitly protesting against Gehlen's philosophical anthropology of utter deficiency: "That man is 'open' is an empty thesis, advanced—rarely without an invidious side glance at the animal—by an anthropology that has 'arrived.' It is a thesis that would pass off its own indefiniteness, its *fallissement*, as its definite and positive side."[76]

Perhaps the best way to summarize the differences in their deployment of nonconceptuality is to foreground the critical potential in each. For Blumenberg, metaphor and myth are expressions of the eternal and unrelenting struggle to orient ourselves in a world forever beyond our ken, a world in which the real, both outside us and in our own bodies, remains elusive and potentially dangerous. Nonconceptual efforts to familiarize the unfamiliar are cultural strategies that blunt the terror of the unknown and orient us in a world lacking natural signposts. As such, they serve self-preservation, a claim that has allowed some critics to argue that Blumenberg's metaphorology reintroduces as instrumental precisely the reductive version of reason that the Frankfurt School was at such pains to discredit.[77]

Be that as it may, Blumenberg argued that when such strategies lose their magic and become useless, we invent new ones, which will themselves be replaced in turn. But never will there be an adequate fit between conceptual knowledge and the world that concepts seek to describe. Never will that "longing" of the concepts themselves, understood in ontological rather than solely epistemological terms, to realize their potential in existence be satisfied. We should remain thankful instead for the insufficient reason of rhetoric and metaphor and myth, never hoping for a more satisfactory alternative. Perhaps, if we follow Robert Savage's reading of Blumenberg, laughter, exemplified by the reaction of the Thracian woman to Thales's famous tumble into the well as he looked up at the stars, may be the quintessential variant of nonconceptuality: "It acts as a reality check to theory whenever it loses sight of the lifeworld, which is to say, whenever it takes its claim to totality seriously."[78] If there is a politics in all this, it would be essentially one of small expectations and limited goals, a politics of accommodation to an unknowable reality that remains forever absolute and unforgiving. If it implies a critique of ideology, it is only directed at the problematic use of language and not the social conditions that might underpin it.[79]

Adorno, in contrast, doggedly maintained a utopian hope, despite the failure of all efforts to realize it, that the domination of the constitutive subject can be ended, allowing access to a reality that is no longer utterly impenetrable and requiring the flawed and temporary compensations of cultural invention. By eschewing the comforting stratagems of metaphoric familiarization and mythic consolation, we can gesture toward a nonconceptuality that points in this direction, thus preparing the appearance of "things beyond resemblance." Against the familiarizing function of metaphor assumed by Blumenberg's metaphorology, Adorno expressed tacit solidarity with the defamiliarization techniques of modern art, as famously described by Viktor Shklovsky and the Russian formalists, and with Brecht's alienation effect.[80]

Rather than a nonconceptuality of mirth, which can draw on laughter to mock the foibles of theoretical overreaching, Adorno's variant is grounded in a self-denying ascesis that refuses to see the joke. However sardonic his irony in such works as *Minima Moralia* or playful he might have been in his private relations with, for example, his parents, Adorno's "science" remained resolutely "melancholy." Robert Savage is right to compare our two protagonists on precisely this issue; he notes that "Plutarch reports that even, as a child, Cato the Younger never laughed and was rarely seen to smile. Among Blumenberg's contemporaries, the theorist who came closest to matching this antique standard of humourlessness, at least in his *ex cathedra* pronouncements, was Adorno."[81] Like Thales, he kept his gaze fixed on the stars, oblivious to the mockery of those who focus only on the abyss into which we can so easily fall. Whether or not this was a privilege of living above the fray in a grand hotel, as Lukács famously sneered, or an attitude that allowed Adorno to fill his mind with ever new and increasing awe and admiration for the stars the more frequently and continuously he reflected on them is, to paraphrase Kant's famous conclusion to the *Critique of Practical Reason*, not for us to decide now. What is clear is that along with Blumenberg, he allowed us to appreciate the value of *Unbegrifflichkeit* in all of its motley variety—indeed, precisely because of it, as a vital star in the constellation of any critical theory worthy of that name.

7

Chromophilia: *Der Blaue Reiter*, Walter Benjamin and the Emancipation of Color

In many respects, Walter Benjamin remained an outlier in the development of Critical Theory, only peripherally involved with the projects Horkheimer and his colleagues pursued collaboratively at the Institute of Social Research. Although he was closest to Adorno, whose work was deeply influenced by him in many respects, they did not always see, as it were, eye to eye. As we have noted, Adorno and Horkheimer found in the Jewish Bilderverbot, if understood more metaphorically than literally, legitimation of their reluctance to picture utopia or represent radical evil. The issue of visuality—Horkheimer's boosterish and underdeveloped remarks on The Family of Man notwithstanding—was rarely central to their work.[1] In Benjamin's case, however, painting, photography, architecture and film were among his primary interests, and he is often acknowledged as a pioneer of the visual culture studies that have blossomed in our own day.

Although Benjamin's greatest impact has been on the discussion of modern technologies of mechanical reproduction, photography and film in particular, he was also fascinated by the implications of what has been called "the emancipation of color" in modernist painting, exemplified by Wassily Kandinsky and the expressionists of the Blaue Reiter. During the second decade of the twentieth century, when he was frenetically pursuing the means to access some deeper, purer, more primordial level of reality than could be reached through conventional philosophical, scientific and theological means, he speculated about the resistance color showed to the restrictive categories imposed on the world by the conceptualizing mind.[2] Although ultimately he would move on from this hope to a no less *speculative investment in the power of language understood in noncommunicative terms as a repository of redemptive yearnings, Benjamin's ruminations about color remain among his most suggestive legacies.*[3]

> Indelible from the resistance to the fungible world of barter is the resistance of the eye that does not want the colors of the world to fade.
>
> Theodor W. Adorno[4]

In 2003, the Wilhelm Hack Museum in the city of Ludwigshafen am Rhein mounted an exhibition entitled "*Der Blaue Reiter: Die Befreiung der Farbe.*"[5] In what follows, I want to focus on the provocative subtitle of that show and ask: what did the "emancipation of color" mean for the Blaue Reiter, in particular for its most prominent figure, Wassily Kandinsky? Other artists associated with the movement, such as Robert Delaunay, Franz Marc, August Macke, Alexander Jawlensky and Paul Klee, were also remarkable chromatic innovators, but Kandinsky was the most articulate spokesman of their more or less common position.[6] The language of "emancipation" is, in fact, one he explicitly adopted.[7] To help us clarify the stakes of his argument, I also examine the fragmentary, posthumously published thoughts on color by a German critic who was himself fascinated by the Blaue Reiter, Walter Benjamin, and whose musings have recently been subjected to sustained analysis by Howard Caygill, Esther Leslie and Heinz Brüggemann.[8]

Histories of early twentieth-century visual modernism routinely foreground the experiments in color performed by avant-garde communities of artists like the Nabis and Fauves in France and Die Brücke in Germany. But perhaps no other group put as much theoretical weight on its importance as did the Blaue Reiter, which, after all, even included a color in its very name.[9] Whether infused with metaphysical, even mystical meaning or understood more in terms of sensual experiences of the profane world—this opposition radically separated Kandinsky and Marc from Jawlensky, Macke and Delaunay[10]—color was to be liberated from its hitherto inferior status in the visual arts. And with its liberation, so it seemed, would come a more profound emancipation of human experience.

To make sense of that hope requires an appreciation of the long-standing debate about the implications of color in Western culture. Occupying a unique place at the intersection of the senses and the psyche, as well as between objects and the subjective experiences we have of them, color has perplexed philosophers, scientists and artists ever since humans first pondered the world around them. The age-old battle in painting between *disegno e colore*, first explicitly articulated in the sixteenth century by Giorgio Vasari and periodically fought between artists like Michelangelo and Titian or Poussin and Rubens, was more frequently won by the former quality.[11] Deemed inferior to form because of its volatility and evanescence, color struggled to defend its honor against the advocates of order, solidity and duration. Contrasted with the purity and calm of whiteness, the prismatic dispersal of color often seemed dangerously unstable, somehow akin to the desire unleashed when men fell from grace.

To be sure, the colorists of Venice sought to assert themselves against the austerity of Florence in Renaissance painting, while lush romantics like Delacroix resisted the power of severe classicists like Ingres. But what David Batchelor has dubbed "chromophobia" underpinned a widespread suspicion of color as merely superficial, cosmetic or ornamental, reinforced by associating it with marginalized or abject cultural phenomena, such as the feminine, the childish, the oriental or the queer.[12] Indeed, since the time of the ancient Greeks, it suffered from its association with seductive rhetoric rather than rigorous dialectic.[13] In the more modern vocabulary of John Locke, it was understood to be a secondary, superficial characteristic of the perceived world, not primary like shape and form, which could be confirmed by another sense, touch. Often it was identified as well with the primitive, the emotional, the untrustworthy and even the pathological. In Latin, *colorem*, it has been argued, is related to *celare*, the verb for hiding or concealing.[14] Color, admitted even the great twentieth-century colorist Josef Albers, "deceives continuously."[15]

And yet, as we know, what is marginal often finds its way back to the center and has its revenge against the hegemonic order. What seems dangerous in one context is redemptive in another. By the late nineteenth century, what might be called "chromophilia" began to emerge in a number of different contexts.[16] In 1884, to take one example from literature, the celebrated mathematical fantasy novel *Flatland*, by British theologian Edwin Abbot, imagined a great Color Revolt led by a pentagon named Chromatistes against the tyranny of the two-dimensional world of orderly lines and regular geometric shapes.[17] Significantly, he called it a "parable of spiritual dimensions."

In the case of the actual visual arts of modern Europe, color asserted itself in the wake of the impressionist exploration of the impact of light playing on objects registered by the eyes of the beholder, rather than on the objects themselves. Here, ironically reversing Abbot's mathematical allegory, it was the move from three to two dimensions that proved liberating. More important than the solid presence of a world to be recorded by the artist, a world understood as intelligible in terms of the formal principles of perspectival space, were the fleeting impressions left on the registering apparatus itself. The familiar story of the retreat from the three-dimensionality of the traditional window-on-the-world version of painting to the two-dimensionality of the flat canvas meant a diminished interest in the solidity of objects and a new fascination with their surfaces; this soon led to a comparable focus on the flatness of the canvases on which they were painted. Although impressionists generally thought of themselves as recording as faithfully and dispassionately as they could their perceptions of the world, the collapse of perspectival space meant an implicit diminution of interest in solid shape and form and a new appreciation of evanescence and impermanence.

When the impressionist passion for sensual accuracy faded and the painter's eye was freed from recording not only enduring objects but also fleeting perceptions, what might justifiably be called the full emancipation of color could follow.[18] Now the somewhat subdued, pastel, even wan pallet of the impressionists could give way to the more intense explosion of vibrant colors on a Fauve, Brücke or Blaue Reiter canvas. Color, no longer serving representation, became its own self-sufficient subject. Now the optical mixing of colors that produced effects of shimmering surfaces reflecting natural light could be replaced by a palette of pure colors that reflected nothing but themselves. In fact, the actual artist's wooden palette on which oil paints were placed before being applied to the canvas gained primacy over the colors of the natural world, either in objects or on the retina of the painter, a trend toward the autonomization of color that was accelerated in the 1960s when color was applied directly from commercial paint cans by many artists seeking even greater chromatic intensity.[19]

A similar phenomenon occurred slightly earlier in the register of music, where Hector Berlioz has been credited with emancipating color from line and preparing the way for the lush chromaticism of Wagner and Schoenberg's *Klangfiguren*.[20] In musical terms, color is a metaphor for virtuoso ornamentation, as in *coloratura* singing, as well as for the variations in timbre and orchestration that give the same pitch different sonorous qualities. As Charles Riley II notes, "color is also related, as in painting, to a dangerous antiformal force that threatens the very fabric of musical symmetry and organization."[21] Against melody and harmony, it allows impurity and imprecision to invade the precincts of musical order, so often understood as analogous to mathematical regularities. Insofar as color has often been seen as more than a metaphorical bridge between the visual and aural worlds, this parallel emancipation is not without its importance, especially for those artists hoping for a synesthetic overcoming of rigid distinctions between senses.

Among their number was Wassily Kandinsky, who himself apparently possessed the ability to mingle senses and sought to duplicate the experience on his canvases.[22] His penchant for musical titles for his works and his friendship with Arnold Schoenberg, the painter/composer who had fostered another celebrated aesthetic emancipation—that of tonal dissonance in musical composition—also testify to his belief that the emancipation of color should be embraced by more than just the visual arts. Significantly, *The Blaue Reiter Almanac* included not only a piece by Schoenberg, but also three other essays on musical themes by Thomas von Hartmann, Leonid Sabaneiev and Nikolai Kulbin, as well as the plan for a "stage composition" by Kandinsky called "The Yellow Sound."[23]

If one interprets the idea of emancipation in more narrowly defined visual terms, however, it meant freedom from three or perhaps four tyrannies. The first, as we have noted, was the priority of the drawn line or distinct form, the primacy of spatial order and relational intelligibility, which was challenged in favor of the messiness, instability, luminosity and vibrancy of hue and tone. Contour was no longer a rigid boundary, coloring outside the lines more than just an error of childish imprecision. The second was the tyranny of mimetic reproduction, the imperative to imitate faithfully the sensed colors of the external world, including the variations caused by changing conditions of light and shadow. The third tyranny was more institutional than practical: the entrenched power of official academies with their prescribed rules for good painting.[24] One final tyranny from which color might be understood to escape, at least for certain of its liberators, was its identification with mere surface appearances, as the impressionists had assumed. Instead, it could be interpreted symbolically as revealing deeper essential truths, either of the world or of the psyche.

Freed from its constraints, color could pursue its own path, either toward a new order of its own or toward the subversion of order itself and the celebration of formlessness as a positive value in its own right.[25]

Here it could be the handmaiden of the parallel revolution known as abstraction, in which the formal elements of a painting were no longer dependent on the representation of a prior world but could be replaced either by purer ideal forms or by deliberate formlessness.[26] Abstractly geometric shapes and allegedly pure colors—neither of which can easily be found in nature—were one possible direction. But there was also another possibility, as we will see when we turn to Walter Benjamin, which involved escaping from fantasies of absolute purity in either register.

Why, we must ask, were lines, forms and mimesis of the given world, the world of appearances, considered tyrannical in the first place? What was implied by the struggle to escape their domination? For champions of linear form and the hegemony of design, the values of clarity, distinctness, boundaried space and an opposition between figure and ground were held dear. Both three- and two-dimensional depictions of form seemed on the side of rationality rather than feeling, balanced order rather than disordered chaos. Traditionally, line was associated with spiritual distinction, while color was identified with base materiality.[27] Even when modernist movements like cubism deconstructed received notions of formal design and ideal form, they did so in the name of a more complex and accurate portrayal of multiple perspectives and temporal transitions simultaneously represented on a flat canvas. As a result, they were often seen less as advocates of the full emancipation of color than as obstacles to it.

Once emancipated from the hegemony of form, color could, of course, itself be subject to the structural imperative to bring order into chaos, with charts, diagrams, scales and many other spatial configurations used to depict relationships of harmony, complementarity and dissonance. Here, imperfect static representations sought to capture the dynamic interactions of colors, which involve issues of saturation, transparency, after-images and lighting, but with results that were rarely satisfactory. The natural spectrum of the rainbow, prismatically refracting white light into its component parts, proved often more evocative than all of the color wheels invented by scientific categorizations, at least for practicing artists.

It is commonplace in art criticism to note that artists who used color effectively were not enslaved by the scientific analysis of color, even if some were stimulated by works on the interactions of neighboring colors, such as Michel Eugène Chevreul's 1839 *De la loi du contraste simultané des couleurs et de l'assortiment des objets colorés* and his 1864 *Des couleurs et de leurs applications aux arts industriels*.[28] Although intended to help tapestry and fabric makers at the Gobelin works, these texts did inspire certain artists as well. Perhaps more genuinely inspirational was Goethe's celebrated *Farbenlehre*, which had explored the psychological as well as perceptual dimensions of color and sought to separate it from the domination of schematic, mathematical optics associated with Newton. Goethe's abandonment of the passive camera obscura model of vision and stress on the role of the observer's eye—he is a central figure in the story Jonathan Crary tells of the subjectivization of vision in the nineteenth century[29]—also opened the door to a more expressionist appreciation of the emotional valences of color.

By the time of Kandinsky's path-breaking treatise *Concerning the Spiritual in Art*, published first in 1911, and *The Blaue Reiter Almanac*, which appeared the following year, the physiological and psychological dimensions of the emancipation of color were supplemented by metaphysical ones, helping to reverse its traditional identification with matter rather than spirit. Not surprisingly, one of Kandinsky's philosophical inspirations was Arthur Schopenhauer, whose theories of color extended Goethe's critique of Newton and whose celebration of music as the art closest to the level of the impersonal will left their mark on Kandinsky. Kandinsky's theories were derived from a hodge-podge of different, more or less dubious strains in Russian and German thought, vitalist, religious, mystical, theosophical and symbolist. At once apocalyptic and cosmogenic, Kandinsky swam in the same turbulent waters as many other intellectuals and artists during the early decades of the twentieth century. His central concept of *Geist*, which can be translated as either spirit or mind, had lost the rationalist connotation it had enjoyed in German idealism. Instead, it was now employed in the service of a neo-romantic ideology of renewal with no fixed political valence. As George Mosse has noted, it was a favorite term of figures like Eugen Diederichs, the publisher of *völkisch* new romanticism. "Earlier romantics had employed a similar concept and the same word to designate human empathy with cosmic vitality. Diederichs used the word in the same way. He styled the *Geist* as the 'longing of the soul towards unity.' "[30] Others with more leftist inclinations like Kurt Hiller, the leader of the so-called activist expressionists who emerged during the war, were also enamored of the term. As August Wiedmann puts it, "*Geist* was the all-embracing and seemingly self-explanatory *principle* for Hiller and his intellectual workers—*Geist* as active, as 'holy' and holistic. And this *Geist* was believed to generate a new dynamic rationalism, one politically alert and aggressively opposed to the Germans' penchant for passive intro-spection. The new rationalism was, however, not that of analytical reason, but of intuitive creative thought which, in Hiller's view, required 'ecstasy' to keep it going."[31]

In this usage, *Geist* came close to signifying what was sometimes construed as its opposite in the German vocabulary of the day, *Seele* (psyche or soul). In fact, in Ludwig Klages's influential 1929 book enti-tled *Geist als Widersacher der Seele*, they were pitted against each other as two incompatible principles. For a *Lebensphilosoph* like Klages, *Geist* still smacked too much of idealist rationalism. But for Kandinsky, there seems to have been no meaningful distinction between them. As he put it in a passage on color that has become one of the most frequently cited from *Concerning the Spiritual in Art*, "Color is the keyboard, the eyes are the hammers, the soul is the piano with many strings. The artist is the hand which plays, touching one key or another, to cause vibrations in the soul."[32]

Along with Kandinsky's yearning for an increasingly vibrating soul went a valorization of primitivism, which included everything from Russian folk art and the masks of Borneo to the fetishes of Africa, Oceana and pre-Columbian America. As David Pan has pointed out, the Blaue Reiter "attempted to understand the primitive as a certain spiritual dimension of all human culture. They did not work with dichotomies of Western versus non-Western or primitive versus modern but with the distinction between spiritual and the material."[33] Kandinsky's primitivism might seem to be in tension with his utopian and apocalyptic fantasies about the imminent arrival of a new, more spiritual age, but it has long been recognized that spiritual renewal after an era of alleged decadence can draw on fantasies of restoring a lost innocence.[34] Rather than evolutionary, his version of primitivism was cyclical, promising a vitalized return rather than an irretrievable past.

A powerful tool to serve that end was the emancipation of color, which Kandinsky understood in dialectical rather than oppositional relation to form, whose liberation from mimetic purposes he also sought.[35] Indeed, color, he conceded, could not exist except as a bound-aryless element in the mind. There was, moreover, an affinity between certain colors and shapes: blue, for example, was linked with circularity, red with squareness and yellow with triangularity.[36] But he cautioned, "we should never make a god out of form. We should struggle for form only as long as it serves as a means of expression for the inner sound."[37] For Kandinsky, color seemed to have a more potent psychological and metaphysical effect, causing a "spiritual vibration." It "provides a whole wealth of possibilities of her own, and when combined with form, yet a further series of possibilities. And all these will be expressions of the inner need."[38]

Colors, to be more precise, seem to be either warm or cold, light or dark, or combinations of these elements. Yellow and blue are the most powerful opposition, as Goethe had argued, followed by white and black. Yellow, an earthly color, initially seems to approach the beholder, then bursts its boundaries and can end by disturbing him through its aggressive, even shrill character. Blue, in contrast, retreats from the beholder, is closer to heaven than earth and ultimately produces a sensation of rest (although not as much as green). Other colors, Kandinsky continued, have their own properties and effects. Even if they seem individual and isolated, they can work together to produce a successful image:

> The strife of colors, the sense of balance we have lost, tottering principles, unexpected assaults, great questions, apparently useless striving, storm and tempest, broken chains, antitheses and contradictions, these make up our harmony. The composition arising from this harmony is a mingling of color and form each with its separate existence, but each blended into a common life which is called a picture by the force of inner need.[39]

In his own artistic creations and those of his Blaue Reiter colleagues, the principles articulated in these works were given vivid and powerful expression, if often only loosely applied.[40]

There were few more appreciative enthusiasts of the Blaue Reiter in general and Kandinsky in particular than Walter Benjamin.[41] In 1920, he eagerly devoured *Concerning the Spiritual in Art*, writing to his friend Gershom Scholem, "This book fills me with the highest esteem for its author, just as his paintings elicit my admiration. It is probably the only book on expressionism devoid of gibberish; not, of course, from the standpoint of a philosophy, but from that of a doctrine of painting."[42] A year later he visited an exhibition by Macke, who had been killed during the war, and wrote an essay about it, which was not published and has since disappeared. In a letter from the same year, expressing his disappointment at a canvas by Chagall, he wrote, "I am coming more and more to the realization that I can depend sight unseen, as it were, only on the painting of Klee, Macke, and maybe Kandinsky. Everything else has pitfalls that require you to be on guard."[43] Benjamin's fascination with Klee is, of course, well known—it was in the spring of 1921 that he bought the painting called *Angelus Novus* that was to be one of his prize possessions[44]—but his interest in the other luminaries of the movement has been less widely appreciated.[45]

Even before the war, the canvases of the Blaue Reiter seem to have held out for the young Benjamin the promise of a renewal of vision itself, the recovery of that "innocent eye" that had existed before the fall into rationalized vision in which subjects looked at objects in an organized perspectival field. Not only did their respect for the so-called primitive art of folk traditions—Russian icons, Bavarian glass paintings, woodblock prints and the like—suggest they were in touch with an earlier stage of visual development, but their fascination with the allegedly uncorrupted vision of the child also meant that they understood its survival despite the transition to modernity. Against Scholem's defense of cubism, which was rooted in the latter's belief in a certain Jewish affinity for spatial and mathematical thinking, Benjamin vigorously extolled the utopian potential he saw in color.[46] In so arguing, Benjamin was following a long tradition that included John Ruskin and extended as far back as the German romantics.[47]

An unpublished fragment entitled "A Child's View of Color," written by Benjamin in 1914–15, begins with an assertion that could have been straight out of Kandinsky:

> Color is something spiritual, something whose clarity is spiritual, so that when colors are mixed they produce nuances of color, not a blur. The rainbow is a pure childlike image. In it color is wholly contour; for the person who sees it with a child's eyes, it marks boundaries, is not a layer of something imposed on matter, as it is for adults. The latter abstract from color, regarding it as a deceptive cloak for individual objects existing in time and space.[48]

Benjamin's fascination with the Blaue Reiter's experiments in color was fueled by his hostility to both the domination of general concepts in German idealism and the fetish of singular objects in the competing worldview of positivist sensationalism. Color, he argued, resisted the reduction of the world to isolated, discrete things, favoring instead a response to it as infinite nuance, alive with shimmering energy. For children, three-dimensionality was ascertained by touch, not sight, which reached its purest state when it was set apart from other senses. Color itself, however, is not at its most powerful when it seeks a homogeneous essence, but rather when it reveals the incessant movement of tone and shade. Above all, in the eyes of an innocent child it refuses to be subordinate to the tyranny of form, which, for Benjamin, then at his most antinomian, was in league with the law:

> The fact is that the imagination never engages with form, which is the concern of the law, but can only contemplate the living world from a human point of view creatively in feeling. This takes place through color, which for that reason cannot be single and pure, for then it remains dull . . . Productive adults derive no support from color; for them color can subsist only under law-given circumstances.[49]

A child's experience of color is purely receptive, operating without the imposition of schematic categories of time and space. As every parent knows, they have to be disciplined to color within the lines. Going beyond the animal senses, color touches the "soul," awakening a nonreflective mood that is open to the spiritual essence of objects, not their abstract forms. There is thus something "paradisiacal" about works of art that emancipate color, art "where the world is full of color in a state of identity, innocence and harmony. Children are not ashamed, since they do not reflect, but only see."[50]

Another fragment written during the same period, "The Rainbow: A Dialogue on Fantasy,"[51] drew on ancient associations between the apparition of the rainbow and heavenly beauty—as manifested, for example, in the haloes around angels in Matthias Grünewald's *Isenheim Altar*. It is cast as a conversation between a painter named Georg and his friend Margarethe, who shares her nocturnal dreams of color with him. He responds to her description of an intense dissolution of the self into color by saying, "I know these images of phantasy. I believe that they are in me when I paint. I mix the colors and see nothing but the color; I can almost say: I am color."[52] Normal painting, he explains, is dominated by form, which involves inscribing a surface, understood as a section of infinite space, an extensive infinity, graphically demarcated. Color is instead more of an intensive infinity, one that expresses a limitless number of potential contrasts with other colors, a fluid, indeterminate flow of nuances. Whereas graphic images are based on the contrast of light and dark, figure and ground, producing the line that separates forms, chromatic images develop the endless configurations of color that are without sharp boundaries from one another or the distinction between figure and ground.[53]

As he put it in yet another unpublished fragment from this period, "Painting, or Signs and Marks" in 1917: "A picture has no background. Nor is one color ever superimposed on another, but at most appears in the medium of another color. But even that is often difficult to determine, so that in principle it is often impossible to say in many paintings where a color is on top or underneath. The question makes no sense, however. There is no background in painting, nor is there any graphic line."[54] Such a generalization about "painting" tout court may seem puzzling until one understands how strongly he identified the most advanced achievements in the medium with the Blaue Reiter. Significantly, the only painter mentioned in one final fragment of 1917, "Painting and the Graphic Arts," is Kandinsky, whose pictures he calls "the simultaneous occurrence of conjuring and manifestation."[55]

Benjamin's rhapsodic celebration of color as a site of utopian fantasy has rightly been interpreted by Howard Caygill as the first manifestation of his challenge to Kant's notion of experience, which was based on intuitions of space and time as a priori, transcendental categories and the placement of objects of experience in them. Kant had, in fact, denigrated color in his aesthetic theory, arguing in Critique of Judgment that in the fine arts, "the design is what is essential . . . The colors which give brilliance to the sketch are part of the charm. They may no doubt, in their own way, enliven the object for sensation, but make it really worth looking at and beautiful they cannot."[56] In contrast, for Benjamin color was prior to the formal categories of the intellect, a more primitive perception than that of the schematizing mind. As he explained in a frequently cited letter to Scholem of October 22, 1917, it was the correlate of the Adamic view of pure noncommunicative language that he had just developed in his 1916 essay "On Language as Such and the Language of Man."[57] In both cases, the target was conceptual thought, with its reified categories and formal distinctions, and an understanding of perception that prioritized form over content. Foreshadowing his 1923 discussion of the utopian "task of the translator," he would describe this transition in his 1916 essay as passing "through continua of transformation, not abstract areas of identity and similarity."[58] Both color and the Adamic

Ursprache—the latter approached by translating from one language of man into another—were avenues of entry into what he called "absolute experience." Both were superior to the imperfect languages of men in the plural, which falter when it comes to finding the adequate term for visual perceptions. No vocabulary is able to discriminate among the endless gradations of chromatic nuance; each reflects the limitations of its cultural origin and semiotic network.[59]

Another way to parse Benjamin's celebration of color is to see it as an anticipation of his distrust of the traditional notion of narrative linearity that characterized his hostility to the historicist tradition. As Jacqueline Lichtenstein has noted, in the teachings of the academy, "drawing is the means of inscribing history in painting. Drawing has primacy—included in the favor granted historical painting, assumed in the definition of painting as discourse, and also imposed by the constitution of a discourse on painting."[60] In contrast, color is on the side of antiauthoritarian disruption and discontinuity, the radical leap of temporality that undermines smooth evolutionary progress. As Charles A. Riley II puts it, "Color and the unique event elude prescriptive guidelines."[61]

It was, in fact, Benjamin's insistence on color defying categorization—either synchronic or diachronic—that suggests a certain distance from Kandinsky, or at least the latter's reflections on what constituted emancipation. As we have noted, Kandinsky sought to discover the spiritual language of colors in which specific ones would have inherent symbolic and psychological implications. Thus, for example, he asserts that "blue is the typical heavenly color. The ultimate feeling it creates is one of rest. When it sinks almost to black, it echoes a grief that is hardly human. When it rises to white, a movement little suited to it, its appeal to men grows weaker and more distant."[62] Because of his desire to crack the semiotic code of color, a code he implied was universal, Kandinsky has been accused of being a chromatic essentialist. Mark Cheetham, for example, writes: "The salient notion of purity incorporated for Kandinsky the ideas of metaphysical immutability, of spiritual as opposed to material being, of essence rather than transitory appearance."[63] His talk of "an inner necessity" invokes an eidetic intuition that reveals more affinities with the theosophy of Rudolf Steiner than Edmund Husserl's phenomenology, but which nonetheless is in the service of a metaphysical absolute manifested in material terms.[64] As David Pan warns, "Kandinsky's spiritual catalog of color effects runs the risk of arbitrarily pinning down the spiritual value of colors according to a private schema that he understands to be universal."[65] The emancipation of color, in other words, threatens to turn into a new tyranny.

In Benjamin's appropriation of Kandinsky, however, this danger is chiefly avoided. Rather than seeking to identify a particular emotion or metaphysical value with a specific color in its pure form, he stressed the nuanced transitions between colors, the infinity of gradations that defied singular categorization. The emancipation of color for Benjamin meant not only freedom from objects and the faithful imitation of the perceived world, but also from rigid semiotic schemes that attributed natural qualities to distinct colors. As in the case of what he would call "language as such" as opposed to the language of man, color's primary function is not to communicate meaning but to manifest the Absolute, dissolving the artificial human categories under which we subsume entities and impose intelligibility onto the world. Its role is thus closer to what might be called "magical nominalism" than to a Platonic search for eternal essences.[66]

How successful Benjamin actually was in linking the emancipation of color with a more fundamental project of emancipation, understood in either metaphysical or social and political terms is not, to be sure, very clear. Howard Caygill rightly calls Benjamin's unpublished fragments on the question an "early ruin,"[67] and notes that he soon turned to language as an alternative locus of his utopian desires.[68] When Benjamin came later to posit "dialectical images" as a model of critical cultural analysis, they had little of the chromatic intensity he had so admired in the Blaue Reiter artists.[69]

The war and the havoc it wreaked may well have muted Benjamin's hopes for the emancipation *of* color as equivalent to human emancipation *via* color. The Blaue Reiter itself had lost two of its major figures in the fighting, Franz Marc and August Macke, and in the words of Marcus Bullock, "saw the seismic pressures of warfare end its vision of a redemption accomplished by a transformation of the senses."[70] But during the immediate postwar years, when the utopian spirit was not yet extinguished, Benjamin could still rhapsodize about Kandinsky's work and his thought.[71] In his unpublished "Notes for a Study of the Beauty of Colored Illustrations in Children's Books," composed in 1921 as reflections on the work of Johann Peter Lyser, he returned to the experience children had of books that contained "the color of paradise." "Children," he wrote, "learn in the memory of their first intuition. And they learn from bright colors, because the fantastic play of color is the home of memory without yearning, and it can be free of yearning because it is unalloyed."[72] But for adults who had come to know what yearning was and had faced the obstacles to its fulfillment, the spiritual optics of the Blaue Reiter indicated, alas, more of paradise irretrievably lost than one that even the most brilliant of paintings might help us regain.

8

Timbremelancholy: Walter Benjamin and the Fate of Philately

There is perhaps no better illustration of Benjamin's remarkable skill in extracting from the apparent minutiae of cultural life lessons of resonant profundity than his scattered remarks on the fate of postage stamps and those who collected them. As in the more familiar cases of his analyses of photography and film, he probed the utopian potential of mechanically reproduced works of art. Here his interest in visual culture focused on the miniature worlds, both imagined and real, on the tiny pieces of gummed paper that so captivated young philatelists, and not them alone. As the surrealists had realized, stamps could open up enchanted worlds that stimulated desire for life beyond humdrum quotidian existence and provincial borders. Benjamin also presciently grasped the looming collapse of the mode of communication that had supported postage stamps and the hobbyists who collected them. As another instance of experiential impoverishment in the modern world, the decline of postage stamps and the collections they enabled were a source of melancholic reflection that resonates with special intensity for those of us who shared his childhood fascination with the world of stamps.[1]

> O philately, philately: you are a most strange goddess, a slightly foolish fairy; and it is you who take by the hand the child emerging from the enchanted forest in which Little Tom Thumb, the Blue Bird, Little Red Riding Hood and the Wolf have finally gone to sleep side by side.
>
> Louis Aragon[2]

In Michael Chabon's 2007 alternative history novel, *The Yiddish Policemen's Union*, a Jewish refuge in Sitka, Alaska, is created during World War II and survives for six decades after the stillborn creation of the state of Israel. In a preliminary essay called "Imaginary Homelands,"[3] which foreshadowed his novel, Chabon mused that such a settlement would boast postage stamps honoring heroes of Jewish history. Among them is one adorned with a portrait of Walter Benjamin, who would have felt moved by the honor, although probably just as much by the location of the tribute as the tribute itself. For Benjamin had a special place in his heart for stamps and all they represented in the modern world. In his 1928 collection of aphorisms, *One-Way Street*, he included an evocative rumination called the "Stamp Dealer," and for a radio broadcast a few years later, he wrote "Stamp Swindles," a script that focused on the issue of postmarks and the chicanery of stamp forgers.[4] Unlike his friend Theodor W. Adorno, who was honored on his centenary in 2003 by an actual German stamp showing him writing at his desk surrounded by a page of his hand-edited text, Benjamin has not been so recognized, as far as I can tell, by any government outside of Chabon's imaginary Alaskan refuge for Jews. This is a pity, for he far outpaced Adorno in his appreciation of the wealth of conflicting meanings condensed in the small, fragile pieces of gummed paper used to send letters and postcards. Indeed, in many respects, his reflections on this theme can themselves serve as a microcosm of much of his own remarkable *oeuvre*.

In the vast literature on Benjamin, however, only two commentators, to my knowledge—Pierre Missac and Jeffrey Mehlman—have paid any serious attention to his thoughts on stamps.[5] The former situates it in his discussion of Benjamin's theories of collecting; the latter introduces it to bolster his claim that Benjamin was a forerunner of deconstruction. I want to build on their insights and offer some reflections, filtered through my own experiences as an amateur philatelist, of the meaning they retain for our own time, when both postage stamps and their collectors are on the wane. Indeed, it is perhaps fitting that Chabon's imagined District of Sitka had a time limit that was on the verge of expiring when the action of his novel transpires, as Benjamin had a premonition that the days of stamps and their collectors were numbered.

Before reflecting on their decline, however, we need to focus on the reasons Benjamin found postage stamps and the hobby of collecting them so rich a lode for his ruminations on modern life. At the most basic level, he suggested in *One-Way Street*, they are monadic exemplars of the eternal struggle between life and death. "A mass of little digits, tiny letters, marks, and spots," he wrote, "they constitute graphic scraps of cell tissues. Everything seethes and teems and, like the lower animals, lives on even when shredded in pieces."[6] But shadowing their vitality is the inevitability of death, for on stamps, "life always carries a whiff of corruption as a sign that it is made up of dead matter." Its mortality is realized when a stamp is canceled, producing a postmark that "is the stamp's nocturnal side." Cancellation is an act of violence, as "no sadistic fantasy comes close to the sinister procedure that covers faces with weals and rips through the soil of whole continents like an earthquake."[7]

And yet, stamps—both mint and canceled—gain the chance for a second life when they enter the world of the collector, who rescues them from their initial use value in delivering mail and resituates them in a new, essentially nonutilitarian context. Decontextualization allows the imaginative reconstellation of objects that Benjamin always thought had allegorical potential. Although in some ways like legal tender—stamps, after all, are backed by the state and sometimes can function to pay debts[8]—they differ from printed or coined money by not retaining their assigned exchange value after they are used. But ironically, unlike other goods whose value disappears when they are consumed, their liberation from their role in their initial system of value can allow them to realize an even greater potential. More precisely, two different potentials are unleashed. For in addition to their entering a secondary commercial market based on their rarity or imperfections, which attracts unsentimental investors, for Benjamin, they also possess a nonutilitarian value that lies elsewhere for true collectors. Especially for the child who starts a collection, stamps contain the ability to awake a yearning to leave mundane routine behind and discover something beyond quotidian experience. "Is there perhaps a glimpse," Benjamin muses, "breaking through in the color sequences of long sets, of the light of some strange sun?" Even tiny stamps—those with no colors, pictures, or indications of their origin and the currency for which they can be purchased—can seem to a child, he argues, just like "fate's real lottery tickets"[9] if they simply have numbers on them.

Not surprisingly, surrealists such as Louis Aragon—who had written about stamp collecting in a work Benjamin revered, *Le Paysan de Paris* (1926)—appreciated their potential through juxtaposition, disparities of scale and unnatural hues to awaken a sense of the marvelous. Like other readymades or *objets trouvés*, they had the potential to spark what Benjamin liked to call "profane illuminations," which miraculously appeared without anyone intending them.[10] As Benjamin's friend Missac put it, "it is easy to see [the stamp] as a suitable vehicle for surrealist imagery based on precision and trompe l'oeil. The routes it opens lead not only to Constantinople or Colombia but to imaginary countries or to planets."[11]

But more than containing generic utopian intimations of a world beyond our own, stamps also open the eyes of children to actual splendors in the real world. They stimulate the imagination, triggering dreams of voyages to exotic destinations, dreams that avoid the commodity fetishism of modern consumerism. For Aragon,

> great adventures have shaken those childhood companions of ours, stamps which a thousand bonds of mystery unite with world history. Here are the newcomers which take into account a recent and incomprehensible reshuffling of global boundaries. Here are the stamps of defeats, the stamps of revolutions. Used, mint—what do I care? I shall never understand the first thing about all this history and geography. Surcharges, surtaxes, your black enigmas terrify me: they conceal from me an unknown sovereign, a massacre, palaces in flames, and the song of a mob marching towards a throne, waving placards and shouting slogans.[12]

Albums of stamps, Benjamin concurred, "are magical reference books recording the number of monarchs and palaces, animals, allegories and states." As if they are looking at countries through the wrong end of an opera glass, children can see a miniature version of the world and can fantasize emulating a great explorer in the Age of Discovery. "Stamps are the visiting cards that the major countries leave in the nursery," Benjamin writes. "Gulliver-like, the child visits the land and people of each stamp,"[13] learning a bit about the institutions, personalities, histories and celebrations of the Lilliputians. Held between your fingers—or in a tweezer, if you're serious about their pristine condition—stamps combined proximity with distance, a combination that Benjamin later claimed was an important source of auratic enchantment.

However, as Benjamin concluded in the aphorism in *One-Way Street*, there is a looming crisis for stamps and their collectors. The practice of putting beautiful flowers on stamps, which he attributes to distinguished nineteenth-century German postal director Heinrich von Stephan, is now in danger, and the cause is technological. "How long will this floral abundance survive between telegraph poles? The big art stamps of the postwar years, with their wealth of color—are they not already the autumnal asters and dahlias of this flora? Stephan, a German, and not by chance a contemporary of Jean Paul, sowed this seed in the summery mid-nineteenth-century. It will not survive the twentieth."[14] Implied in that scenario of impending doom fostered by technological "progress" is the fear that the art of writing letters is also in jeopardy, a mark of the decline of bourgeois culture in the age of information.[15]

Benjamin, to be sure, was never simply nostalgic for that culture, nor did he express Luddite contempt for the depredations of technology. In fact, his ruminations on the potentially emancipatory transformation of art in the age of mechanical (or technological) reproduction, expressed in 1936 in his most widely influential essay,[16] are anticipated in his fascination for stamps, those mass-produced miniature images that in some ways foreshadow the films whose revolutionary potential he extolled in his great essay. Unlike unique works of auratic art, they do not gain their value through being unique and authentic originals, but from the very beginning are always already duplicated. Yet, ironically, as Benjamin was well aware, it is when they regain a certain rarity, either by virtue of the disappearance of most of their exemplars or by a flaw in the execution of a few of them, that an aura can emerge, as well as enhanced monetary value. But the irony does not end there, as he noted in his radio script "Stamp Swindles," for some states deliberately duplicated what had become rare stamps in order to sell them to collectors, implicitly acting as forgers of their own postal currency. Then, to compound the irony, collectors became suspicious of these pseudo-originals and began trusting only stamps that had been canceled (or, as it were, "stamped"). But the spiral does not end there, for cancellations could themselves be even more easily forged than actual stamps, undermining the latter's value in the secondary market of collectors. It is thus easy to see why Jeffrey Mehlman could read Benjamin's essay as proto-deconstructionist, because "the two maxims proffered in the text—the postmark as both validating supplement or completion and seal of inauthenticity—are kept in suspension throughout the text, endowing it with an unresolvable ambiguity."[17]

That productive ambiguity was in danger of being lost with the evolution in postal practices that Benjamin foresaw in predicting the decline of the stamp. He anticipated the waning of the importance of physical stamps, those colorful stimulants of childhood reveries, with postmarks sufficient unto themselves. Not only did this decline happen through the advent of postage meters and prepaid mailers, but it intensified with the radical dematerialization following the replacement of snail with electronic mail. Traditional postage stamps, of course, still exist and rare stamps still command substantial prices in the marketplace—the 1868 American Benjamin Franklin "Z Grill" was acquired by financier Bill Gross in 2005 for a block of four 1918 "Inverted Jenny" stamps worth $3 million—but there are clear signs that the heyday of collecting is now over. The "timbremania" that began soon after the first stamp was printed in 1840 and evolved into the more elevated pursuit called *philatélie*—a term coined by one Georges Herpin in 1864 from the Greek words meaning "the love of prepayment or tax"—is now irreversibly turning into "timbremelancholy." The Internet is filled with articles expressing alarm at the imminent demise of the hobby and how the investment value of most collections seems to have declined with the inexorable shrinkage of demand, especially after the bursting of a bubble in the 1970s.[18] Organizations for junior collectors, such as Kidstamps, now have a fraction of the members enjoyed by comparable groups a generation ago. Always a hobby more for boys than for girls— even the most famous female collector of the twentieth century, Louise Boyd Dale, was carrying on a collection started by her father—it has never managed to spread vigorously across the gender line.[19] The time when famous leaders like King George V and Franklin D. Roosevelt were also renowned collectors is past, and it is unlikely that fans of their more recent successors like John Lennon, Freddy Mercury or Ron Wood would swoon over their stamp collections rather than their music, if they even knew the former had existed. Truth be told, the decline probably began after World War I, symbolized by France's seizure of Philipp von Ferrary's vast collection, often called the greatest of all time, to help pay war reparations. But the full extent of the downswing has only been apparent in our own century. Philately is now increasingly a hobby for old men, who wonder anxiously what will become of their collections once they pass from the scene.

As one of their number, albeit whose collecting days are long over, I cannot help being gripped by a certain twinge of regret for the decline of what once kept me so happily busy as a child.[20] The feeling, however, is ironically appropriate, for nostalgia for something lost was always part of the fascination of stamps, which reflected not merely an exotic new world waiting to be explored, but also an old one on the wane. Salvaged from history's famous dustbin, they were numinous relics of *temps* irrevocably *perdu*. Aragon insightfully noted the ability of stamps to render the recent past archaic: "Edward VII already looks like a monarch from ancient times."[21] My initial interest in stamps had, in fact, been piqued when I was about twelve and inherited an older cousin's half-filled album that dated from the 1930s. Not only were many of the stamps it contained from the interwar era, a period that seemed very remote in the 1950s, but a good number of the countries or provinces from which they had come were no longer in existence, or had lost whatever autonomy they once enjoyed. Some—Cilicia, Epirus, Ubangi, Cyrenaica, Roumelia—sounded to my ears no more real than Shakespeare's Illyria in *Twelfth Night*, while others—Fiume, Danzig— still conjured up their unhappy fate in the recent past. World War II had rearranged the map, a process accelerated by the rapidly unfolding process of decolonization. It was eye-opening to see how ephemeral nation-states or the lesser entities that had minted postage stamps could be.

No less jolting than the stamps of obliterated countries were those that had honored leaders or regimes that had passed into history, none more so than the Weimar Republic and the Third Reich. It was easy in the 1950s to come by German stamps from the early 1920s, with successive overprints reflecting the runaway inflation of those years: ten marks turning into a thousand turning into a hundred thousand in the blink of an eye, or rather on the same flimsy piece of gummed paper. My favorite had "2 million" imprinted over its original 200 mark value. The giddy explosion of prices captured on the faces of stamps was a reminder that the stability of a currency could be no less ephemeral than the sovereignty of a state. Benjamin, it turned out, had himself written about the sinister effects of the postwar inflation in *One-Way Street* in a section on the "Kaiserpanorama," a drum-shaped series of stereoscopes with scenes of passing life. He had bemoaned the loss of human warmth and intimacy, the shame induced by sudden impoverishment, and the crushing ambiguity of a future that was anything but secure. Metaphorizing his title, he darkly warned, "The air also teems with delusions, mirages of a radiant cultural future that, despite everything, will dawn tomorrow: because everyone is committed to the optical illusions of his own isolated standpoint."[22]

My twelve-year-old self could not, of course, know of Benjamin's ruminations or even fully understand the human consequences of hyperinflation, but I had no trouble connecting to the delusory future of the Germany that followed. In the stamps bearing the face of General Hindenburg and the once obscure corporal who succeeded him as

Germany's chancellor, it was chillingly evident. Others from that period were decorated with swastikas or heroes of the Third Reich, little material residues of a history that was still very raw in my imagination and printed on pieces of paper, I realized with a shudder, likely bearing traces of the spittle of Nazi letter writers. Especially sinister were my Hitler heads with the words "Ukraine" or "Ostland" printed over them, the latter referring to the occupied territories of the Baltic States and parts of White Russia and Poland, the very territories from which my grandparents had luckily fled in the late nineteenth century.

Equally redolent of the recent past were the stamps from erstwhile British colonies, many of which had gained or were in the process of gaining sovereignty. Stamps and their collectors had always had a special place in the British imperial imaginary, which reflected the need to communicate over vast distances of the globe that were ruled from London. The first adhesive postage stamp, the Penny Black, was, in fact, printed in Britain in 1840, with the Tuppence Blue following two days later. Affordable and plentiful—more than 68 million of the former were ultimately printed—they revolutionized the delivery of mail, which had previously been paid for by the recipient. The central role of Britain in the history of postage stamps is nicely symbolized by the fact that theirs never explicitly named the country from which they were issued, remaining the unmarked norm in a sea of marked rivals. There was no need to do anything but include a picture of Queen Victoria or her successors to insure the provenance of the stamp (the first nonroyal to appear on a British stamp was Shakespeare in 1964). At times, the word "imperium" was added to make clear that they were issued from one colony or another, whose individual identities were less important than their inclusion in the larger community subjected to the British Crown. Although the creation of the Commonwealth in 1949 put a fig leaf over the transition, it was clear even to a young stamp collector that the days of British hegemony were over.

When it came to the stamps of my own country, whose often whitewashed official history I had no reason to question as a boy, there was also something backward-looking about the exercise. American stamps had been introduced in 1847 during the Polk administration and quickly spread with the increased geographical mobility spawned by the gold rush and the Civil War. The next twenty-five years, according to historian David Henkin, saw a democratic revolution in communications that rivaled the rapidly growing transportation network knitting together remote parts of the expanding country.[23] When personal letters replaced newspapers as the major cargo paid for by modestly priced stamps, a new culture of epistolary intimacy spread down the social ladder.

With the invention and dissemination of the telephone, however, alternative means of long-distance communication began to rival those of stamped letters; thus, expedients had to be designed to maintain post office profits. The first commemorative issues were introduced with the Columbian Exposition of 1893. The US Post Office Department established the Philatelic Agency in 1921 to handle requests from collectors for commemoratives (something, it might be noted, that the Treasury Department never did for coin collectors). Thus began a revenue-generating practice that culminated with the most successful commemorative stamp of all time, that honoring the popularly chosen "young" Elvis Presley in 1993, well after I had stopped adding to my own collection. By then celebrities were replacing more conventional heroes, as the post office sought to boost its sagging sales, a practice that reached its nadir in 2011 with the controversial decision to issue millions of stamps with images of a non-American, fictional character, Harry Potter, and his friends.[24] For my own generation, the most recent commemorative stamps had celebrated FDR's New Deal programs, as well as the military victories of the war. Although there were oversized, lavishly colored and stunningly designed stamps to acquire, often ironically from "postage stamp-sized" countries like Monaco or San Marino, most American stamps of that era exhibited the gravitas of a country that saw itself as the responsible leader of the free world.

The stamps I and countless others of my generation collected were, of course, only the fragile material residue of a vast new network of practices and institutions that were deliberately nurtured by the growing modern state. If newspapers and novels were means of fostering the "imagined community" that was the modern nation-state, as Benedict Anderson famously argued,[25] the postal service was no less important. And yet, paradoxically, it could also function as an engine of international cooperation, especially after the volume of long-distance mail increased with air delivery. The postal convention of 1874 in Bern, Switzerland, spawned a general postal union that ultimately became known as the Universal Postal Convention, which included most of the world by 1914. Although the League of Nations had issued a few stamps, mostly Swiss ones with "SND" (*Société des Nations*) overprinted, the

United Nations realized they could profit from the souvenir trade and began minting their own in 1947; several of these stamps found their way into my boyhood collection. After 1981, though, when they produced one celebrating the "inalienable rights of the Palestinian people," demand seems to have plummeted.

Political sensitivities have, of course, been only a minor reason for the secular decline of stamps and their collections. As Benjamin had foreseen, the classic letter, taking a while to compose and write out by hand, was in trouble well before the new technologies delivered the coup de grâce. Slow food may have made a modest comeback, but snail mail is not likely to duplicate its revival. The introduction of self-adhesive glue rather than water-activated gum in the 1970s made it much harder to detach canceled stamps from their envelopes, a process that now requires obtaining special solvents like Bestine.[26] The arrival of generic "forever stamps" diluted the specificity of traditional ones proudly broadcasting their particular historical moment. But perhaps most damaging of all, the dematerialization of communication media—email itself being now rapidly overshadowed by texting, tweets, Snapchats and the like—means that the tactile presence of stamps, their tangibility as durable things in the world whose existence can be "redeemed" for Benjamin by their collection, has evaporated. Most of the stuff we now receive by traditional mail delivery is rightly classified as "junk" that we have no reason to touch delicately with tweezers and is the last thing anyone wants to collect.

Stamp collecting has, of course, by no means entirely vanished and it is still possible to examine potential additions "on approval" from dealers trusting in their customers' honesty. Some shrewd investors can turn a profit and some forgers can make a modest killing at the expense of others. But most of us will enjoy no monetary gain from the collections we have held on to for half a century, nor, alas, find anyone to cherish them after we are gone. The future of philately, as Benjamin prophesied almost a century ago, like that of postage stamps in general, is not rosy. The world out of which it emerged seems to have a terminal date, like Chabon's imagined "district of Sitka," and it is likely to end before Walter Benjamin gets his face on a stamp. But perhaps there is some justice in that outcome, for no one was as sensitive to the critical potential lurking in melancholy as Benjamin himself.[27] Timbremania is indeed over, but rather than mourning its end, achieving closure and moving on, we might appreciate what we've lost—or, rather, not yet gained—by refusing to be consoled for its passing.[28] Interminable timbremelancholy, in other words, may have its uses. Philately, as the easy pun has it, may indeed get you nowhere. But perhaps we can also say, with a nod to William Morris, that it still may bring us the news from that nowhere, news from imaginary planets lit by strange suns that had once so captivated and enchanted our long-buried childhood selves.

9

The Little Shopgirls Enter the Public Sphere: Miriam Hansen on Kracauer

Among the most vexed legacies of Critical Theory was its characteriza-tion—and denunciation—of what Horkheimer and Adorno called "the culture industry" in Dialectic of Enlightenment.[1] *Central to their analy-sis was the role cinema played in the modern world as both ideological mass entertainment and a potential medium of emancipation. No one probed the implications of their complicated reactions to film more trench-antly than German-American film theorist and historian Miriam Bratu Hansen, whose long-awaited masterwork,* Cinema and Experience, *appeared shortly after her premature death at the age of 61 in 2011.[2] Hansen insisted on including Siegfried Kracauer along with Walter Benjamin and Theodor W. Adorno in her expanded definition of Critical Theory, and the payoff was a richer appreciation of the full range of ways cinematic experience might be understood.*

A conference of international scholars in film studies was held at Columbia University in 2012 to commemorate Hansen's life and work, resulting in a special issue of the journal New German Critique, *on whose editorial board she served for many years.[3] My own contribution probed the implications of her attempt to mobilize the concept of an oppositional public sphere, developed by sociologist Oskar Negt and filmmaker Alexander Kluge, to rescue cinema from the sour analysis of it in* Dialectic of Enlightenment. *While acknowledging the power of her arguments on its behalf, I was skeptical of the ways in which Negt and Kluge replaced Habermas's notion of the public sphere as a locus of communicative rationality and discursive validity testing with one that saw it as a space for shared sensually mediated experiences. Although such experiences*

might well stimulate discussion and awaken critical impulses, they were
not sufficient by themselves to foster the problem-solving, value-testing
culture of egalitarian argumentation that the classic public sphere, at least
as an ideal telos, can provide.

In a series of eight short articles that ran in the *Frankfurter Zeitung* in
1927, collectively entitled "The Little Shopgirls Go to the Movies,"
Siegfried Kracauer fleshed out his claim that "stupid and unreal film
fantasies are the *daydreams of society*, in which its actual reality comes
to the fore and its otherwise repressed wishes take on form."[4] Each of
the film vignettes he examined exemplified how those wishes were
discharged harmlessly through ideological consolations for the real
injustices of class and gender that the films only appear to address.
Kracauer's scorn for such films' function is matched only by his conde-
scension toward their victims—why are they "little" and why "girls"?—
who are unable to generate any critical distance from the spectacles that
lull them into complacency. It was thus far from a compliment when,
many years later, Adorno, in the barbed tribute that so infuriated his
friend, wrote that Kracauer "himself had something of the moviegoer's
naive delight in viewing; he found an aspect of his own mode of response
even in the little shopgirls who amused him. For this reason, if no other,
his relationship to the mass media was never as harsh as his reflections
on their effects would have led one to expect."[5]

If this were true for Kracauer, whose work ambivalently explored
both the ideological and critical potential in cinema, it was arguably no
less the case for one of his most trenchant commentators, Miriam
Hansen, whose richly nuanced reception and application of Kracauer's
legacy, along with that of Benjamin and Adorno himself, culminated in
Cinema and Experience.[6] Hansen, to be sure, was anything but naive,
and her palpable delight in viewing was buttressed by a well-developed
theoretical defense of the critical potential in cinema as well as a sober
recognition of its possible repressive functions. One source of her theorizing was an acute understanding of the ways in which movies affected
viewers on a level that was deeper than the content, ideological or
otherwise, of the stories they typically told. Distancing herself, however,
from the psychoanalytically inflected, technologically determinist
"apparatus theory" that had so powerfully captured film studies in the
1970s, Hansen looked for inspiration in the anthropological materialism—to adopt Benjamin's term—of her Weimar heroes, who alerted
her to the potentially liberating somatic and perceptual transformations

wrought by movie spectatorship. Here she brought into play their complicated theories of mimetic comportment and the renewal of experience in the robust sense of *Erfahrung* rather than the impoverished alternative of *Erlebnis*.

But in addition to her appreciation of these aspects of the Weimar film theory legacy, Hansen drew heavily on a notion developed by a later Frankfurt School theorist, Jürgen Habermas—that of the "public sphere" or, more precisely, on a version of it refracted through the critique of Alexander Kluge and Oskar Negt. Kluge, a protégé of Adorno and a leading participant in the new German cinema that produced the Oberhausen Manifesto in 1962, had taught a series of seminars on film and media in 1975–6 in Frankfurt, which Hansen attended.[7] He and Negt, who had studied with Adorno and was Habermas's assistant in Frankfurt, had published in 1972 a study contrasting the bourgeois with the proletarian public sphere, the latter of which stressed the importance of the role of experience.[8]

A few years later, in a special double issue of *New German Critique* devoted to New German Cinema, Hansen published an essay on the theme of "Cooperative Auteur Cinema and Oppositional Public Sphere," which focused on Kluge's contribution to the collective film *Germany in Autumn*. The same issue of the journal included her and Thomas Levin's translation of excerpts from his *Die Patriotin* entitled "On Film and the Public Sphere."[9] Her first book on film, *Babel and Babylon* of 1991, began with an assertion of the importance of the public sphere, understood in Negt and Kluge's terms, in any historical consideration of spectatorship that wants to avoid the passive implications of ideological or technological determinism.[10] She continued her interest in the theme in such later essays as "Early Cinema, Late Cinema: Permutations of the Public Sphere," which appeared in *Screen* in 1993. When Negt and Kluge's book was finally translated into English in 1993, it was, fittingly, Miriam Hansen who wrote an extensive introduction.[11]

Hansen took from Negt and Kluge an expanded notion of the public sphere that went beyond Habermas's both in terms of the groups involved—often, those marginalized and disempowered—and the substance of their participation. She also endorsed their reversal of his narrative of decline in *The Structural Transformation of the Public Sphere*, a *Verfallsgeschichte* that was too heavily indebted to the bleak analysis of the culture industry Habermas had taken from Horkheimer and Adorno. Instead of claiming that mass media spelled the death of the public sphere, understood in terms of a narrow Enlightenment model of discursive communication, they had argued that it opened up new possibilities for a "counter public sphere" based on the shared experiences of those who inhabited it. Included in these were experiences of production as well as consumption, which allowed them to speak—at least for a while—of a specifically proletarian variant.[12] They had also contended that unlike the "face-to-face communication" that they saw as the model of the bourgeois public sphere endorsed by Habermas, new photographic and electronic technologies made it possible to invent forms of distanced interaction that had not yet been developed in the heyday of the bourgeoisie or, more precisely, the *Bildungsbürgertum*.[13] "This expansion of the category of the public," Hansen wrote, "involves a shift from the formal conditions of communication (free association, free speech, equal participation, polite argument) to the more comprehensive notion of a 'social horizon of experience,' grounded in what Negt and Kluge call 'the context of living' (*Lebenszusammenhang*), in material, psychic and social reproduction."[14] Open both in terms of inclusion and in terms of the open-endedness of its temporality, this expanded version of *Öffentlichkeit* was more of a process than a space, even a spherical one.

Central to this expanded version of the public sphere was the mass medium of the cinema, to which Kluge paid special attention as a politically involved filmmaker of considerable ambition. Bracketing the ideologically affirmative films typical of the classical age of Hollywood cinema, he sought inspiration in the heyday of silent films, which had exploited the disruptive potential of montage and mobilized viewers' fantasies to subvert conventional modes of experiencing the world. By locating the film in the head of the spectator rather than in a technological apparatus that inevitably generated a passive and supine subject, Kluge avoided the ahistorical fatalism that had characterized recent French cinema theory. Hansen followed him in constructing a critical constellation of pre- and postclassical filmmaking:

> Both periods are characterized by a profound transformation of the relations of cultural representation and reception, by a measure of instability that makes the intervening decades look relatively stable by contrast, anchored in and centered by the classical system. Both stages of media culture vary from the classical norm of controlling reception through a strong diegetic effect, ensured by particular textual strategies and a suppression of the exhibition context; by contrast, pre-classical and post-classical forms of spectatorship give the viewer a greater

leeway, for better or worse, in interacting with the film, a greater awareness of exhibition and cultural intertexts.[15]

Drawing on Benjamin's stubbornly utopian reading of the implications
of the modern arts of mechanical reproduction, Kluge had sought to
"salvage the experiential possibilities of the disintegrated aura for a
secularized public context . . . The reciprocity between the film on the
screen and spectator's stream of associations becomes the measure of a
particular film's use value for an alternative public sphere: a film either
exploits the viewer's needs, perceptions and wishes or it encourages
their autonomous movement, fine-tuning and self-reliance."[16]

Stressing the importance of cinema for women, urbanized workers
and new immigrant groups in early twentieth-century America,
Hansen's *Babel and Babylon* also adopted Foucault's notion of a "hetero-
topia," an alternative space for those groups to resist the full lure of
consumer culture, at least potentially. The new medium allowed these
groups to organize their own experience, "not only by creating a space
for the actualization of involuntary memory, of disjunctive layers of
time and subjectivity, it also offered a collective forum for the production of fantasy, the capability of envisioning a different future."[17]
Although conceding the industry's gentrification of the viewing experience, the rise of classical narrative cinema and the updating of the traditional domestic ideology for women spectators had blunted the transgressive implications of this new medium, Hansen nonetheless
cautioned against a wholesale abandonment of its critical potential:
"The alignment of female spectatorship with a gendered hierarchy of
vision was as complex and contradictory a process as the implementation of the classical system in general, neither as instantaneously effective nor as complete as film theorists have made it seem."[18]

In *Cinema and Experience*, the public sphere, understood largely in
Negt and Kluge's terms, remains a key category. In the book, Hansen
projected the realization of its importance back to Kracauer's work in the
1920s and his appreciation of the potential in the heterogeneous new
audience flocking to the movies, including those little shopgirls whose
daydreams inspired and were inspired in turn by the films and film stars
they worshipped. Although in *Babel and Babylon*, Hansen had pitted the
more skeptical Kracauer against the overly optimistic Benjamin,[19] she
later concluded that he also understood the critical implications of the
new medium. Despite his lamenting the ideological function of certain
films, Kracauer, she argues, had also realized that filmgoers "constitute a

new form of *public* (*Öffentlichkeit*) . . . a specifically modern public sphere that resists thinking of the masses and the idea of the public as an opposition (as upheld by Jürgen Habermas in his 1962 *Structural Transformation of the Public Sphere*)."[20] Although acknowledging that while Kracauer was not claiming they constituted a self-conscious "counter-public sphere" in Negt and Kluge's sense, she contends that he "sees in the cinema a blueprint for an alternative public sphere that can realize itself only through the destruction of the dominant, bourgeois public sphere that draws legitimation from institutions of high art, education and culture no longer in touch with reality."[21] An anti-elitist democrat believing in popular self-determination, Kracauer was

> materialist enough to know that these principles do not miraculously emerge from the rational discourse of inner-directed subjects, let alone from efforts to restore the authority of a literary public sphere. Rather, cognition has to be grounded in the very sphere of experience in which modernization is most palpable and most destructive—in a sensory perceptual, aesthetic discourse that allows for a "self-representation of the masses subject to the process of mechanization."[22]

Kracauer's appreciation for the importance of shock and chance as a "signature" of modern life, she argued, betokens "the emergence of a new kind of public sphere that is unpredictable and volatile."[23] Even in his postwar *Theory of Film*, Hansen contends, Kracauer was in touch with a heterogeneous *Lebenswelt* (lifeworld) disrupting the smooth workings of the narrative diegesis of classical cinema, and it is here that "we can hear an echo, albeit muted, of his early vision of cinema as an alternative public sphere, a sensory and collective horizon for people trying to live a life in the interstices of modernity."[24]

In her consideration of Benjamin's contribution to film theory, Hansen concedes that he had fully appreciated the dangerous potential in the mass ornaments that film so powerfully depicted during the fascist era: "In the giant rallies and processes, mass sporting events, and above all war, 'the mass looks itself in the face.' This technologically amplified mirror effect, however, is far from enabling the masses 'to reason with itself,' as Benjamin postulates in a text of the same period. The fascist phantasmagoria of national self-expression forecloses any reflection and discussion as to which end, in whose interest, and at whose cost these events are stated."[25] Benjamin, she admits, knew that "the collective assembled in the movie theaters was hardly that of the heroic proletariat; rather, he considered the cinema audience in tendency part of the 'compact mass'—the blind, destructive and self-destruction formation of the masses that were the object of political organization by fascism."[26]

However, at least in some of his essays or, more correctly, in drafts for essays that were not always retained once published, Benjamin mused on the transgressive potential of distraction and what he called "the collective innervation of technology," which involved spectators on a psychosomatic level. Compared with the later apparatus theoreticians, who one-sidedly damned the ideological effects of classical cinema, Benjamin, she writes, "sees the cinematic crossing of supreme artificiality with physiological immediacy as a chance—a chance to rehearse technological innervation in the medium of the optical unconscious."[27] But clearly it was a long shot, and Benjamin, who dropped many of the more hopeful expressions of the argument in the published versions of his work, knew it. Thus, Hansen concludes with the warning that

> we can no less assimilate Benjamin's prescient speculations to a naive digital utopianism (such as flourished during the 1990s) than to an understanding of cinema as intrinsically progressive. He would more likely have shared the concern of critical media theorists regarding global systems of surveillance, information, and control; the vastly increased imbrication of play, labor and consumption, and an unproblematic valorization of social networks as an egalitarian, democratic, alternative public sphere.[28]

If Benjamin was thus a reluctant witness for the defense of Negt and Kluge's version of the public sphere applied to film, the third figure in Hansen's triumvirate, Adorno, was even less willing. Adorno's skepticism about communication in general is, of course, well known, as is his distaste for the Hollywood culture in whose proximity he lived during the 1940s.[29] The man who sourly commented in *Minima Moralia* that "every visit to the cinema leaves me, against all my vigilance, stupider and worse"[30] was no obvious friend of the experiential value of this new public sphere. Although Adorno thought very highly of Kluge and seems to have modified his earlier blanket condemnation of contemporary cinema as a result, Hansen acknowledges that "Kluge's thinking about cinema as a public sphere, and as a space in which different and multiple temporalities can be articulated and experienced, was dialectically prompted by the critique of the culture industry."[31]

Nonetheless, Hansen imaginatively reads a number of Adorno's arguments against the grain, extrapolating from others that he developed in a musical context, to show that in certain respects he could be mobilized in favor of a more sympathetic analysis of the medium's critical potential. In particular, his complicated musings on the role of mimesis might serve that purpose. But the links with a robust concept of the public sphere, even one understood on Negt and Kluge's terms, were harder to forge. "Like Benjamin and Kracauer," she wrote, "Adorno observes a transformation of sensory perception and subjectivity in modernity. But where the former stress the collective nature of this transformation, Adorno insists on the mediation of collective experience by the idiosyncratic individual in whose art pre-individual mimetic impulses take refuge."[32]

By the end of *Cinema and Experience*, one must admit, the plausibility of the concept of the public sphere as developed by Negt and Kluge seems somewhat diminished, particularly compared with its role in *Babel and Babylon*. One reason is historical. Whereas that earlier book focuses on the era of silent films, when the case for its applicability was strongest, the more recent one looks at theorists whose work spanned a much longer era, including the heyday of classical cinema. Although Hansen tries to make a case for the postclassical era, exemplified by Kluge's own work, it does not really have the conviction of her earlier analysis of the silent film era. Ironically, her analysis of the public sphere mimics that of Habermas in *The Structural Transformation* in that both posit an early era of relative robustness followed by one of decline in which the emancipatory potential of the public sphere wanes.

But perhaps a more telling reason for the loss of power of the concept becomes apparent if we return to Habermas's notion, which Negt and Kluge claimed they had surpassed. Several of their criticisms have been accepted by most observers. By expanding the scope of *Öffentlichkeit* beyond the predominantly male bourgeoisie, they joined a large number of other critics who have questioned Habermas's focus on its narrow class and gender origins.[33] Although the idea of a specifically proletarian variant now seems dated—and indeed was dropped by Kluge—the notion of counter-public spheres uneasily vying for whatever is left of a dominant one is not. Their reading of the emergence of such counter-publics in the era of mass culture, where Habermas, overly beholden to the culture-industry pessimism of the classical Frankfurt School, had located only collapse, has also been affirmed by others, including a chastened Habermas himself. Or, at least, the idea is now widely shared that segmented publics, such as those coalescing around new social movements, may be thriving without an overriding public to bring them all together. Whether or not they will ever meld into a larger solidarity—Hansen briefly alludes to Michael Hardt and Antonio Negri's vague notion of the "multitude" and says it was anticipated in part by Kracauer[34]—remains to be seen.

Habermas's overly dismissive attitude toward the so-called "representative" publicness of the ancient regime, in which theatrical ceremony and courtly ritual serves the power of the feudal class on display, has also been open to challenge.[35] Although it would be a mistake to conflate the theater and the cinema, for reasons that have been widely discussed,[36] both generate visually mediated experiences that cannot be reduced to the passive acceptance of the spectacle or simulacrum. The tacit Protestant distrust of the image, itself indebted to the Jewish *Bilderverbot* so often invoked by the first generation of Critical Theorists, may well inform Habermas's distrust of representation.

However, it is in the overly schematic contrast of the two versions of the public sphere that problems arise. Negt and Kluge were opposed to Habermas's idealized version of the public sphere because they saw an inextricable relationship between its class origins and its pretensions to rational universality. Thus, rather than a disintegration of a classical public sphere with the rise of mass culture, it was already fatally compromised from the beginning. As Hansen paraphrases their position in her foreword to *Public Sphere and Experience,*

> In its abstractness, this principle of generality (the bracketing of social status and special interest) is no more human or democratic—and no less violent—than the universalizing tendency of the liberal-capitalist market that it presumes to set aside. Thus, from its inception, the bourgeois public's claim to represent a general will functions as a powerful mechanism of exclusion.[37]

But this argument is itself ideologically reductive, failing to acknowledge that social origins do not exhaust the critical potential of the ideologies they generate. The idea, after all, that the proletariat is inherently an embryonic universal class, which is at the basis of their notion of a proletarian public sphere, depends precisely on this distinction. For the actual existing working class has never been anything more than one class in an antagonistic social order, even if it may be a prefiguration of something more. Thus, it is deeply problematic to say that the ideal of rational communication based on the inclusion of all relevant parties, the validity testing of arguments on their own merits and the willingness to revise conclusions based on new evidence is somehow equivalent to the violence of the capitalist exchange principle. At best, it is an example of the genetic fallacy; at worst, an instance of the very process it calls into question: the commensuration as identical of what is in fact qualitatively distinct.

If it is too hasty to dismiss the counterfactual ideal of communicative rationality as merely ideological, what of the alternative posited by Negt and Kluge in their attempt to salvage a post-bourgeois notion of the public sphere? Can their notion of experience do the work they assign it in providing a model of publicness, which can be extended, as we have seen Hansen do, to the realm of cinema? The basic semantic shift they suggest is from the idea of public sphere as a site—as much metaphorical as literal—for the rational discussion of both cognitive and normative claims to one in which shared experience in the sense of *Erfahrung* is paramount. According to Hansen's gloss, it is a

> rather complex theory of experience in the tradition of Adorno, Kracauer and Benjamin: experience as that which mediates individual perception with social meaning, consciousness with unconscious processes, loss of self with self-reflexivity, experience as the capacity to see connections and relations (*Zusammenhang*), experience as the matrix of conflicting temporalities, of memory, and hope, including the historical loss of these dimensions.[38]

A great deal, of course, can be said about the concept of experience, as I discovered when I wrote a book on it a few years ago,[39] but what is especially striking about this passage is the departing concession Hansen makes to the larger argument of the Frankfurt School. That is, rather than seeing the modern media, film included, as a locus of genuine experience extended to the masses, they understood it largely in terms of the impoverishment of experience, even its threatened extinction. Although Hansen imaginatively labored to rescue more hopeful signs of a regenerated experience in cinema, at least during certain periods of its development, she was going against the grain of their analysis, broadly speaking. Although it is never easy to prove or disprove contentions about the ultimate power of any medium like film to challenge the status quo, it is hard to say that the optimists are winning the battle.

In addition, what may be lost by the too-rapid jettisoning of the

Habermasian version of the public sphere is implied by a distinction he made in terms of language, which might also be applied to cinema. Borrowing terms from Humboldt and Heidegger, Habermas talks of a "world-making" or "world-disclosing" function of language.[40] Prior to any cognitive reflexivity or validity testing, language generates meaning, imbuing our lives with value. In the aesthetic use of language in particular, new worlds are revealed that had hitherto been hidden from us. As Hansen claims, drawing on Negt and Kluge's celebration of experience, the cinema at its most creative can also open up worlds of meaning, making us emotionally richer, allowing us to get in touch with our needs, desires and fears in direct and immediate ways. It can also unsettle the received meanings of our conventional world and disclose possibilities hitherto unimagined.

But there is also a second function of language, which fits more clearly with the public sphere as Habermas developed it. This is the use of language to solve problems, test the validity of arguments and make collective decisions. It is the discursive rather than disclosable use of language, the one that operates in what the American philosopher Wilfred Sellers famously called "the space of reasons." It connects the idea of the public sphere with the capacity to learn from errors and argumentation about the new experiences that are disclosed by media like the cinema. Although a counterfactual ideal that has never been realized in any pure form and is never likely to be, it can serve as a motivating force behind and beyond the limited class or gender matrix out of which it historically emerged. Rather than damned as a vestige of a discredited liberalism, mocked as a utopian fantasy of perfect communicability or relegated to the dust heap of a history that has moved to more visually immediate and emotionally charged forms of experience, it can still model what a public sphere in a democratic society must approach. At a time when the prospects of genuine democratization are increasingly dim, we need all the varieties of public spheres we can get. To play a bit on what Kant famously said about concepts and percepts, "a rational public sphere without experience is empty, but experiences without the reasons to assess and validate them are blind."

10

Irony and Dialectics:
One-Dimensional Man and 1968

Critical Theory, reflecting its roots in historical materialism, has always stressed the importance of accounting for temporality in any theoretical endeavor, including the specific historical location of the actual theorist. Although eschewing a simplistic historicism in which every idea is relative only to its context, it has argued that a negotiation always takes place between past and present, involving a constantly changing constellation of values and forces. Appropriately, in 2014, Herbert Marcuse's One-Dimensional Man, a seminal contribution to the American reception of Frankfurt School ideas, became the topic of a fiftieth-anniversary conference organized at Brandeis University, where he'd spent a good part of his career. Bringing together scholars of my generation—including Andrew Feenberg, Douglas Kellner, Russell Jacoby and Marcuse's son, Peter, who had been influenced by the book when it first appeared—with a younger cohort of scholars discovering it for the first time, the conference sought to assess its continuing relevance in a very changed environment.

Drawing on a general interest in the role irony plays in historical analysis,[1] I used the occasion to remark not only on the ironic distance between the book's pessimistic arguments and its own historical moment at the cusp of the New Left's heyday, but also on the ways in which irony functioned in the text itself. Rather than reducing irony to the forms it takes in postmodern or liberal relativism, or hastily absorbing it into a comforting but dubious world-historical narrative with a telos of reconciliation, the book tacitly argues for a more nuanced notion of ironic action that acknowledges the resistance of the world to the realization of one's aims and yet promotes engagement to change it nonetheless. As such, it transcends the limitations of its original moment, a moment of apparent calm just before the storm of the 1960s. With all of its limitations, it still has something that speaks to us today.[2]

The joke played by history on Herbert Marcuse's *One-Dimensional Man* was almost immediate. Written in the early 1960s, although arguably in preparation for the previous thirty years, the book expressed a profound pessimism about the chances for meaningful discontent in a culture that had lost its critical edge, a society that no longer had a revolutionary subject in the working class and a politics that pretended to be democratic while tacitly continuing the totalitarianism it ostensibly opposed. Whatever promise there might be in the technological advances of modern industrial society to alleviate suffering and share abundance would be thwarted, so Marcuse argued, by the fetish of a purely instrumentalized reason that masked the irrationality of the capitalist system as a whole. The passage from Critical Theory to liberating practice was blocked, making it impossible to honor Marx's injunction in the eleventh Thesis on Feuerbach to no longer interpret, but instead to change society. "The critical theory of society," Marcuse grimly concluded, "possesses no concepts which could bridge the gap between the present and future; holding no promise and showing no success, it remains negative."[3] The only alternative he could envisage was a vague gesture of solidarity with those who remained marginalized by the system, the outcasts who quixotically devote their lives to what he called, somewhat melodramatically, "the Great Refusal."

Although Marcuse had already introduced the distinction between one- and two-dimensionality as early as the 1930s, the book also made available to an American audience for the first time many of the arguments of his former colleagues at the Institute of Social Research, in particular Max Horkheimer and Theodor Adorno's *Dialectic of Enlightenment*, a work not yet translated—indeed, no longer even in print in German—and thus virtually unknown in the English-speaking world.[4] It also tacitly drew on the contention of Friedrich Pollock that "state capitalism"—or what was sometimes called "organized capitalism"—had somehow contrived to suspend the contradictions that Marx had insisted would create a terminal crisis that would culminate, as Luxemburg famously put it, either in "socialism or barbarism."

But, whereas the analyses of Horkheimer, Adorno and Pollock had been conceived in the desperate years of World War II, at what arguably was the nadir of modern Western civilization, *One-Dimensional Man* appeared at a very different historical juncture, a time when despera-tion had given way to a certain complacency about the superiority of "the American way of life" to totalitarianisms of the right and left. A great deal of its power was derived from the relentless and unqualified way Marcuse debunked that assumption, daring to question the value of the welfare state, denouncing the "end of ideology" thesis as itself ideological and linking trends in academic philosophy with those in society as a whole. If, as Adorno famously said in *Minima Moralia*, "in psychoanalysis nothing is true except the exaggerations,"[5] *One-Dimensional Man* also seemed to get to truths that were hitherto occluded because its author was willing without apology to push his arguments to hyperbolic extremes. His was certainly not the vision of America that most of its citizens shared in 1964; indeed, the point of the book was precisely that they had been prevented from seeing through it by the mystifying ruses of our culture. But in its very intransigent exces-siveness, it hoped to open a tear in the fabric of the bland consensus that still prevailed. This expression of hope, to be sure, was still more of a "message in a bottle" (*Flaschenpost*) for an uncertain posterity than a clarion call to immediate action, but it was still meant as an act of defi-ance against impotent resignation.[6]

The joke history had in store for Marcuse was, of course, that almost immediately after he had declared critique exhausted and practical intervention in the world fruitless, the upheaval of the 1960s proved him, at least to many observers, woefully wrong. It became possible for some to say, as Douglas Kellner was able to do as late as 1988, that "Marcuse exaggerated the stability of capitalism and failed to analyze adequately its crisis-tendencies and contradictions. Consequently, his theory of 'one-dimensional' society cannot account either for the erup-tion of social revolt on a global sale in the 1960s, or for the global crisis of capitalism in the 1970s and 1980s."[7] In the works that followed *One-Dimensional Man*, especially the 1969 *Essay on Liberation*, Marcuse himself cautiously acknowledged he had been deaf to the rumblings beneath his feet.

But, if perhaps less than precise in the short run, it is not so clear that *One-Dimensional Man* was mistaken in its general observations about the ways in which capitalism had succeeded in blunting or containing forces that purported to subvert it. When Kellner goes on to say that Marcuse "failed to perceive the extent to which his theory articulated a stage of historical development that was soon coming to a close and that would give way to a new era marked by a world crisis of capitalism and by social revolt and revolutionary struggles both within and without advanced capitalist societies,"[8] it is hard not to wonder who has been proven the better prophet.

It is not, however, my intention here to assign marks for prescience or to play the tired game of making solemn pronouncements about where we are in the never-ending story of the terminal crisis of capitalism, pronouncing the glass half empty or proclaiming it instead half full. It is perhaps better to rehearse the now familiar lament—was it first voiced by Russell Jacoby?—that the problem with late capitalism is that it is never late enough, and then move on to other questions. The one in particular I want to address is not how we can explain the ironic reversal of *One-Dimensional Man*'s analysis, or to ponder why the reversal itself was not to last, but rather the role of irony itself in *One-Dimensional Man*. What, I want to ask, is its relationship to the concept of two-dimensionality, which Marcuse inherited from Hegel? Is there a difference between an ironic distinction between surface and depth and the dialectical one posited by Marcuse and other Hegelian Marxists? Must we furthermore differentiate among varieties of irony to do justice to its dialectical potential?

But before we address these questions, we must pause to consider a troubling possibility: that irony, in any and all of its forms, may have become impotent in the modern world, losing whatever subversive potential it may once have had. It was precisely this threat that Adorno had considered in an aphorism in *Minima Moralia* titled "Juvenal's Error,"[9] composed in 1947. The title refers to the Roman poet's claim that it was "difficult not to write satire," which Adorno claims is no longer the case in the modern world, and he extends this denial to irony as well. Irony, Adorno argues, "convicts its object by presenting it as what it purports to be; and without passing judgment, as if leaving a blank for the observing subject, measures it against its being-in-itself. It shows up the negative by confronting the positive with its own claim to positivity."[10] It thus needs no conceptual mediation or even interpretation, but rather relies on an intersubjective consensus about values, which it can then tacitly employ as a standard by which to measure and find wanting the status quo. It is thus comparable to what the Frankfurt School liked to call "immanent critique," which drew its critical edge from invoking a society's noble ideals against the bleak reality that dubiously claimed to embody them. The critical ground of irony and immanent critique alike is thus outrage at the actual betrayal of laudable ideals, ideals shared by all in a society, that are woefully unrealized. For irony, like immanent critique, must take seriously the ideologies that are falsely claimed to describe a reality that fails to live up to them, ideologies that nonetheless contain values and goals worth striving to realize.

However, writing in the shadow of World War II, Adorno sourly concluded that both satire and irony are no longer possible:

> Irony's medium, the difference between ideology and reality, has disappeared. The former resigns itself to confirmation of reality by its mere duplication. Irony used to say: such it claims to be, but such it is; today, however, the world, even in its most radical lie, falls back on the argument that things are like this, a simple finding which coincides, for it, with the good. There is not a crevice in the cliff of the established order in which the ironist might hook a fingernail.[11]

Here, we get an anticipation of Marcuse's claim that flat one-dimensionality is now the order of the day. Neither irony nor immanent critique is possible when no yawning gap between ideology and reality exists to produce the necessary outrage to motivate them. Instead, all that is left is a dull affirmation of a status quo by disillusioned and passive observers who have utterly lost whatever hope they might once have harbored that there is any meaningful alternative. The indignation that fueled satire and irony from Juvenal to modern times is now a fading memory; we have learned, Adorno seems to be saying, to love the culture industry in the same way the citizens of Orwell's Oceana loved Big Brother—is it a coincidence that the aphorism "Juvenal's Error" was composed the same year as *1984*?—and we can no longer rely on a tacit consensus that something better is both desirable and possible.

Was irony still operative in *One-Dimensional Man*? Is it something Marcuse validated in itself or merely used as a tool in the service of a post-ironic alternative? Does he in fact have a consistent attitude toward its function in the world whose bleak prospects he laments in his book? The first thing that must be acknowledged is that Marcuse's rhetoric often derives its power from his indignant insistence that what claims to be the case is in fact reversed by reality. In the very first paragraphs of the book's preface, we are told, inter alia, that "we submit to the peaceful production of the means of destruction, to the perfection of waste, to being educated for a defense which deforms the defenders and that which they defend," and that "the political needs of society become individual needs and aspirations, their satisfaction promotes business and the commonweal, and the whole appears to be the very embodiment of Reason. And yet this society is irrational as a whole."[12] Reading passages like this in 1971, Ronald Aronson, one of Marcuse's most devoted students, could claim that they are "rich with irony, joining terms and concepts kept apart by the mass media: perfection *and* waste; productivity *and* destruction, growth *and* repression, peace *and* war, capabilities *and* domination."[13] Irony, in this sense, indeed remains a central tool of Marcuse's analysis as the book develops, one celebrated example being his critique of repressive or controlled desublimation, in which unconstrained libidinal energy serves the smoother functioning of a still unfree social and cultural order rather than the liberation it promises (an argument that appears, in another form around the same time, in his critique of repressive tolerance).

Marcuse's reliance on irony indeed was evident in the surface rhetoric of his argument. In fact, in 1970, an orthodox Marxist critic, philosopher of law Mitchell Franklin, could contribute an essay to *Telos* titled "The Irony of the Beautiful Soul in Marcuse," lamenting the ways in which romantic notions of subjective irony had allegedly infected Marcuse's entire philosophy with an impotent idealism that was the opposite of a robust dialectical materialism.[14] The term "beautiful soul" was, of course, taken from Hegel, whose critique of romantic irony as "infinite absolute negativity"[15] informed Franklin's claim that Marcuse had fallen prey to an existentialist fetish of ambiguity, nihilation and endless displacement that failed to acknowledge the still vibrant role of the working class as the revolutionary subject of history. Franklin's confidence that orthodox dialectical materialism could still serve as an antidote to the disengaged "beautiful souls" of romantic ironists unable to throw their lot in with the progressive forces of history was misplaced in 1970—as even the editors of *Telos* themselves acknowledged[16]—and seems even more so today. But his sensitivity to the central role of irony in Marcuse's oeuvre is worth noting.

The question, of course, is what kind of irony was it and did it have the nefarious implications that orthodox dialecticians like Franklin claimed it did? To answer this question, let me distinguish among three kinds of irony, which I will call 1) cynical, 2) paradoxical or unstable and 3) dramatic or world historical, and then offer some thoughts on what might be seen as a fourth alternative. Cynical irony, expressing a loss of confidence in a meaningful gap between ideal and reality, was already accelerating in the interwar era, especially during the heyday of the "new objectivity" in the Germany out of which the Frankfurt School had emerged. It shows itself in the "cool conduct," to borrow Helmut Lethen's phrase, that collapsed the distinction between interiority and exteriority, producing a self that is an armored shell with no soft core of authenticity beneath.[17] It has even been discerned in the plays and poetry of Bertolt Brecht by, for example, Peter Sloterdijk in his *Critique of Cynical Reason*. Noting that Brecht urged his public not to live off the "good old values," but to start with the "bad new reality," he writes,

> Obviously, a new quality of irony and a nonaffirmative form of affirmation makes itself felt here. In this irony, it is not a subject that has "stayed clean" that reveals itself, who, distanced, above the fronts, the melee, and the tumult, tries to save its integrity. It is rather the irony of a bashed ego who has got caught up in the clockwork (rather like Charlie Chaplin in *Modern Times*) who makes its hands as dirty as the circumstances are and who, in the midst of the goings-on, only takes care to observe alertly what it encounters.[18]

With Brecht, Sloterdijk contends, "the pugnacious irony appropriate to modernity makes itself felt: cynical irony. It does not resist reality with 'imagined fantasies' but exercises resistance in the form of unresisting accommodation."[19]

Such cynical irony might still be at home in the world described by Adorno in *Minima Moralia*, in which there is no crevice in the cliff of the established order to allow ironic distance to gain a critical foothold. It also reappeared in the heyday of postmodernism in the 1990s[20]— when imbued with melancholic affect, it could imply impotent surrender to the incoherence of a world that defied both understanding and transformation. But it is certainly hard to reconcile with the frankly utopian impulse—whether or not fleshed out by "imagined fantasies"— that could still motivate Marcuse to write *One-Dimensional Man*. For all his respect for Brecht, whose "estrangement effect" he praises in that book and elsewhere, Marcuse did not embrace this kind of tactic, which risked the loss of any critical distance from that entangling clockwork in which it is enmeshed.

Another alternative, which we might call "paradoxical" or "unstable" irony, is more closely allied with the "beautiful soul" often identified with the German romantics, in particular Friedrich Schlegel, who developed it in the 1790s in his *Kritische* and *Athenäums Fragmente*. It operates on an essentially philosophical level. From its perspective, there are two stubbornly constant obstacles to attaining the full truth.

The first arises from the inadequacy of language to communicate the content of thought or the intention of the speaker, what in a later vocabulary would be the gap in every sign between signifier and signified. All language is thus only a fragment of or a limited perspective on a perpetually inaccessible totality. Irony expresses this transcendental condition of language, in which subjects are always fractured, at once empirical and ideal, never at one with their authentic selves. As Schlegel famously put it, "irony is a permanent parabasis,"[21] referring to the trope in Greek tragedy in which the dramatic action is interrupted by the chorus stepping to the front of the stage and directly addressing the audience. What parabasis implies, in other words, is the denial of seamless narrative, nonreflective immediacy and unity of action without something happening to undermine it. Parabasis is permanent because the apparent immediacy of the chorus's address is itself open to reflective interruption, and so on down. Every intended meaning is thwarted, or at least distorted, by the imperfect medium of its expression, which is in excess of what is deliberately meant. In addition to parabasis, the favored trope of unstable irony is catachresis, in which, among other things, words fail to mean or refer unambiguously to one thing in particular.

In addition to the ironic implications of language's unsublatable self-contestation, unstable irony drew on another, more metaphysical assumption: the paradoxical impossibility and yet necessity of questing after the Absolute. Any attempt to know the Absolute, to reach the unconditioned foundation of meaning and express it adequately, is bound to fail because such knowledge would necessarily falsify it in the very act of conditioning it—as shown in vain attempts to define God's characteristics in a positive way—but we cannot *refrain* from searching for it. Thus, Socratic questioning is the model of infinite striving for a knowledge that is always just out of the questioner's reach. Both poetry and philosophy for the romantic believer in paradoxical irony are forever becoming and never finished, always striving and never reaching a state of satiation.

It was, of course, this version of radical, destabilizing irony that attracted the critical attention of later commentators like Kierkegaard in the nineteenth century and the admiration of poststructuralists in the twentieth. To cite a typical formulation from Kevin Newmark's *Irony on Occasion*, written in the tradition of Derrida and de Man, irony is "this self-resisting—that is, infinitely, although nonreflexively *repetitive*—truth about the literary structure of all possible philosophical meaning."[22] Here we have an essentially transcendental argument about the human condition, the inevitably rhetorical cum literary refraction of even the most stringently philosophical reasoning, and the impossibility of ever escaping from the ensuing ambiguities. Shorn of the anxiety that infused the romantic worldview, it could evolve into a staple of popular culture. As one student of "the ironic" in more recent history has noted, whereas the romantics were still in search of authenticity in one form or another, we have become "comfortable with the artifices of mass culture, and the phantasmagoria of symbols and representations that accompany a capitalist economic order."[23] Not much of this version of irony can obviously be found in Marcuse's worldview.

How congenial was he instead to a third variant, which can be called dramatic or world-historical irony? In dramatic irony, the audience is given knowledge of foretold outcomes or at least hidden meanings that are denied the characters in the play, allowing its members a critical distance from the action as it unfolds. We have early awareness that is denied to, say, Oedipus and Othello, until the end of the play. Likewise, in what might be called "world-historical irony," we benefit from a kind of proleptic hindsight, which grants us a superior, more total knowledge in comparison with that of the characters in a drama whose outcome they cannot foretell. Their intentions, we can appreciate as they cannot, have unintended consequences. That is, we adopt in advance the position of the last historian, an omniscient narrator who can see the shape of the metanarrative after it has fully unfolded.

Hegel's critique of the romantics, which, we have noted, was invoked by orthodox dialectical materialists like Mitchell Franklin against Marcuse, sought to historicize what had been transcendentalized by Schlegel in precisely this way. As in the case of the melancholic "unhappiness consciousness" itself, Hegel saw paradoxical irony as a necessary but ultimately surpassable moment in a dialectical process that he believed would have a comic rather than ironic outcome, revealing itself as more of a good totality than a bad infinity. The pluralism of partial viewpoints, expressing irreconcilable subjective perspectivalism, that fueled the romantic distrust of the Absolute were all folded into one metasubjective standpoint that sublated rather than abolished them. The romantics' ironic detachment, ultimately frivolous for Hegel because of its escape from the serious business of living a meaningful life, was overcome in a synthesis of subject and object, in which engagement rather than distance defined human investment in the world into which we were thrown. For Hegel, in short, each individual moment in the dialectical process, however negative, contradictory or partial, should be understood as a necessary stage in a historical theodicy.

Kierkegaard shared Hegel's insistence that aesthetic detachment—hovering above the world, as in the case of romantic "beautiful souls" who refused to get their hands dirty—was an inadequate response to the challenges of our existence, ultimately lacking in the seriousness that true commitment entailed. Where he differed, however, was in his refusal to embrace the positive sublation of the ironic standpoint, the submersion, we might say, of the figure of Socrates, the critical questioner, in the speculative truth of Platonic reason.[24] As one commentator has put it, Kierkegaard honored "the uniquely personal contribution of Socrates to the foundations of the dialectical imagination."[25] But it was more of a negative than positive version of the dialectic. Despite the unintended consequences of subjective actions, the self for Kierkegaard is not to be dissolved into an objective process ruled by the "cunning of Reason." For Kierkegaard, the arrow of irony is reversed. All moments of apparent positivity should be understood ironically as illusory consolations for the inherently unsublatable distance between subject and object, individual and collectivity, human and divine.

Where, to return to our main question, does Marcuse stand in this shifting terrain of attitudes toward irony? At his bleakest, he echoes the bitter complaint of Adorno in *Minima Moralia* that there is no space for ironic distance in the present one-dimensional world. It is, he tells us, a world "in which ideas, aspirations, and objectives that, by their content, transcend the established universe of discourse and action are either repelled or reduced to terms of this universe."[26] The "total mobilization" of all media to defend the status quo has made communication of "transcending contents . . . technically impossible . . . the impossibility of speaking a non-reified language, of communicating the negative . . . has materialized."[27] Even the potentially productive discontent of the "unhappiness consciousness" has been blunted by the rise of the pseudo-happiness produced by "repressive desublimation." Indeed, the very concept of reason, which remained for Marcuse a standard by which social injustice and oppression could be measured, was in danger of losing its critical edge: "In this society, the rational rather than the irrational becomes the most effective vehicle of mystification."[28]

With pronouncements like these, Marcuse demonstrated how much in the early 1960s he still shared with the Horkheimer and Adorno of the late 1940s. It may thus seem, as critics like Franklin argued, that this attitude brought him close to the unengaged "beautiful soul" decried by Hegel—but it is not because he, or they, saw the world through the subjective irony of romantic infinite unsublatable reflexivity. Nor, as we have argued, did he adopt the Brechtian ironic cynicism that dove into the "bad new reality" and never found a way to come up for air. Instead, Marcuse's mobilization of both the rhetoric of irony and the contention that it was evident in the objective workings of the world in which he lived was based on the Hegelian belief—now more desperate hope than self-confident certainty—that, despite everything, a second dimension was still at least a potentiality in a one-dimensional world. *Pace* Franklin, he too anchored his own position in a redemptive metanarrative in which the negativity of the Great Refusal would somehow, some day, be turned into the utopian positivity of a world in which art and technology, reason and the libido, freedom and democracy were reconciled without contradiction.

If, therefore, we have to identify the type of irony present in *One-Dimensional Man*, it is neither that of the "beautiful soul" hovering above the world in order to keep his hands clean nor the cynical realist fully immersed in it, but that of the chastened but still hopeful historical materialist who believes the future can redeem the promises of the past, however much they are now thwarted. It is the irony of a narrator of an unfolding story that, against all odds, he thinks still has a chance of ending happily. But, because he has no faith in any immanent force, movement or agency to serve as the heroic protagonist of the story, it is also the irony of an impatient spectator who has the honesty not to identify himself with a Promethean pseudo-agent able to make rather than suffer his fate.

At the end of the book, Marcuse locates the feeble repository of whatever promise of a future alternative there might be in the realm of art, which he claims is the enclave of a genuinely emancipatory rationality that defies the irrationality of instrumental reason. He already asserts that the "aesthetic dimension,"[29] elaborated in his last work, is the only plausible answer, at least for now, to one-dimensional society, even going so far as to assert that "the more blatantly irrational the society becomes, the greater the rationality of the artistic universe."[30] In what is a final ironic gesture, he concludes that "the advancing one-dimensional society alters the relationship between the rational and irrational. Contrasted with the fantastic and insane aspects of its rationality, the realm of the irrational becomes the home of the really rational—of the ideas which may 'promote the art of life.' "[31] But because it is ultimately life that must be changed, rather than art serving as a permanent refuge from it, Marcuse refused the aesthetic escape from engaged commitment to transforming life that Kierkegaard and Hegel alike had condemned in romanticism.

Marcuse, in short, maintained a position that cannot be identified with the elevated irony of the "beautiful soul" perpetually hovering above the world or with the cynical irony of the armored subject striving to survive amid its ruins, let alone with the radical irony of the postmodernist skeptic who places us eternally in the prison-house or reflecting hall of mirrors of language. It is, rather, the irony of a latter-day Hegelian, stubbornly holding on to a world-historical perspective, who believes we can ultimately move beyond the stage of "infinite absolute negativity" into a more positive "comic" reconciliation beyond irony of any kind. His pessimism about doing so in the immediate future thus never descended into the interminably melancholic lassitude that Kierkegaard for one identified with the ironic attitude at its most self-abnegating.

Another way to characterize the ironic moment in *One-Dimensional Man* is to identify it with what is sometimes called "stable irony," which J. M. Bernstein describes in *The Philosophy of the Novel* as dividing the "readership into 'us' and 'them,' aligning the knowing reader with the author in a space of truth, a space free from vanity and self-deception . . . The epistemic effect of a stable irony is to establish a community between author and reader, a community of the undeceived, a community of truth whose authority is the authorial separation of appearance and reality which only the knowing can recognize."[32] As in the case of Socratic irony, it can employ temporary dissimulation in the service of ultimately moving us toward virtue. For all its apparent despair, *One-Dimensional Man* was in fact written with the faith that such a community, however small, could exist and grow. And as the success of the book in stimulating its expansion shows, it was, for a while at least, a viable assumption. In fact, given that we still read it today, more than fifty years later, suggests that such a community of readers who largely agree with its arguments has not entirely vanished.

But I also think we would be fooling ourselves if we did not take seriously the intervening changes, what at the beginning of this chapter I described as the ironic jokes played by history on many of those arguments. As a result, it is increasingly difficult to mobilize the confidence that we are part of a meaningful "community of the undeceived" who really know which way history is going or even should be going and who can make sense of the forces or agencies that will help us move in the right direction.[33] For we may well be closer to a situation already characterized by Jürgen Habermas back in 1985 as "*die neue Unübersichtlichkeit*," the "new unsurveyability,"[34] in which we cannot plausibly adopt the position of a world-historical narrator capable of the stable irony based on an imagined community of the enlightened, as was adopted by Marcuse in *One-Dimensional Man*. It was perhaps Richard Rorty who most cogently expressed the sobering implications of this loss through his defense of liberal "ironists" in his 1989 collection, *Contigency, Irony, and Solidarity*. According to Rorty, they realized "that anything can be made to look good or bad by being redescribed" and thus lacked any faith in their ability to choose final vocabularies and pledge serious allegiance in a world of contingency and uncertainty.[35] Not only did they acknowledge the impossibility of firm and unimpeachable value commitments, but they also admitted the tentative and revisable quality of all attempts to write definitive narratives by which we might orient ourselves in a world of rapid change.

The question that I want to address in conclusion is thus the following: is there a more promising notion of irony, latent in *One-Dimensional Man*, that avoids the limitations of disinterested distance, cynical compromise and the dizzying mise en abyme of postmodern irony or the anything-goes relativism of liberal irony, and yet does not rely on the dubious security of a discredited world-historical narrative that is harder and harder to endorse? Perhaps the answer lies in that aesthetic dimension into which Marcuse poured so many of his utopian aspirations. One place to begin is the suggestive discussion of irony in theater from Sophocles to Beckett by a third-generation Frankfurt School theorist, Christoph Menke, in his *Tragic Play*, first published in 2005 and translated four years later.[36]

In discussing *Oedipus Rex*, Menke borrows Connop Thirlwall's distinction between the "irony of the action" and "poet's irony." The former means that the tragic hero is not merely the passive victim of an externally mandated fate, but rather unintentionally brings it about himself. In the case of Oedipus, his fate is unwittingly brought about through the curse he hurls on the unknown murderer of his wife's late husband, a curse he hopes will lift the plague of infertility that has struck the city of Thebes. As a result, his own miserable destiny is self-inflicted, for he inadvertently had cursed himself, not knowing that he had been that very murderer. The "poet's irony," which is another term for "dramatic irony," is that of the playwright, expressed by the chorus and grasped by the audience, which knows from the outside what is unfolding before its eyes. It is the irony of the distant spectator, not the protagonist in the drama, a bit like the world-historical ironist who can anticipate the outcome of the story and knows the narrative as a whole, a knowledge not yet available to the characters in the action.

Now, what makes this suggestive for our purposes is Menke's argument that the two ironic positions are in fact integrated in the case of Oedipus, whose curse unintentionally brings about his downfall.

> In his ironic-equivocal speech [his curse] Oedipus knows of the tragic-ironic reversal of his prosperity into adversity because he stands in relation to himself at the ironic distance of the spectator. And by means of this ironic-equivocal speech Oedipus brings about the tragic-ironic reversal of his prosperity into adversity because he stands in relation to himself at the ironic distance of the author [in the sense of unwittingly authoring his own fate].[37]

In other words, the subject positions of an ironic reversal's unwitting author, who is responsible for doing the deed, and that of the knowing spectator, who understands its meaning from afar, merge in the end. Much can be said about this merger, but what is important for our purposes is that it precludes the "cool conduct" of both the cynical ironist and the beautiful but detached soul hovering above the world. Instead, it embodies at least in part that engagement in existence that both Kierkegaard and Hegel defended, each in his own way, an engagement that implies that irony need not be without practical implications in the way we confront the challenges of life, even if we cannot always bring about exactly what we intend.

The implication of all this will, I hope, become clearer if we turn to yet another commentator on the meaning of irony, philosopher and psychoanalyst Jonathan Lear, who titled the Tanner Lectures on Human Values he gave at Harvard in 2008 "A Case for Irony."[38] Drawing on Kierkegaard's analysis of Socratic irony but distancing himself from the Dane's negative interpretation, at least in his early writings, of its dangers, Lear argues that an ironic existence can be a productive path toward what he calls the pursuit of human excellence. To the extent that it is a form of detachment, it is detachment from social pretense, alienation from given social roles, but it is also accompanied by a kind of uncanny longing for what is lost. Thus, "developing a capacity for ironic disruption may be a manifestation of seriousness about one's practical identity. It is not merely a disruption of one's practical identity; it is a form of loyalty to it."[39] That is, although the pretense of already living up to ideals needs to be shattered, the ideals themselves can still function to impel us forward. Is there a way in which this personal quest reverberates beyond the self, an effect that might even be understood as political? Lear contends that the point of irony correctly understood is

> not simply to destroy pretenses, but to inject a certain form of not-knowing into polis life . . . it shows the difficulty of becoming human: not just the arduousness of maintaining a practical identity in the face of temptation, but the difficulty of getting the hang of a certain kind of playful, disrupting existence to understand—that is, to grasp practically—the limits of human understanding of such excellence.[40]

Rather than leading to the superficial relativism of Rorty's liberal ironist, who distrusts all final vocabularies and refuses to see any narrative as definitive, Lear claims that this kind of irony can lead to a more serious and intense engagement with what turns out to be one's own final vocabulary.

Taking off his philosopher's hat and putting on his psychoanalyst's, Lear then argues that unconscious psychic fantasies are a source of the ideal for which we still yearn when we realize the inadequacy of social pretense and allow the uncanny return of what is repressed, an *unheimlich* refusal to be "at home" in our present world and identities. Rather than understanding psychic unity on the basis of ego strength to be the ultimate goal of our lives, he argues that experiencing the ironic disruption produced by this return is a much clearer sign of a life well lived. Instead of seeking to tame our desires and relinquish our fantasies in the name of ego strength or rational mastery, "it would seem to be rational to call into question the ultimate rationality of the picture of rationality as simply consisting in my ability to step back and reflect on how well or badly items of consciousness conform to my conscious practical identity."[41]

Irony, therefore, allows us to remain within the unresolved tension between what Christoph Menke introduces in his discussion of tragedy as the "irony of agency" and "the poet's irony," in the sense that it involves a certain responsibility for our destinies alongside an awareness that at times we must surrender to forces or desires outside of that control. But unlike the tragic outcome of *Oedipus Rex*, in which both ironic reversals conspire to turn our prosperity into disaster, it has the opposite potential: to move us toward more meaningful lives well spent in the pursuit of ideals worth pursuing. In short, we know we are not fully in control, but we do not relinquish the responsibility of acting as if our actions are meaningful in determining outcomes.

And so we arrive in conclusion back at *One-Dimensional Man* with an enriched understanding of the role of irony in its underlying makeup. For if we concede the untenability of the larger world-historical narrative that Marcuse himself could not entirely abandon, we can still find in his insistence on the superiority of a two-dimensional understanding of the human condition over its one-dimensional alternative something akin to what Jonathan Lear calls the committed pursuit of personal excellence, albeit with the potential to transcend the purely personal. As an ironic attitude that is neither cynical nor disengaged, it instead resists accommodation to social pretense and draws on the unfulfilled fantasies of our unconscious to fuel our striving beyond the status quo. Like the irony Menke discerns in Greek tragedy, it acknowledges the force of both external circumstances and the vagaries of fortune, as well as helping us to see that we are responsible at least in part for our fate. It may not provide the reassurance of Socratic or dramatic irony at its most knowing, but in a world that will not grant us such knowledge, it keeps alive the negative power of two-dimensionality that Marcuse so eloquently defended. It may not lead to a melodramatic Great Refusal intransigently rejecting the totality of oppressive circumstances in our lives, but it may give us the resilience to keep marshaling all the little refusals that can make even damaged lives worth living. And, in so doing, it may inspire a meaningful political engagement, one that moves beyond the pursuit of personal excellence to something larger. In that pursuit, there may well be a positive role for irony with all of its inherent two-dimensionality and resistance to settled meanings, rather than rejecting it as merely a marker of impotent cynicism, aesthetic escapism or the reveries of a beautiful soul hovering above a fallen world it cannot hope to change.

11

Dialectic of Counter-Enlightenment: The Frankfurt School as Scapegoat of the Lunatic Fringe

---

If history is often a tale of ironic narrative reversals, perhaps no reversal in the Frankfurt School's story is quite as astounding as its transformation from a marginalized group of esoteric intellectuals, often belittled by leftist activists who lamented their alleged political pusillanimity, into sinister puppet-masters responsible, according to the alt-right, for virtually all of the ills of contemporary "politically correct" culture. Even more ironically, this underground counterhistory of the Frankfurt School—or, rather, an impoverished cartoon version of it—first came to my attention through a newspaper account of no less a giant of the left than Fidel Castro, who was hoodwinked into accepting it as an explanation not for political correctness but, even more bizarrely, for the suppression of class conflict. Castro's confusion ultimately had no long-term effects, but the same cannot be said for the adoption of a similar argument by right-wing critics of so-called "cultural Marxism."

What began as a subterranean rivulet of conspiratorial scapegoating in the 1990s was amplified into a raging river and given international currency by the Internet in the decades that followed. Based on the brain-numbing repetition of a small number of caricatured and ill-informed characterizations of its work, the Frankfurt School was turned into a meme gone viral in the no longer shadowy world of half-baked radical right cultural critique. My entry into the melee, which began as one of my "Force Field" Salmagundi columns in 2011, was itself frequently duplicated on a number of websites hoping to contain the damage, and it even helped spawn a competition on Wikipedia between debunkers and defenders of what became known as "the Frankfurt School conspiracy theory."[1]

But it was woefully ineffective as an antidote to the meme's continued dissemination and, alas, disastrous practical consequences, which are still reverberating today.

On August 18, 2010, Fidel Castro contributed an article to the Cuban Communist Party paper *Granma* in which he endorsed the bizarre allegations of an obscure Lithuanian-born conspiracy theorist named Daniel Estulin in a 2005 book entitled *The Secrets of the Bilderberg Club*.[2] In an Associated Press wire story written by Will Weissert, which was quickly picked up by scores of sites online, Castro's infatuation went viral and suddenly Estulin was unknown no more. Soon after, he was invited to Havana for a meeting with his new admirer, who was untroubled by Estulin's ambiguous political affiliations, and before the day was out, the aging Cuban leader and his unexpected friend had declared that Osama Bin Laden was really a secret CIA agent and the United States was planning to destroy Russia's still-potent military forces, by nuclear means if necessary.[3]

Estulin's claim in the book that captivated Castro goes something like this: beginning with a meeting in 1954 in the Bilderberg Hotel in the Dutch town of Oosterbeek, a group of powerful men—heads of state, economic tycoons, even the occasional monarch—have gathered annually in order to decide the fate of the world. Among the usual suspects, the Rockefeller family, the Rothschilds, Prince Bernhard and Henry Kissinger are prominent éminences grises. With the ultimate goal of installing a world government—or more precisely, a "one-world corporation"—under their control, they pull the strings of the economy, aiming to create chaos and plot to narcotize the population by any means possible. Perhaps their most effective gambit has been the concoction and dissemination of mass culture, in particular the rock and roll that turned potential social revolutionaries into countercultural stoners.

After decades of battling actual conspiracies dedicated to overturning his revolution, the eighty-four-year-old Castro is, I suppose, as entitled as anyone to paranoid fantasies. But what makes his embrace of Estulin's book especially risible is the subordinate argument—and this is the part that most concerns me here—that the inspiration for the subversion of domestic unrest came from Max Horkheimer, Theodor W. Adorno, Herbert Marcuse, Leo Löwenthal and their colleagues at the Institute for Social Research in the 1950s. To cite the Associated Press's condensed version: "The excerpt published by Castro suggested that the esoteric Frankfurt School of socialist academics worked with members of the Rockefeller family in the 1950s to pave the way for rock music to 'control the masses' by diverting attention from civil rights and social injustice."[4] The Radio Research Project, under Paul Lazarsfeld's direction, had hired Adorno when he came to America in 1938 and had, after all, been funded by the Rockefeller Foundation. It was here that the techniques for mind control via pop music had been developed. And then, according to Estulin, the task of realizing their sinister potential was given to no less a luminary than Walter Lippmann(!), who was somehow able to engineer the Beatles' conquest of the American media in the 1960s. What followed was a new and more powerful opium of the people (although, to be sure, opium or its substitutes were doing a pretty good job as well). After all, didn't John Lennon admit as much when he so memorably sang, "You say you want a revolution . . . you know you can count me out, don't you know it's gonna be all right, all right, all right."

Here we have clearly broken through the looking glass and entered a parallel universe in which normal rules of evidence and plausibility have been suspended. It is a mark of the silliness of these claims that they were subjected to ridicule by Rush Limbaugh on his August 20, 2010, radio show. Even he had to point out that the Beatles were on the side of social change, not opposed to it. Limbaugh, to be sure, ignored the other most blatant absurdity in Estulin's scheme, which was attributing to the Frankfurt School a position precisely opposite to what its members had always taken. That is, when they discussed the "culture industry," it was with the explicit criticism, ironically echoed here by Castro, that it functioned to reconcile people to their misery and dull the pain of their suffering. Whether or not the Frankfurt School's argument is fully plausible is not the issue here; it is, rather, the pathetic miscomprehension of Estulin and the credulity of Castro in seeing them as agents of the Bilderberg project to make the world safe for capitalist elites. The even weirder fantasy about their assigning Lippmann the job of reconciling theory and practice is so outlandish that it is impossible even to guess how it might have been concocted.

I have no stake in exonerating or blaming the Bilderberg gang for ruining the world. Until this episode, I had, in fact, never heard of them. Like other candidates for the role of chief conspiratorial clique—the Freemasons, the Illuminati, the Trilateral Commission, the denizens of Bohemian Grove, take your pick—they can surely take care of themselves. Moreover, anyone who believes, to take one of Estulin's sillier claims, that Watergate was a frame-up devised by Bilderberg kingpin Kissinger to get rid of Nixon because he was failing to carry out their orders is not going to convince many sober-minded observers. What concerns me here, instead, is the transformation of "the Frankfurt School" into a kind of vulgar meme, a charged unit of cultural meaning that reduces all the complexities of its intellectual history into a sound-bite-sized package available to be plugged into a paranoid narrative able to sucker no less a figure than Fidel Castro.

Although the process was foreshadowed in the 1960s when Herbert Marcuse became the media's favorite "guru" of the New Left and was often portrayed in simple-minded terms, it was not really until a decade or so ago that the School as a whole entered the netherworld of garbled memedom and began circulating in a wide variety of narratives, such as that promoted by Estulin and Castro. Most of these, to be sure, came from a very different political direction. Patrick Buchanan's 2001 best-selling screed against the nefarious impact of immigration, *The Death of the West*, was one major source, stigmatizing as it did the Frankfurt School for promoting "cultural Marxism" (a recycling of the old Weimar conservative charge of "cultural Bolshevism" aimed at aesthetic modern-ists).[5] But the opening salvo had, in fact, been fired a decade earlier in a lengthy essay by one Michael Minnicino called "New Dark Age: The Frankfurt School and 'Political Correctness,'" published in 1992 in the obscure journal *Fidelio*.[6] Its provenance is particularly telling: it was an organ of the Lyndon LaRouche movement *cum* cult, one of the less savory curiosities of nightmare fringe politics.

Larouche and his followers have, to be sure, always remained on the fringe of the fringe, too confused in their ideology to be taken seriously by either radical left or right, with little if any significant impact on the real world. But the seed sown by Minnicino was ultimately to bear remarkably poisonous fruit. The harvester was the Free Congress Foundation, a paleoconservative Washington think tank founded by Paul Weyrich, who was also in on the creation of the Heritage Foundation and the Moral Majority movement. Much of the financial support came from his collaborator Joseph Coors, who knew how to turn all that pure Rocky Mountain water into a cash flow for the radical right. The FCF sponsored a satellite television network called National Empowerment Television, which churned out slickly produced shows promulgating its various opinions.

In 1999, it broadcast an hour-long, skillfully crafted exposé, "Political Correctness: The Frankfurt School," which was put together largely by William Lind, one of Weyrich's colleagues at the foundation and head of its Center for Cultural Conservatism. Weyrich himself appeared only at the end, during a question-and-answer session with viewers who called in. In addition to Lind, a number of the usual suspects—right-wing pundits Roger Kimball and David Horowitz, and former football star and homophobic religious preacher Reggie White—commented on the School's history. There is, in addition, one anomalous figure: the author of the first history of the Frankfurt School, *The Dialectical Imagination.* The book itself was displayed at the end of the show and recommended to anyone interested in the full story, albeit with the cautionary reminder that its author was himself a dangerous apologist for the School's philosophy. Later, Lind would crow in a column in *The American Conservative,* "The video is especially valuable because we interviewed the principal American expert on the Frankfurt School, Martin Jay, who was then the chairman of the History Department at Berkeley (and obviously no conservative). He spills the beans."[7]

Since that lamentable broadcast, I have often been asked how I fell among such dubious characters, and so let me beg the reader's indulgence for a moment to explain before moving on to the larger issues at hand. When I was approached for the interview, I was not informed of the political agenda of the broadcasters, who seemed professional and courteous. Having done a number of similar shows in the past on one or another aspect of the history of the Frankfurt School, I naively assumed the end results would reflect my opinions with some fidelity, at least within the constraints of the edited final product. But what happened instead was that all my critical remarks about the hypocrisy of the right-wing campaign against political correctness were lost and what remained were simple factual statements confirming the Marxist origins of the School, which had never been a secret to anyone. Interweaving my edited testimony into the larger narrative may have given it an unearned legitimacy, which I now, of course, regret, but it is likely the effect would have been pretty much the same without my participation as "useful idiot." Those beans I allegedly spilled had already been on the plate for a very long time, and it would have taken no effort at all to confirm that, yes, they were Marxists, and yes, they thought cultural questions were important, and yes, they—or at least Marcuse—worried about the effects of "repressive tolerance."

In any event, the "documentary," soon available on the net, spawned a number of condensed textual versions, which were reproduced on a number of radical right-wing sites. These in turn led to a welter of new videos, now available on YouTube, which feature an odd cast of pseudo-experts regurgitating exactly the same line. The message is numbingly simplistic: all the ills of modern American culture, from feminism, affirmative action, sexual liberation and gay rights to the decay of traditional education and even environmentalism are ultimately attributable to the insidious influence of the members of the Institute for Social Research who came to America in the 1930s. The origins of "cultural Marxism" are traced back to Lukács and Gramsci, but because they were not actual émigrés, their role in the narrative is not as prominent. Nor do most of the commentators attribute responsibility to the Communist International, although occasionally, as in the case of *Cry Havoc!*, a 2007 book by a founder of the *National Review*, Ralph de Toledano, the crackpot claim is actually advanced that the Frankfurt School was a Commie front set up by Willi Münzenberg.[8]

There is a transparent subtext in the original FCF program that is not hard to discern and has become more explicit with each telling of the narrative. Although there is scarcely any direct reference to the ethnic origins of the School's members, subtle hints allow the listener to draw their own conclusions about the provenance of foreigners who tried to combine Marx and Freud, those giants of critical Jewish intelligence. At one point, William Lind asserts that "once in America they shifted the focus of their work from destroying German society to attacking the society and culture of its new place of refuge," as if the very people who had to flee the Nazis had been responsible for what they were fleeing![9] Airtime is also given to another of Weyrich's colleagues at the FCF, Laszlo Pasztor, who is innocently identified as a "leader of the Hungarian resistance against Communism," but had already been discredited a decade earlier as a former member of the pro-Nazi "Arrow Cross," who had to leave the Bush campaign in 1988 when he was outed.

A number of years later an unapologetic neo-Nazi website called "Stormfront" could boldly express what had hitherto only been insinuated, and in so doing really spill some foul-tasting beans:

Talking about the Frankfurt School is ideal for not naming the *Jews as a group* (which often leads to a panicky rejection, a stubborn refusal to listening anymore and even a "shut up") but naming the *Jew by proper names*. People will make their generalizations by themselves—in the privacy of their own minds. At least it worked like that with me. It was my lightbulb moment, when confusing pieces of an alarming puzzle suddenly grouped to a visible picture. Learn by heart the most important proper names of the Frankfurt Schoolers—they are (except for a handful of minor members and female "groupies") ALL Jews. One can even quite innocently mention that the Frankfurt Schoolers had to leave Germany in 1933 because "*they were to a man, Jewish*," as William S. Lind does.[10]

Now that the real origins of political correctness in the cultural Marxism devised by a clever bunch of foreign-born Jews had been revealed, the full extent of the damage they had caused could be spelled out. Here is a list cited verbatim from many of the websites devoted to the question:

1. The creation of racism offences
2. Continual change to create confusion
3. The teaching of sex and homosexuality to children
4. The undermining of schools' and teachers' authority
5. Huge immigration to destroy identity
6. The promotion of excessive drinking
7. Emptying of churches
8. An unreliable legal system with bias against victims of crime
9. Dependency on the state or state benefits
10. Control and dumbing down of media
11. Encouraging the breakdown of the family[11]

Well, I suppose at least the second plank has been realized, with perhaps the self-inflicted help of the sixth. In this confused world, it is only a short step to blaming everything from Roman Polanski's lust for underage girls and the allegedly liberal curriculum at the Naval Academy to Obama's health care initiative—these are among many of the wild assertions one can find online—on the sinister influence of Horkheimer and his friends. One site even asserts that the Fabian Society, the group of reformist intellectuals of late nineteenth-century British socialism, was "a division of the Frankfurt School," which suggests that linear chronology can be swept aside when it comes to exposing the work of the devil. The ultimate goal of "cultural Marxism," in their telling, is thus far more than the leftist thought control that denies alternative positions under the guise of restricting hate speech. It is the subversion of Western civilization itself.

It is, frankly, very difficult to know what to make of all of this—and even harder to imagine a way to counter it. The radical left, it has to be conceded, has, at times, also scapegoated émigré intellectuals for their sinister, covert influence. After Bush's invasion of Iraq, the neoconservatives supposedly inspired by Leo Strauss and his followers were blamed for inspiring a foreign policy that was ultimately in Israel's interest. Here, too, a certain anti-Semitic subtext could easily creep into the discourse.[12] And as we see in the unholy alliance of Castro and Estulin, the Frankfurt School could be assigned the same role by leftists fighting against the shadowy string-pullers allegedly running the universe. Indeed, if we go back to Estulin's original Spanish text and look for the source that he cites to make his absurd claim that was swallowed whole by the gullible Castro, we find the very same 1992 essay by the Lyndon LaRouche minion Michael Minnicino that was the source of the Free Congress Foundation video![13] But the vast majority of accusations of this sort come out of a swamp of shockingly ill-informed, logically challenged demagogues on the radical right, whose easy access to the Internet allows them to blithely spread the most egregious nonsense.

Does the sheer quantity of sites devoted to disseminating it, almost always drawing on the same obsessively repeated pseudo-facts and unfounded speculations, suggest a genuinely widespread phenomenon? Although it may be hard to gauge its real extent, the momentum of the dissemination has certainly accelerated in the past few years. What began as a bizarre Lyndon LaRouche coinage has become the common currency of a larger and larger public of addled *enragés*. As the case of Pat Buchanan shows, it has entered at least the fringes of the mainstream. Indeed, if you include right-wing radio demagogues with sizeable audiences like the thuggish Michael Savage, it has now become their stock in trade as well.[14] Can it be doubted that if you polled the crowds at Tea Party rallies about the influence of "cultural Marxism" on the decline of American culture, which they want to "take back" from immigrants, recent and otherwise, you would find significant familiarity with this discourse?

Only very recently—and then only in passing—has the radical right's obsession with "cultural Marxism" and the Frankfurt School even been noticed, let alone systematically analyzed.[15] There has, in contrast, been sustained scholarly interest in the ways in which Critical Theory has been received in America, including scrupulously researched and judiciously argued new books by David Jenneman and Thomas Wheatland about the ways in which they interacted with American culture during their actual time as émigrés.[16] But only their influence on and interaction with other intellectuals has attracted real attention. There is little, if any, connection between this reception and the one detailed above. The latter functions instead on the far lower level of the demagogic propaganda spewed by the very "prophets of deceit," to cite the title of Löwenthal's contribution to the Institute's series of *Studies in Prejudice* who were analyzed sixty years ago by the Frankfurt School itself.[17]

It is very disheartening to see how robust this phenomenon remains today and a source of bitter irony to observe how the School itself has become its explicit target. But if there is one positive implication of these developments, it is the perverse tribute today's radical right pays to the School's acuity in revealing the workings of their deplorable ideology and its origins in their political and psychological pathologies. In looking for a scapegoat for all of the transformations of culture to which they cannot abide, they have recognized the most acute analysts of their own condition. In the fog of their blighted understanding, they have discerned a real threat. But it is not to some phantasm called "Western civilization," whose most valuable achievements they themselves routinely betray, but rather to their own pathetic and misguided worldview and the dangerous politics it has spawned in our climate of heightened fear and despair.

The answer should not be to replace one scapegoat with another and trace all critiques of political correctness and the anxieties of those who level them back to the machinations of an extremist cult. Only a solution that reduces the deeper sources of those anxieties will lessen the attraction of such theories to the people who find them persuasive. But perhaps at least exposing the paper trail leading from Lyndon LaRouche to both Paul Weyrich and Fidel Castro can cause some of the more gullible to pause before they leap into the abyss. If not, at least we can always fall back on those death panels mandated by our former foreign-born Muslim socialist president, himself a tool of the Frankfurt School,[18] to keep those who resist our plot to destroy Western civilization in line. Oops, sorry, more beans spilled . . .

ADDENDUM 2019

Eight years after "Dialectic of Counter-Enlightenment" appeared, the Frankfurt School conspiracy theory has become increasingly potent in the age of Donald Trump. Rather than merely denouncing the conspiracy theory's confused understanding of a tradition whose subtleties it was too clueless to grasp and ridiculing its exponents as marginalized cranks, it may now be necessary to step back and think about it more seriously and with more nuance. For if the Enlightenment needs to be analyzed dialectically, with all of the awareness of contradictions that it entails, so too does the counter-Enlightenment. It too demands an immanent rather than transcendent critique, one that reads it against the grain, tries to understand its appeal from within and is sensitive to its critical impulses along with its ideological functions. There is ample precedent for this approach in the Frankfurt School's own history, as evidenced, for example, by Benjamin's interest in Carl Schmitt and Ludwig Klages, Löwenthal's writing on Franz von Baader and Adorno's reading of the legacy of Oswald Spengler against the grain ("Spengler is one of the theoreticians of extreme reaction whose critique of liberalism proved itself superior in many respects to the progressive one").[19]

What follows is by no means a full analysis. But it opens up several questions that are pertinent for understanding the endurance and appeal of the meme. What role, for example, does the sometimes tacit, sometimes overt anti-Semitic impulse behind the scapegoating of Critical Theory play? Does it merely confirm the anxieties that we have seen expressed by, among others, Max Horkheimer and Felix Weil that were triggered by even mentioning the Jewish backgrounds of many of the Frankfurt School's members? But if so, how do we understand the disturbing support given to the conspiracy theory by a meaningful number of right-wing Jewish commentators, some with considerable political clout? Is there some other dynamic at work that is itself screened by the evocation of anti-Semitic clichés that may hide as much as they reveal? Can nativist populism be voicing a distorted protest against the effects of the capitalist globalization that leftist critics of neoliberalism were so vociferous in denouncing a short time ago?

Another potential issue to be probed concerns the limits of the denunciation of alt-right populism by evoking the category of the "authoritarian personality," which draws on the exclusively cognitive reading of psychoanalysis we noted in Adorno, in particular in the sour reading of therapy in *Minima Moralia*. Does the protest against being pathologized by this diagnosis on the part of many alt-right critics of Critical Theory contain a kernel of validity in their resistance to being subsumed under a psychological category that denies any political value to their ideas? Is there a tension between the protest so often launched by the Frankfurt School against the domination of concepts, which rendered the nonidentical identical, and the application of such a concept to the individuals whose nativist or populist inclinations are reduced to a symptom of a personality syndrome? Although there is some power to the riposte that the reduction is not the fault of the critical observer but of a society that has itself already turned the nonidentical into the same, we must also recall the lessons drawn earlier from the role of exaggeration in Critical Theory. That is, there is always something in excess of the categories we need to describe a world that is never fully describable through them, something that always transcends the power to homogenize what is heterogeneous.

Another way to make this point is to return to the guiding image of this enterprise: the splinters in our eyes produced not only pain but also cognitive magnification. There is clearly pain in the eyes of those who have scapegoated the Frankfurt School as the source of virtually all the evils of contemporary, "politically correct" culture. But, contrary to the implication of Adorno's metaphor, the magnification it has produced, no serious student of the Frankfurt School would deny, is of a distorted and misunderstood reality. Yet if we examine the results more closely, there may well be something revealed about the legacy of Critical Theory—and, more importantly, about the current society that can turn it into a simplistic meme—than has hitherto been occluded. What that may be is still to be determined, but it may well require stereoscopic vision, in which both eyes—and the discomforts in them—are needed to see through the darkness that now threatens to engulf us.

Although the alt-right Frankfurt School meme may seem too absurd, too blatantly contrary to a sober understanding of its history and intellectual achievement, to warrant serious attention, the disturbing real-world consequences that soon followed cannot be so easily dismissed. They did not come, however, from followers of Castro, as his confused adoption of Estulin's crackpot theories had absolutely no resonance on the left. The outcome on the right was entirely different, as demonstrated by a horrific event that happened between the original publication of my essay in *Salmagundi* and its German translation in *Westend* a few months later.[20] On July 22, 2011, a neofascist Norwegian terrorist named Anders Behring Breivik set off a car bomb explosion, killing eight people in Oslo, and then went to a socialist youth camp on the island of Utøya and ruthlessly gunned down sixty-nine more. That morning he had distributed online a 1,503-page manifesto, titled *2083: A European Declaration of Independence*, which he had prepared well before his horrific act. In addition to the predictable racist rant against Islam and immigration to Europe, muddled defense of "Christian civilization" and borrowings from the Unabomber's screed against modern technology, the document recycled—more accurately, plagiarized—all of the charges made against the Frankfurt School as the fount of political correctness discussed in this essay. In fact, its introductory chapter attacking "cultural Marxism" is lifted almost entirely from *Political Correctness: A Short History of an Ideology* by William Lind of the Free Congress Foundation. In it, Breivik railed against the invasion of Europe by Islamic and other foreign cultures, attributing a considerable amount of the blame to cultural Marxism and its alleged Frankfurt School progenitors. Much to my chagrin, Breivik even followed Lind in urging his audience to turn to *The Dialectical Imagination* for relevant information, while warning his audience that it was written by a left-wing sympathizer of Critical Theory.[21]

It might be thought that the horrific Breivik massacre would make exponents of the Frankfurt School conspiracy theory think again about the veracity of their accusation and the baleful effects it might engender in the real world. In fact, the original source of the fantasy, the Lyndon LaRouche acolyte named Michael Minnicino, did come to see the error of his ways. Having in the interim left the LaRouche cult, he was now appalled by the results of his essay and put out a statement of regret:

> I still like to think that some of my research was validly conducted and useful. However, I see very clearly that the whole enterprise—and especially the conclusions—was hopelessly deformed by self-censorship and the desire to in some way support Mr. LaRouche's crack-brained world-view. So, in that sense, I do not stand by what I wrote, and I find it unfortunate that it is still remembered. I might also note that over the years my published writings on culture have been cited, as well as shamelessly plagiarized, by a wide and weird group of authors, ranging from Communist dictators (Fidel Castro, himself!) to conspiraphiles from both the left and the right, and on to outright neo-Nazis. Breivik is the latest tragic addition.[22]

Minnicino's awkward self-repudiation seems itself, alas, to have fallen on deaf ears. And although my own *Salmagundi* column was often recycled online and cited in a number of later essays on the subject, the spread of the vilification of the Frankfurt School has only intensified in the years since.[23] In addition to a flood of new videos by an international cast of conspiracy theorists, who repeat ad nauseum virtually the same narrative with all of the same clichéd talking points, it has been recycled in ever more bizarre contexts, including a conspiracy theory about the choice of a black hero for the latest Star Wars episode and the claim that the Frankfurt School was somehow responsible for the Orlando, Florida, mass shooting in 2016.[24]

Even more ominously, this outlandish conspiracy theory has surfaced in the writings of several very influential figures in contemporary American politics. Among the most powerful of these was journalist Andrew Breitbart, who launched a radical right-wing news service bearing his name.[25] After his untimely death in 2012, it was taken over by Steve Bannon and emerged during the Trump era as a major force in alt-right politics in America and beyond. Shortly before he died, Breitbart published a best-selling book titled *Righteous Indignation: Excuse Me While I Save the World,*[26] which included a chapter on cultural Marxism and the Frankfurt School. In it, Breitbart displayed appalling ignorance of the actual history and ideas of the School while blithely rehearsing all of the garbled conspiracy theory that had been floating around for two decades. In an interview on July 14, 2011, available on YouTube,[27] his simplistic understanding of their ideas and history is revealed the minute he opens his mouth. Italian Communist theoretician Antonio Gramsci, he asserted, had been a founding member of the School, who had come to America "in the middle of World War II" to spread the cultural Marxist virus, which spawned everything from women's liberation, queer studies, and multiculturalism to Saul Alinsky's community organizing, the inspiration for Obama's political career. After Breitbart left the scene, another pseudo-intellectual tribune of the alt-right, his friend Ben Shapiro, recycled exactly the same line with all of the same crude simplifications and simplistic misunderstandings.[28] Unsurprisingly, Breitbart News lavishly praised the latest recycling of the alt-right's obsession with the pernicious influence of the Frankfurt School by journalist Michael Walsh in a 2015 book whose very title, *The Devil's Pleasure Palace: The Cult of Critical Theory and the Subversion of the West,*[29] betrayed its intention to demonize the School.

No less symptomatic of the alt-right's obsession with Critical Theory is the bizarre fact that one of the most outspoken purveyors of white supremacist racism in America today, Richard Spencer, wrote his master's thesis at the University of Chicago on Adorno. Spencer is infamous for greeting the outcome of the 2016 election by shouting "Hail Trump, hail our people, hail victory!" and being one of the featured speakers at the notorious Charlottesville, Virginia, "Unite the Right" rally in 2017. In his thesis, he claimed that despite appearances, Adorno was afraid to admit how much he actually admired Wagner's music because the composer was an anti-Semite loved by the Nazis.[30] Spencer may be a particularly shrill voice in the alt-right chorus, but a sinister premise of the conspiracy theory, noted as early as Bill Berkowitz's 2003 article in the Southern Poverty Law Center's journal, has been, in fact, its unmistakable anti-Semitic coloration.[31] My article of 2011 cited several explicit examples of the connection, including a long statement by neo-Nazi site Stormfront praising William Lind for his implicit insinuation that Jews were to blame for political correctness. In 2002, Lind himself had informed a Holocaust denial conference organized by the insidious *Barnes Review* that, "these guys were all Jewish."[32] Perhaps the most unfiltered expression of the linkage can be found in the voluminous writings of psychologist Kevin MacDonald. Unlike more sober attempts to analyze the complex impact of Jewish experience and intellectual traditions in the development of Critical Theory—the most recent being Jack Jacobs's thoughtful book, *The Frankfurt School, Jewish Lives and Anti-Semitism*[33]—MacDonald and his ilk introduce it with only one goal: to discredit the ideas themselves. One need only look at his critique of Breivik's manifesto, which he attacks for not being sufficiently hostile to the Jews, to see how deep the anti-Semitism runs in certain precincts of the alt-right.[34]

What must also be acknowledged, however, is the puzzling and uncomfortable fact that several purveyors of the alt-right slander themselves have Jewish backgrounds. Toledano, author of *Cry Havoc!*, came from a Moroccan Sephardic family. Breitbart and Shapiro, as well as David Horowitz, one of the main talking heads in William Lind's film, are from European Jewish stock. So too is right-wing radio ranter and author Michael Savage. Even more interesting is the case of Paul Gottfried, another paleoconservative critic of cultural Marxism who was briefly a student of Marcuse as well as, oddly enough, a friend of Richard Nixon after his fall from the presidency. A more serious scholar than any of the other figures mentioned above, he was associated for a while with the journal *Telos*, which went from being a conduit of European New Left theory, in particular the Frankfurt School, to a defender of Carl Schmitt, Alain de Benoist and the Italian Northern League.[35] Gottfried has been called the "Alt-right's Jewish Godfather"[36] and has had to acknowledge, with some discomfort, his influence on outright Nazis like Richard Spencer.[37] In a response to the warring entries in Wikipedia on the Frankfurt School conspiracy theory, where he defends his "friend of many years, Bill Lind," Gottfried explicitly criticized attempts, my own included, to discredit the alt-right attack on

Critical Theory as colored by anti-Semitism.[38] Likewise, after Breitbart's death, the new agency he founded felt it necessary to defend him against the charge, made in the Israeli newspaper *Ha'aretz*, that he was, despite his background, a tacit anti-Semite.[39]

Unlike earlier so-called "neoconservatives" of Jewish descent—such as Irving and William Kristol, Norman and John Podhoretz, Gertrude Himmelfarb, Paul Wolfowitz, Elliott Abrams and Charles Krauthammer, who reached the apex of their influence and power during the George W. Bush administration—they have made common cause with a resurgent paleoconservative alternative whose time once seemed past. Whereas the neocons were often converts from liberal or even socialist commitments and were vigilantly opposed to signs of a revival of anti-Semitism (which they often too easily conflated with anti-Zionism), their alt-right Jewish successors blithely embrace the radical right's traditional insensitivity—or worse—to that threat. No one exemplifies their rise to prominence more alarmingly than Stephen Miller, the young right-wing militant from a California Jewish family, who advises President Trump on immigration policy and once denounced CNN reporter Jim Acosta with the familiar anti-Semitic slur of "cosmopolitanism."[40]

Mentioning Stephen Miller alerts us to an even more disturbing aspect of the Frankfurt School/cultural Marxism conspiracy theory's stubborn popularity: the fact that it has reached the highest levels of the current American government. In May 2017, shortly before the deadly white supremacist rally in Charlottesville, which drew an appallingly evenhanded response from Trump, an aide in the strategic planning office of the National Security Council named Rich Higgins wrote a memo called "POTUS and Political Warfare," which blamed the opposition to the president on the "cultural Marxism" spawned by the Frankfurt School.[41] Although Higgins was soon fired by then national security advisor General H. R. McMaster, who saw him as a remnant of his predecessor Michael Flynn's team of ideological zealots, unnamed sources have claimed that "[Donald] Trump Jr., at that time in the glare of media scrutiny around his meeting with a Russian lawyer at Trump Tower during the presidential campaign, gave the memo to his father, who gushed over it."[42] The president was then apparently livid when he discovered that Higgins had been sacked without his knowledge. Within a year, McMaster was himself gone.

If there is any doubt that Trump, who has been so quick to adopt and disseminate the demonization of "political correctness," has been close enough to the Frankfurt School conspiracy theory to have been infected, in the spring of 2016, while running for the Republican Party nomination for president, he met with William Lind. In a picture taken at the meeting, they hold copies of Lind's coauthored book with Paul Weyrich, *The Next Conservatism*, published in 2009. It contains a lengthy account of the Frankfurt School's alleged responsibility for "cultural Marxism" and its effects.[43] Later, Lind crowed, "Trump's views on avoidable foreign wars, free trade, political correctness and a number of other subjects have much in common with *The Next Conservatism*. If he reads it, our book might be helpful to him in fleshing out his agenda." In the picture, Trump flashes a maniacal grin and gives the thumbs-up sign, but it is not clear he actually opened the book, as he lacks the patience to read anything longer than a page or two of bullet points.[44] Nonetheless, the ideas in it do seem to have found their way into his worldview and the disastrous policies to which it has led. When he was elected, not surprisingly, his victory was immediately declared by one commentator as "a real movement, a true counter-revolution against Cultural Marxism and the Frankfurt School."[45]

The tenacity of this new variant of the counter-Enlightenment and its ability to survive attempts, such as my 2011 *Salmagundi* column, to discredit it, suggest that any serious attempt to come to terms with it would require as much of a dialectical account as the one Horkheimer and Adorno devoted to the Enlightenment itself. Only then might we understand the overdetermined appeal of alt-right populist movements that channel contempt for traditional elites and their power and yet yearn for strong new leaders who will somehow resolve their grievances. Only then might we appreciate the ways in which the alt-right has accepted the New Left's challenge to shift the focus to the struggle for cultural hegemony from questions of economic interest. Only then might we begin to make sense of such baffling phenomena as the willingness of certain paleoconservative Jews to defend what so blatantly draws on anti-Semitic impulses, a contradiction that reflects the growing quarrel dividing the Jewish community over the Zionist embrace of an ethnonationalist rather than cosmopolitan universalist agenda. And only then might we come to grips with the utter reversal of the New Left's frequent denunciation of the Frankfurt School's first generation for its retreat from concrete political action into a purely theoretical "strategy of hibernation," as Habermas famously called it, into the alt-right's contrary assertion that its actual influence on contemporary culture and politics has been enormous.

To do justice to the dialectic of the current counter-Enlightenment as expressed in the Frankfurt School conspiracy theory is clearly beyond the scope of an essay. But one useful way to begin would be to focus on the complicated and ambiguous role played by the School's analysis of "the authoritarian personality."[46] Explored in a study jointly conducted with the Berkeley Public Opinion Study Group in the years after World War II, it was the centerpiece of a series of "Studies in Prejudice" commissioned by the American Jewish Committee.[47] Extending the Institute's work, conducted as early as the Weimar period, on the psychology of authoritarianism—specifically, the disparity between the overt ideological commitments of workers and their covert psychological inclinations—it was a prime example of the complicated integration of Freudian psychoanalysis into the essentially Marxist analysis of Critical Theory.[48] The study created considerable controversy at the time and, although often acknowledged as a landmark in the social scientific analysis of prejudice, its methodological shortcomings and focus on right-wing rather than left-wing authoritarianism led to its growing marginalization in mainstream social science.

The nascent alt-right, however, was aware of its implicit threat to the legitimacy of their ideas. As early as the 1991 article by Minnicino, it was singled out as a dangerous weapon in the arsenal of cultural Marxism and instrumental in the dissemination of political correctness. "The authors," Minnicino writes,

> were able to tease together an empirical definition of what Adorno called 'a new anthropological type,' the authoritarian personality. The legerdemain here, as in all psychoanalytic survey work, is the assumption of a Weberian 'type.' Once the type has been statistically determined, all behavior can be explained; if an anti-Semitic personality does not act in an anti-Semitic way, then he or she has an ulterior motive for the act, or is being discontinuous. The idea that a human mind is capable of transformation is ignored.[49]

Not only was the methodology flawed, he continued, but because some members of the Frankfurt School had been involved in governmental war efforts against the Nazis, it had had an impact on postwar politics as well: "Part of the influence of the authoritarian personality hoax in our own day also derives from the fact that, incredibly, the Frankfurt School and its theories were officially accepted by the US government during World War II, and these Cominternists were responsible for determining who were America's wartime, and postwar, enemies."[50] Although it would have come as a great surprise to those Institute members helping the American war effort against the Nazis—in particular, Marcuse, Neumann and Löwenthal—to discover how the School's theories were "officially accepted by the US government" or that they were "Cominternists" doing the Soviet Union's work, the exaggeration of their influence, including the alleged popularity of the "authoritarian personality" analysis, only grew as the alt-right demonization developed.

Comparable attention to the putatively nefarious impact of the authoritarian personality analysis can be found in later exemplars of the Frankfurt School conspiracy theory, such as Kevin MacDonald's *Culture of Critique*, with its lengthy and detailed chapter "The Frankfurt School of Social Research and the Pathologization of Gentile Group Allegiances."[51] By imputing a latent ethnic agenda that was nowhere to be found in the text, he bizarrely claimed that all of the negative traits attributed to gentile groups—excessive in-group solidarity, fear of external influences, social climbing, etc.—could just as easily be assigned to their Jewish counterparts, and that the study's hostility to strong patriarchal family relations was intended to undermine the dominant family patterns of Western Christian culture. Concluding that "the entire program of research of *The Authoritarian Personality* involved deception from beginning to end,"[52] he bemoaned its influence on detractors of later populist movements such as McCarthyism, claiming that it had inspired multiculturalist and postmodernist ideologies. As recently as April 3, 2018, MacDonald's screed was reproduced by a European fascist site called "European Defence League" under the title "The Authoritarian Personality: The Frankfurt School's Attack on White Identity."[53]

For all its confusion about the ethnic agenda motivating the "Studies in Prejudice," the preemptive strike against the "the authoritarian personality" diagnosis was prescient, as the latter was, in fact, revived as a ready-made tool in the response to the populist onslaught against liberal globalization earlier in this decade. It was perhaps most prominently deployed in a piece published just after the 2016 presidential election in *The New Yorker* magazine by Alex Ross titled "The Frankfurt School Knew Trump was Coming," which contended that "with the election of Donald Trump, the latent threat of American authoritarianism is on the verge of being realized, its traits already mapped by latter day sociologists who have up-dated Adorno's F-scale for fascist tendencies."[54] The following September, a symposium on "Reading Adorno's Fascist Propaganda Essay in the Age of Trump," held at the New School for Social Research with papers by Jay M. Bernstein, Chiara Bottici, Lucas Ballestín, Jamieson Webster and Vladamir Pinheiro Safatle.[55] A month later, the Leo Baeck Institute convened another panel discussion, borrowing Ross's title, "The Frankfurt School Knew Trump was Coming," with papers by Jack Jacobs, Liliane Weissberg and Anson Rabinbach.[56] Although there was some resistance to the accuracy of the fit between Trump's supporters—many of whom prided themselves on being rebels against conventional pieties—and the syndrome defined by Adorno and his colleagues, the consensus, at least among leftists trying to make sense of his support, was that its revival as a diagnostic tool was merited.[57] In fact, Trump himself was explicitly condemned by Bernie Sanders for having "a strong authoritarian personality."[58]

Perhaps the most nuanced and trenchant consideration of the implications of *The Authoritarian Personality* was published by Harvard intellectual historian Peter E. Gordon.[59] Despite the frequent reproach made against *The Authoritarian Personality* that it elevated a psychological over a sociological explanation—or Freud over Marx—and did so by reifying ahistorical character types, Gordon noted that

> for Adorno, it was misleading to identify a new "anthropological type" alongside others that could be ranked on a scale of differing styles of psychology or "character" (the latter being the term Adorno preferred). After all, the drive to identify psychological types was itself a symptom of typological thinking and therefore betrayed the very same penchant for standardization that it claimed to criticize in social reality. At the same time, however, such a research agenda corresponded to emergent patterns in contemporary social reality.[60]

That is, modern society was itself the ultimate source of the reification of discrete character types through its relentless promotion of standardization, most explicitly apparent in the commodification of the "culture industry." These were then introjected into the (pseudo-)individuals whose subjectivities were "subjected" to conformist pressures by the objective spirit of the times. For Adorno, the ultimate locus of the problem was thus not psychological, but in modern capitalist society itself.

In other words, although the pathologization of "the authoritarian personality" could be seen as another instance of the broader movement to explain deviant politics in terms of mental illness, recently traced by Sander L. Gilman and James M. Thomas,[61] it went beyond it. It was rooted instead in a sweeping critique of the *social* pathology that underlay individual psychological patterns of behavior.[62] It was also of a piece with Adorno's explicitly selective appropriation of the Freudian tradition, which he valued for its epistemological insights rather than its therapeutic intentions.[63] In *Minima Moralia*, in particular, he had scorned psychotherapy as functioning entirely in the service of adapting neurotic deviants to the conformist norms of contemporary society. There could be no individual "cure" in a sick society, no "right life" in a "wrong world."[64] "The therapeutically much-lauded transference," he contended, is "already the pattern of the reflex-dominated, follow-my-leader behavior which liquidates, together with all intellect, the analysts who have betrayed it."[65]

Adorno's disdain for individual therapy had a political as well as personal implication, which carries over to the current characterization of right-wing populists as authoritarian personalities. It implied that those whose problematic politics reflected their underlying characterological pathologies would be unresponsive to deliberative persuasion. Even an appeal to their more benign emotions, such as empathy, or a transferential investment in a less noxious kind of political leader or ego ideal would be unlikely to succeed. Being more than the product of their individual socialization in families that spawned authoritarian children, they passively replicated patterns of social conformism that had deeper and more intractable roots.

Although consistent with Adorno's deeply pessimistic prognosis about the future of our "administered world," such an argument has a cost. As in the case of the stigmatization of some of Trump's supporters as "deplorables" by Hillary Clinton in the 2016 American presidential election, it counterproductively forecloses treating those it categorized as anything but objects of contempt, with little hope of rescue beyond the radical restructuring of society as a whole. Or if it does sanction the collective re-education—emotional as well as ideological—of the deluded, it veers dangerously close to the abuse of psychiatric clinics for political purposes by the Soviet Union and Maoist China.[66]

Ironically, a further danger was noted by no less a pioneer of the Frankfurt School's psychoanalytically informed critique of fascism than Erich Fromm. In a 1943 review he wrote of American analyst Richard Brickner's *Is Germany Incurable?*, which had denounced the putatively paranoid underpinnings of Nazi ideology and called for a reeducation program for its victims after the war, Fromm noted that in addition to serving as "rationalizations for political slogans," psychiatric concepts "become a substitute for valid ethical concepts ... they weaken the sense for moral values, by calling something by a psychiatric term when it should be called plainly evil."[67] In other words, to the extent that an exculpatory implication could follow from the use of a clinical category to explain problematic behavior, it denies the free will and responsibility of those who engaged in it.

A more nuanced approach had, however, informed a later Frankfurt School attempt to integrate Freud into Critical Theory: that of Jürgen Habermas in *Knowledge and Human Interests*.[68] Rather than advocating psychoanalytic theory as merely a way to explain pathological behavior externally—in which the analyst takes the observer position to examine and label an object from afar—he argued that the application of theories from the outside must be combined with a hermeneutic interaction in which two subjects participate together. Without the latter, in which affective transference can take place and be worked through, no therapeutic outcome was possible. Extrapolating from individual psychoanalysis to a broader socioanalysis, Habermas claimed that, however much we might explain the problematic behavior of our adversaries and subsume them under theoretical categories—like "the authoritarian personality"—it was also imperative to listen to them, treat them with dignity and interact with them intersubjectively. Or, in Habermas's terms, instrumental reason had to be supplemented by its communicative alternative.

Critics were quick to point out that the extrapolation from individual to social therapy ignored the difference between a patient who desires to change and thus shares a goal with his or her therapist and social adversaries who are committed to different outcomes. In other words, it is not merely being labeled from the outside "deplorables" or "authoritarian personalities" that prevents at least some alt-right demonizers of the Frankfurt School from seeing the light. Their ideological commitment is deep enough and personal investment in the righteousness of their cause strong enough that no amount of therapeutic work will effect a change. And yet, there may well be others whose devotion may be more volatile and whose motives may be more ambivalent. For them, it would be counterproductive to pathologize their politics too quickly and subsume them under theoretical categories that rob them of any critical self-reflexivity or ability to alter their views or behavior. Instead, a willingness to empathize with their dilemmas and hear their grievances may well be a more constructive way to address the increasing polarization of our body politic in the age of Trump.[69] There is, after all, nothing designed to harden prejudices more effectively than calling those who hold them mentally defective or passive dupes of a social pathology beyond their control.

It would, of course, be extremely naive to hope that the Anders Breiviks of the world would be amenable to any psychologically informed, voluntarily motivated transformation, no matter how mindful we might be of the need to respect their dignity and take their ideas seriously. We lack the tools, alas, to reform those benighted souls in the grip of what can justifiably be called radical evil. But for those whose personalities might be too glibly dismissed as "authoritarian" and their political opinions unthinkingly pathologized, it is necessary to acknowledge that the counter-Enlightenment, as well as the Enlightenment, has to be grasped dialectically. It has to be understood as more than a one-dimensional negation of all that calls itself progressive in the world, more than one antipode in a polarized polity that can find no way out of its current dilemma. It too requires the application of a Critical Theory that knows how to ask the right questions, including ones that contravene the conventional pieties of leftist thought, but does not pretend to have all the answers in advance.

Notes

Introduction

1 Theodor W. Adorno, *Minima Moralia: Reflections from Damaged Life*, trans. E. F. N. Jephcott, London: Verso, 1974, 50.

2 A standard translation is as follows: "Was siehst du aber den Splitter in deines Bruders Auge, und wirst nicht gewahr des Balkens in deinem Auge? Oder wie darfst du sagen zu deinem Bruder: Halt, ich will dir den Splitter aus deinem Auge ziehen, und siehe, ein Balken ist in deinem Auge?"

3 For a consideration of this claim, see Raymond Geuss, "Suffering and Knowledge in Adorno," *Constellations* 12: 1, 2005, 3–20.

4 Elsewhere, Adorno goes so far as to make the general claim that "knowledge is, and by no means *per accidens*, exaggeration." Introduction to Adorno, *The Positivist Dispute in German Sociology*, trans. Glyn Adey and David Frisby, London: Heineman, 1976, 35. For a subtle analysis of the role of exaggeration in philosophy, see Alexander Garcia Düttmann, *Philosophy of Exaggeration*, trans. James Phillips, New York: Continuum, 2007.

5 Adorno, *Minima Moralia*, 39.

6 For a critique of the premise of such a coherent "world history" in the work of Georg Lukács, a premise that still informed some of the Frankfurt School's earliest writing, see Martin Jay, "Fidelity to the Event? Lukács' *History and Class Consciousness* and the Russian Revolution," *Studies in Eastern European Thought* 70, 2018, 195–213.

7 That "truth" is a normative concept with more than only epistemological implications is indicated by Adorno's remark that "the idea of scientific truth cannot be split off from that of a true society. Only such a society would be free from contradiction and lack of contradiction." Introduction in Adorno, *The Positivist Dispute in German Sociology*, 27. For a discussion of his reversal of Hegel's belief that "the whole is the true," see Martin Jay, *Marxism and Totality: The Adventures of a Concept from Lukács to Habermas*, Berkeley: University of California Press, 1984, chapter 8.

8 Theodor W. Adorno, *Prisms*, trans. Samuel and Shierry Weber, London: Neville Spearman, 1967, 164.

9 Herbert Marcuse, *Eros and Civilization: A Philosophical Inquiry into Freud*, Boston: Beacon Press, 1955, 156, where he identifies it with the Orphic and Narcissistic negation of the current psychosocial order. Jürgen Habermas, "Consciousness-Raising or Redemptive Criticism: The Contemporaneity of Walter Benjamin," *New German Critique* 17, 1979, 43.

10 This question is explicitly raised by Fabian Freyenhagen, "What Is Orthodox Critical Theory," *world picture* 12, 2017. He seeks an answer by defining it as an inherent interest in social justice and freedom, which needs no justification. This definition is aimed at rendering the second and third generation of critical theorists, who stressed the importance of justification and giving reasons, no longer "orthodox."

11 Leo Löwenthal, *An Unmastered Past: The Autobiographical Reflections of Leo Löwenthal*, ed. Martin Jay, Berkeley: University of California Press, 1987, 60. Dubiel's study was *Theory and Politics: Studies in the Development of Critical Theory*, trans. Benjamin Gregg, Cambridge: MIT Press, 1985. After moving to the United States, Löwenthal dropped the umlaut from his name, but it has been retained in this book.

12 For example, Gershom Scholem, who wrote that when he met Benjamin in February 1938 in Paris, "I told him that Horkheimer's programmatic essays about what was now being circulated under the code word 'Critical Theory' (for the word Marxism, which, as Benjamin explained to me, was now taboo for political reasons) had failed to enlighten me in this regard. (Only in New York did I learn from Adorno that they had realized in the meantime the flimsiness of this bulky concoction)." *Walter Benjamin: The Story of a Friendship*, trans. Harry Zohn, New York: Schocken Books, 1981, 210.

13 For more on this development, see Martin Jay, "Positive and Negative Totalities: Implicit Tensions in Critical Theory's Vision of Interdisciplinary Research," in *Permanent Exiles: Essays on the Intellectual Migration from Germany to America*, New York: Columbia University Press, 1985.

14 See Martin Jay, "The Frankfurt School's Critique of Karl Mannheim and the Sociology of Knowledge," *Permanent Exiles*.

15 Martin Jay, *The Dialectical Imagination: A History of the Frankfurt School and the Institute of Social Research, 1923–1950*, Boston: Little, Brown, 1973, 2nd edition, Berkeley: University of California Press, 1996; *Adorno*, Cambridge: Harvard University Press, 1984; *Reason after Its Eclipse: On Late Critical Theory*, Madison: University of Wisconsin Press, 2016, as well as sections of *Marxism and Totality: The Adventures of a Concept from Lukács to Habermas*, Berkeley: University of California Press, 1984; and *Permanent Exiles: Essays on the Intellectual Migration from Germany to America*, New York: Columbia University Press, 1985. For other synthetic narratives, see Rolf Wiggershaus, *The Frankfurt School: Its History, Theories and Political Significance*, trans. Michael Robertson, Cambridge: MIT Press, 1994; and Stuart Jeffries, *Grand Hotel Abyss: The Lives of the Frankfurt School*, London, Verso, 2016.

16 In an attempt to counteract the effects of Fromm's ostracism by his former colleagues, especially Marcuse and Adorno, his defenders have sought to reassert his importance in the initial effort of the Institute to marry Marx and Freud. See, for example, Michael Keller and Rainer Funk, eds., *Erich Fromm und die Frankfurter Schule*, Tübingen: A. Francke Verlag, 1992. For a balanced recent account, see Lawrence J. Friedman, *The Lives of Erich Fromm: Love's Prophet*, New York: Columbia University Press, 2013.

17 Theodor W. Adorno, "A l'écart de tous les courants," *Über Walter Benjamin*, Frankfurt : Suhrkamp Verlag, 1970. The title, to be fully accurate, was chosen for the French translation of the essay by the translator when it first appeared in 1969, but Adorno adopted it as his own when it was published in German in this volume.

18 Perhaps the most perceptive comparison of Kracauer with core members of the Frankfurt School is the one Miriam Bratu Hansen attempted in chapter 9 of *Cinema and Experience: Siegfried Kracauer, Walter Benjamin, and Theodor W. Adorno*, Berkeley: University of California Press, 2012. For other considerations, see Gerd Gemünden and Johannes von Moltke, eds., *Culture in the Anteroom: The Legacies of Siegfried Kracauer*, Ann Arbor: University of Michigan Press, 2012.

19 See, for example, William E. Scheuerman, *Between the Norm and the Exception: The Frankfurt School and the Rule of Law*, Cambridge: MIT Press, 1994, and Scheuerman, ed., *The Rule of Law under Siege: Selected Essays of Franz L. Neumann and Otto Kirchheimer*, Berkeley: University of California Press, 1996.

20 See, for example, the issue of *History and the Human Sciences* 29: 2, 2016, dedicated to "The Frankfurt School: Philosophy and (Political) Economy."

21 Detlev Claussen, "The American Experience of the Critical Theorists," in *Herbert Marcuse: A Critical Reader*, eds. John Abromeit and W. Mark Cobb, New York: State University of New York Press, 2004, 51.

22 See David Jenemann, *Adorno in America*, Minneapolis: University of Minnesota Press, 2007, and Thomas Wheatland, *The Frankfurt School in Exile*, Minneapolis: University of Minnesota Press, 2009, for refutations of this assumption.

23 Siegfried Kracauer, *History: The Last Things before the Last*, New York: Oxford University Press, 1969, chapter 5.

24 Adorno was fond of citing Benjamin's *aperçu*, "in any case the eternal is more like lace trimmings on a dress than like an idea," to support the micrological method of juxtaposing unique elements in a dynamic constellation or force field, which he preferred to the subsumption of examples under concepts. See, for example, his "A Portrait of Walter Benjamin," *Prisms*, 231. But as the difficulty Benjamin had in completing his ambitious *Passagenwerk* shows, it was not easy to capture a historical epoch, let alone "the eternal," in details, however assiduously collected and imaginatively juxtaposed.

25 Theodor W. Adorno to Walter Benjamin, March 18, 1936, in Adorno and Benjamin, *The Complete Correspondence, 1928–1940*, ed. Henri Lonitz, trans. Nicholas Walker, Cambridge: Polity Press, 1999, 130. He was alluding to the complicated relationship between autonomous works of art and technologically reproduced entertainment (such as the cinema), each of which bears the "stigmata of capitalism" and yet "contain elements of change."

26 Theodor W. Adorno, "Extorted Reconciliation: On Georg Lukács' *Realism in Our Time*," *Notes to Literature*, vol. 1, ed. Rolf Tiedemann, trans. Shierry Weber Nicholsen, New York: Columbia University Press, 1991.

27 Most recently, Jay, *Reason after Its Eclipse*. For a previous consideration of the tension between such totalizing narratives and the extraneous material they necessarily leave out, see the introduction to Martin Jay, *Essays from the Edge: Parerga and Paralipomena*, Charlottesville: University of Virginia Press, 2011.

1. Ungrounded: Horkheimer and the Founding of the Frankfurt School

1 This chapter originally appeared in *"Politisierung der Wissenschaft"; Jüdische Wissenschaftler und ihre Gegner an der Universität Frankfurt am Main vor und nach 1933*, eds. Moritz Epple, Johannes Fried, Raphael Gross and Janus Gudian, Frankfurt: Verlag Wallstein, 2016; and in Spanish in *Teoría crítica: Imposible Resignarse*, ed. Stefan Gandler, Mexico: Miguel Ángel Porrúa/Universidad Autónoma de Querétaro, 2016.

2 For an appreciation of the importance of other explicitly anti-Hegelian thinkers in the existentialist and phenomenological traditions, at least for Adorno, see Peter E. Gordon, *Adorno and Existence*, Cambridge: Harvard University Press, 2016.

3 Georg Lukács, *The Theory of the Novel*, trans. Anna Bostock, Cambridge: MIT Press, 1962, 22.

4 Georg Lukács, "Grand Hotel 'Abgrund,'" in *Revolutionäres Denken—Georg Lukács Eine Einführung in Leben und Werk*, ed. Frank Benseler, Darmstadt: Luchterhand, 1984.

5 Willem van Reijen and Gunzelin Schmid Noerr, eds., *Grand Hotel Abgrund: Eine Photobiographie der Frankfurter Schule*, Hamburg: Junius, 1990. More recently, the title has been used for two books: Vladimir Safatle, *Grand Hotel Abyss: Desire, Recognition and the Restoration of the Subject*, trans. Lucas Carpinelli, Leuven University Press, 2016, and Stuart Jeffries, *Grand Hotel Abyss: The Lives of the Frankfurt School*, London: Verso, 2016.

6 Karl Korsch, "Der Standpunkt der materialistische Geschichtsauffassung," in *Kernpunkte der materialistischen Geschichtsauffassung* (1922) in Korsch, *Gesamtausgabe, Marxismus und Philosophie: Schriften zur Theorie der Arbeiterbewegung 1920–1923*, vol. 3, ed. Michael Buckmiller, Amsterdam, 1923, 163–89.

7 In *History and Class Consciousness: Studies in Marxist Dialectics*, trans. Rodney Livingstone, Cambridge: Cambridge University Press, 1971, Lukács had argued that although the empirical class consciousness of the proletariat might be subjectively nonrevolutionary, it was possible for a dialectician to impute to it an essential class consciousness that was objectively revolutionary. The Leninist party was the expression of that deeper consciousness.

8 For a discussion of the role Vico's principle played in the Marxist tradition, see Martin Jay, "Vico and Western Marxism" in *Fin-de-Siècle Socialism and Other Essays*, New York: Routledge, 1988.

9 Max Horkheimer, "Ein neuer Ideologiebegriff?," *Archiv für die Geschichte des Sozialismus und der Arbeiterbewegung*, XV, 1930. For a discussion, see Jay, "The Frankfurt School's Critique of Karl Mannheim and the Sociology of Knowledge," in *Permanent Exiles*.

10 For a judicious consideration of Horkheimer's claim that both rootedness and floating freely were inadequate, see John Abromeit, *Max Horkheimer and the Foundations of the Frankfurt School*, Cambridge: Cambridge University Press, 2011, chapter 4.

11 Insofar as foundations are built before the rest of the buildings on which they stand, there is perhaps always a temporal dimension to any notion of grounding.

12 Only well before he was in the Institute's orbit was Walter Benjamin drawn to Schmitt's idea of a law-constituting violent power that was prior to legality. See his discussion in "Critique of Violence," (1920-1) in *Reflections: Essays, Aphorisms, Autobiographical Writings*, ed. Peter Demetz, trans. Edmund Jephcott, New York: Schocken Books, 1978. There is little evidence that this essay influenced his later colleagues.

13 Robert Hullot-Kentor, *Things beyond Resemblance: Collected Essays on Theodor W. Adorno*, New York: Columbia University Press, 2006, 230.

14 Theodor W. Adorno, *Against Epistemology: A Metacritique*, trans. Willis Domingo [revised translation], Cambridge: MIT Press, 1983, 5, 25.

15 Theodor W. Adorno, *Minima Moralia: Reflections from Damaged Life*, trans. E. F. N. Jephcott, London: Verso, 1978, 211-12.

16 For a consideration of these arguments from a different perspective, see Hans Blumenberg, *Care Crosses the River*, trans. Paul Fleming, Stanford: Stanford University Press, 2010, 67-90.

17 Max Horkheimer, *Eclipse of Reason*, New York: Oxford University Press, 1947: "If one were to speak of a disease affecting reason, this disease should be understood not as having stricken reason at some historical moment, but as being inseparable from the nature of reason in civilization as we know it. The disease of reason is that reason was born from man's urge to dominate nature" (176).

18 The most extensive discussion can be found in Ulrike Migdal, *Die Frühgeschichte des Frankfurter Instituts für Sozialforschung*, Frankfurt: Campus Verlag, 1981, which contains a long section on Hermann and Felix Weil. See also Helmuth Robert Eisenach, "Millionär, Agitator und Doktorand: Die Tübinger Studienzeit des Felix Weil (1919)" in *Bausteine zur Tübinger Universitätsgeschichte*, Folge 3, Werkschriften des Universitätsarchiv Tübingen, Reihe 1, Heft, 12, n.d.; and Jeanette Erazo Heufelder, *Der argentinische Krösus: Kleine Wirtschaftsgeschichte der Frankfurter Schule*, Berlin: Berenberg Verlag, 2017.

19 See Paul Kluke, *Die Stiftungsuniversität Frankfurt am Main 1914-1932*, Frankfurt: Kramer, 1982.

20 Bertolt Brecht, *Arbeitsjournal 1938-1942*, ed. Werner Hecht, vol. 1, Frankfurt: Suhrkamp Verlag, 1973, 443. Hermann Weil actually died in 1927, after the founding of the Institute.

21 Eisenach, "Millionär, Agitator und Doktorand," 185. He draws on Weil's unpublished memoirs for this and other details.

22 Eisenach, "Millionär, Agitator und Doktorand," 207.

23 The most extensive account of it can be found in Michael Buckmiller, "Die 'Marxistische Arbeitswoche' 1923 und die Gründung des 'Institut für Sozialforschung,'" in van Reijin and Schmid Noerr, eds., *Grand Hotel Abgrund*. Weil had misremembered the date as 1922, which was the source of my own mistake in the first edition of *The Dialectical Imagination: A History of the Frankfurt School and the Institut für Sozialforschung, 1923-1950*, Boston: Little, Brown, 1973, corrected in the second in 1996.

24 Abromeit, *Max Horkheimer and the Foundations of the Frankfurt School*, 62.

25 They even signed a "friendship contract," affirming their allegiance to one another for life, which in fact lasted until Pollock's death in 1971.

26 Fritz Ringer, *The Decline of the German Mandarins: The German Academic Community, 1890-1933*, Cambridge: Harvard University Press, 1969. Ringer

noted that the University of Frankfurt, along with those of Hamburg and Cologne, had been founded to concentrate on more current problems than the traditional universities. Based on earlier privately and municipally supported institutes for medicine, the physical sciences and commercial and social sciences, it was more modern in its outlook than many others (75–6).

27 Adorno, "Offener Brief an Max Horkheimer," *Gesammelte Schriften*, vol. 10, part I, Frankfurt: Suhrkamp, 1986, 156.

28 Max Horkheimer, "The Current Condition of Social Philosophy and the Task of an Institute of Social Research," *Between Philosophy and Social Science: Selected Early Writings*, trans. G. Frederick Hunter, Matthew S. Kramer and John Torpey, Cambridge: MIT Press, 1993.

29 For an intriguing explanation of the choice of the new name, which unearths evidence of its possible imitation of the name of a comparable institute in Japan, the Ohara Institute for Social Research, whose existence was transmitted to Felix Weil by Fukumoto Kusuo, see Kiichiro Yagi, "Was *Sozialforschung* an Aesopian Term? Marxism as a Link between Japan and the West," in *The Dissemination of Economic Ideas,* eds. Heinz D. Kurz, Tamotsu Nishizawa and Keith Tribe, Cheltenham: Edward Elgar, 2011.

30 Adorno, *Against Epistemology*, 6. For a trenchant overview of Adorno's hostility to a philosophy of origins, see John Pizer, *Toward a Theory of Radical Origin*, Lincoln: University of Nebraska Press, 1995, chapter 3.

31 Adorno, *Minima Moralia*, 152–4; *The Jargon of Authenticity*, trans. Knut Tarnowski and Frederic Will, London: Routledge, 1973. For an analysis of Adorno's critique of authenticity, see Martin Jay, "Taking on the Stigma of Inauthenticity: Adorno's Critique of Genuineness," in *Essays from the Edge: Parerga and Paralipomena*, Charlottesville: University of Virginia Press, 2011.

32 Adorno, *Minima Moralia*, 155.

33 For an argument that Schelling's thought warrants a reconsideration in light of several contemporary philosophical trends, see Andrew Bowie, *Schelling and Modern European Philosophy*, London: Routledge, 1993.

34 Herbert Marcuse, *Reason and Revolution: Hegel and the Rise of Social Theory*, Boston: Beacon Press, 1960, 324.

35 The fragment and important commentaries on it are available in Christoph Jamme and Helmut Schneider, eds., *Mythologie der Vernunft: Hegels "altestes Systemprogramm" des deutschen Idealismus*, Frankfurt: Suhrkamp Verlag, 1984. In English, it can be found in H. S. Harris, *Hegel's Development: Toward the Sunlight, 1770–1801*, Oxford: Oxford University Press, 1972. There is still uncertainty over the roles Hegel and Schelling played in composing it. Adorno noted that "even after the split between Schelling and Hegel one finds in both of them—in the *Ages of the World* in Schelling's case, in the *Phenomenology* in Hegel's—formulations and whole trains of thought in which it is just as difficult to identify the author as it was in the writings of their youth." *Hegel: Three Studies*, trans. Shierry Weber Nicholsen, Cambridge: MIT Press, 1993, 60. The importance of this text for Benjamin's work is spelled out in Gerhard Richter, *Benjamin's Ghosts: Interventions in Contemporary Literary and Cultural Theory*, Stanford: Stanford University Press, 2002, 30.

36 See Frederick C. Beiser, *The Fate of Reason: German Philosophy from Kant to Fichte*, Cambridge: Harvard University Press, 1987, chapters 8 and 10, for a discussion of Reinhold's and Maimon's roles in the transition from Kant to the speculative idealism of Fichte, Hegel and Schelling.

37 Jürgen Habermas, "Das Absolute und die Geschichte. Von der Zwiespältigkeit in Schellings Denken," PhD dissertation, Bonn, 1954. Part of the argument was published in *Theorie und Praxis*, Frankfurt: Suhrkamp, 1972, as "Dialektischer Idealismus im Übergang zum Materialismus— Geschichtsphilosophische Folgerungen aus Schellings Idee einer Contraction Gottes." Unfortunately, it is left out of the English translation of that volume. According to Thomas McCarthy, Habermas's distrust of ultimate foundations can be traced back to his dissertation, in which he "dealt historically and systematically with the repeated attempts by Schelling and his contemporaries to resolve it. He is quite clear there about the failure of transcendental idealism, *Naturphilosophie* and *Identitätsphilosophie*, as well as of more traditional approaches, to deal with it." *The Critical Theory of Jürgen Habermas*, Cambridge: MIT Press, 1978, 403. Helmut Peukert adds that "starting from Schelling's analyses, Habermas tried to show that Feuerbach and Marx in their critique of metaphysics and theology had voiced a major suspicion: namely, that the construction of an Absolute is the projection of a human being who is not yet free from illusion and able to find a place in a contradictory historical and social reality." "Enlightenment and Theology as Unfinished Projects," in *The Frankfurt School on Religion: Key Writings of the Major* Thinkers, ed. Eduardo Mendieta, New York: Routledge, 2005, 359. For an attempt to defend Schelling, see Peter Douglas, "Habermas, Schelling and Nature," in *Critical Theory after Habermas*, eds. Dieter Freundlich, Wayne Hudson and John Rundell, Leiden: Brill, 2004.

38 Jürgen Habermas, "The Unity of Reason in the Diversity of its Voices," *Postmetaphysical Thinking: Philosophical Essays*, trans. William Mark Hohengarten, Cambridge: MIT Press, 1992, 123. Habermas had earlier characterized Bloch as a Marxist Schelling. See his 1960 essay reprinted in *Philosophical-Political Profiles*, trans. Frederick G. Lawrence, Cambridge: MIT Press, 1984.

39 For a thorough discussion of this work, see Abromeit, *Max Horkheimer and the Foundations of the Frankfurt School*, 111–24.

40 Slavoj Žižek, *The Abyss of Freedom* and F. W. J. von Schelling, *Ages of the World*, trans. Judith Norman, Ann Arbor: University of Michigan Press, 1997.

41 As David Farrell Krell notes, with reference to another Schelling work of this period, "The primal, primordial, incipient, or original ground and the nonground are brought as close together as possible: only a single letter distinguishes them, and not even an entire letter inasmuch as it is here merely a matter of prolonging a single stroke of one, of one letter extending the arc of the r in *Urgrund* to the n of *Ungrund*. The one stroke alters origins to nihilations," "The Crisis of Reason in the Nineteenth Century: Schelling's Text on Human Freedom," in *The Collegium Phenomenologicum: The First Ten Years*, eds. John C. Sallis, Giuseppina Moneta and Jacques Taminiaux, Dordrecht: Kluwer, 1988, 25–6.

42 Schelling, *Ages of the World*, 149.

43 Žižek, *The Abyss of Freedom*, 15.

44 In April, 1918, Rosenzweig wrote to his mother; "I am an anti-Hegelian (and anti-Fichtean); my holy protector among the four is Kant—and above all— Schelling. That I have just found Schelling's work [*das Schellingianum*] is a completely remarkable coincidence." Franz Rosenzweig, *Briefe*, ed. Edith Rosenzweig with Ernst Simon, Berlin: Schocken, 1935, 299.

45 Franz Rosenzweig, *Philosophical and Theological Writings*, trans. and ed. Paul

W. Franks and Michael L. Morgan, Indianapolis: Hackett, 2000, 42. See also John R. Betz, "Schelling in Rosenzweig's *Stern der Erlösung*, *Neue Zeitschrift für systematische Theologie und Religionsphilosophie* 45: 2, 2003; and Robert Gibb, *Correlations in Rosenzweig and Levinas*, Princeton: Princeton University Press, 1992, 40–56.

46 Slavoj Žižek, *The Invisible Remainder: On Schelling and Related Matters*, London: Verso, 1996. See also David L. Clark, " 'The Necessary Heritage of Darkness': Tropics of Negativity in Schelling, Derrida and de Man," in *Intersections: Nineteenth-Century Philosophy and Contemporary Theory*, eds. Tilottama Rajan and David L. Clark, Albany: State University of New York Press, 1995.

47 But before assuming too proto-Freudian a version of the unconscious in Schelling, it should be remembered, as Jerrold Seigel has pointed out, that "Schelling's unconscious was different: its roots lay outside the individual in a metaphysical absolute whose incompatibility with self-consciousness allowed it to appear in life, outside of art, only as unwilled fate." *The Idea of the Self: Thought and Experience in Western Europe since the Seventeenth Century*, Cambridge: Cambridge University Press, 2005, 390.

48 For a discussion, see Manfred Frank, *What Is Neostructuralism*, trans. Sabine Wilke and Richard Gray, Minneapolis: University of Minnesota Press, 1987, 276–8.

49 Peter Dews, *Logics of Disintegration: Post-Structuralist Thought and the Claims of Critical Theory*, London: Verso, 1987, 25.

50 It may, however, be possible to discern debts to Schelling in Schopenhauer himself. See Icilio Vecchiotti, "Schopenhauer e Schelling: Problemi Metodologici e Problemi di Contenuto," *Schopenhauer Jahrbuch* (1987).

51 Susan Buck-Morss, *The Origin of Negative Dialectics: Theodor W. Adorno, Walter Benjamin, and the Frankfurt Institute*, New York: Free Press, 1977, 5. He was, however, not drawn to the Frankfurt Lehrhaus, which Rosenzweig directed before his illness, nor did he respect Rosenzweig's collaborator, Martin Buber. See Stefan Müller-Doohm, *Adorno: A Biography*, trans. Rodney Livingstone, Cambridge: Harvard University Press, 2005, 20.

52 For an attempt to explore some of the possible connections, see Howard Caygill, "Critical Theory and the New Thinking: A Preliminary Approach," in *The Early Frankfurt School and Religion*, eds. Margarete Kohlenbach and Raymond Geuss, New York: Palgrave Macmillan, 2005. He notes the importance of Schelling's middle and later work for Rosenzweig: "In place of the Hegelian adventure of thinking the absolute, bringing it within reason, the 'absolute' becomes unthinkable—the dark ground—that lowers itself into the historical world through revelation but whose meaning cannot be grasped from within the historical world—God being 'before all relation' " (150).

53 Theodor W. Adorno, *Critical Models: Interventions and Catchwords*, trans. Henry W. Pickford, New York: State University of New York Press, 1998, 34.

54 Gershom Scholem, *Walter Benjamin—Die Geschichte einer Freundschaft*, Frankfurt: Suhrkamp, 1975, 33. He says that Benjamin was more impressed by Franz von Baader than Schelling, but later acknowledges the importance of Franz Joseph Molitor, a student of Schelling and Baader who had studied the Kabbala, for Benjamin.

55 Jürgen Habermas, "Dual-Layered Time: Personal Notes on Philosopher Theodor W. Adorno in the '50s," *Logos* 2/4, 2003, logosjournal.com.

56 Tilottama Rajan, " 'The Abyss of the Past': Psychoanalysis in Schelling's *Ages of the World* (1815)," *Romantic Circles,* rc.umd.edu.

57 Robert Hullot-Kentor, "Introduction to Adorno's 'Idea of Natural History'," *Telos* 66, 1984, 106.

58 Bowie, *Schelling and Modern European Philosophy*, 58.

59 Adorno, *Minima Moralia*, 15. For a discussion of melancholy in Schelling, see Clark, " 'The Necessary Heritage of Darkness,' " 109–15.

60 Theodor W. Adorno, *Kant's Critique of Pure Reason*, ed. Rolf Tiedemann, trans. Rodney Livingstone, Stanford: Stanford University Press, 2001, 16. For a history of the architectural metaphors underlying such a quest in German philosophy and literature, see Daniel Purdy, *On the Ruins of Babel: Architectural Metaphor in German Thought*, Ithaca: Cornell University Press, 2011.

61 Theodor W. Adorno, *Negative Dialectics*, trans. E. B. Ashton, New York: Continuum, 1973, 202.

62 Herbert Schnädelbach, "Dialektik als Vernunftkritik Zur Konstruktion des Rationalen bei Adorno," in *Adorno-Konferenz 1983*, eds. Ludwig von Friedeburg and Jürgen Habermas, Frankfurt: Suhrkamp, 1983, 75.

63 Lambert Zuidervaart, *Adorno's Aesthetic Theory: The Redemption of an Illusion*, Cambridge: MIT Press, 1991, 136; and Andrew Bowie, *From Romanticism to Critical Theory: The Philosophy of German Literary Theory*, London: Routledge, 1997.

64 For a fuller consideration of this issue, see Martin Jay, *Marxism and Totality: The Adventures of a Concept from Lukács to Habermas*, Berkeley: University of California Press, 1984.

65 For a comparison of Adorno's defense of nonidentity with Schelling, which stresses differences as well as similarities, see Andrew Bowie, " 'Non-Identity': The German Romantics, Schelling and Adorno," *Intersections*, eds. Rajan and Clark. While agreeing that both Schelling and Adorno distance themselves from Hegel's attempt to assimilate being to thought, he argues they understand "reflexivity" differently: "Adorno thinks that by hanging on to an inverted conception of the relation between subject and object he can avoid a construction that entails 'being which is absolutely independent of thinking,' " a mystical and irrationalist conclusion he identifies with Heidegger (253). He thus misses "the nonreflexive ground of the difference of subject and object that emerges via the failure of reflection to ground itself" (257). Bowie concludes, however, that in his aesthetic theory as opposed to his philosophy, Adorno approaches an understanding of this Schellingian insight. But there is evidence as well in his philosophical texts that he avoids the simple reversal that Bowie attributes to him, preferring a constellation of subject and object to the total domination of one by the other (even if object is to be given "priority"). See, for example, "On Subject and Object" in *Critical Models: Interventions and Catchwords,* trans. Henry W. Pickford, New York: Columbia University Press, 1998.

66 Jürgen Habermas, "The Unity of Reason in the Diversity of its Voices," *Postmetaphysical Thought: Philosophical Essays*, trans. William Mark Hohengarten, Cambridge: Polity Press, 1992, 121.

67 Hannah Arendt, *On Revolution*, New York: Viking, 1965.

68 Ibid., 166.

69 For a discussion, see Pizer, *Toward a Theory of Radical Origin*, 138–48. He

argues against Adorno's depiction of Heidegger's work as based on an identity theory of singular origins. What Heidegger did resist, however, was the transition from *Grund* as a foundational point of origin to *Grund* as a reason given by a discursive justification of truth claims, which was Habermas's move. Thus, for example, he could write in *The Principle of Reason*, trans. Reginald Lilly, Bloomington, Indiana University Press, 1996, that "the unique unleashing of the demand to render reasons threatens everything of humans' being-at-home and robs them of the roots of their subsistence, the root from out of which every great human age, every world-opening spirit, every molding of the human form has thus far grown" (3).

70 Buckmuller, "Die 'Marxistische Arbeitswoche' 1923 und die Gründung des 'Instituts für Sozialforschung,' " 145.

2. "The Hope That Earthly Horror Does Not Possess the Last Word": Max Horkheimer and *The Dialectical Imagination*

1 Theodor W. Adorno, Max Horkheimer, *Briefwechsel 1927–1969*, vol. 4: 1950–1969, eds. Christoph Gödde and Henri Lonitz, Frankfurt: Suhrkamp, 2006, 846.

2 Martin Jay, "The Ungrateful Dead," *Refractions of Violence*, New York: Routledge, 2003.

3 Wolfgang Kraushaar, ed., *Frankfurter Schule und Studentenbewegung: Von der Flaschenpost zum Molotowcocktail, 1946 bis 1995*, 3 vols., Hamburg, 1998. Adorno had infamously said: "When I made my theoretical model, I couldn't have guessed that people would try to realize it with Molotov cocktails." Quoted in the *Süddeutsche Zeitung*, April 26–27, 1969, 10.

4 Cited in Matthew G. Specter, *Habermas: An Intellectual Biography*, New York: Cambridge University Press, 2010, 31.

5 Max Horkheimer, *Kritische Theorie*, ed. Alfred Schmidt, 2 vols., Frankfurt: Fischer, 1968. In the introduction, he carefully warned against the uncritical adoption of his earlier positions.

6 See Theodor Adorno, Herbert Marcuse, "Correspondence on the German Student Movement," *New Left Review* 1/233, 1999. The public face is evident in the encomium that Adorno wrote for Marcuse's seventieth birthday to the Philosophy Department at the University of California, San Diego, on September 18, 1968. See Herbert Marcuse, *The New Left and the 1960s*, ed. Douglas Kellner, *Collected Papers of Herbert Marcuse*, vol. 3, London: Routledge, 2005, 120–1.

7 Theodor W. Adorno to the author, Frankfurt, November 11, 1968, in the author's collection.

8 For accounts of their complicated relationship, which began when Adorno joined the Radio Research Project at Princeton in 1938, see David E. Morrison, "Kultur and Culture: The Case of Theodor W. Adorno and Paul F. Lazarsfeld," *Social Research* 45: 2, 1978: 331–55; Isabell Otto, "Empirie als Korrektiv: Adorno, Lazarsfeld und er Eigensinn des Medialen; Fiktionenen objektiver Wahrscheinlichkeit," *Zietschrift für Medienwissenschaft* 5: 2, 2011. As it turned out, Lazarsfeld was very helpful in sharing his archive with me and was generous in his estimation of Adorno's position, even if he did not share it.

9 For evidence of Adorno's continuing animus toward Löwenthal at this time,

see his letter to Horkheimer, Frankfurt, January 24, 1969, in which he advised against mentioning Löwenthal's role in the Institute in Horkheimer's foreword to *Kritische Theorie*. See Horkheimer/Adorno, *Briefwechsel*, vol. 5, 838–9.

10 Max Horkheimer to author, Montagnola, November 22, 1968, in the author's collection.

11 Butler's motivations are not very clear. Lewis Feuer attempted to argue that he had been duped by Horkheimer, who hid the Institute's real agenda. See his "The Frankfurt Marxists and the Columbia Liberals," *Survey* 25: 3, 1980, and my rebuttal "Misrepresentations of the Frankfurt School," *Survey* 26: 2, 1982, and Feuer's response: "The Social Role of the Frankfurt Marxists," *Survey* 26: 2, 1982. For a later critique of Feuer's claims, see Thomas Wheatland, *The Frankfurt School in Exile*, Minneapolis: University of Minnesota Press, 2009, chapter 1.

12 Max Horkheimer to the author, Montagnola, December 11, 1969, in the author's collection.

13 Gretel Adorno to the author, Frankfurt, January 27, 1970, in the author's collection. The article was "The Permanent Exile of Theodor Adorno," *Midstream* 15: 10, 1969.

14 The construction of the two houses is discussed in Nicola Emery, *Per il Non Conformismo: Max Horkheimer e Friedrich Pollock: l'altra Scuola di Francoforte*, Rome: Castelvecchi, 2015. Through his kind intervention, I was able to revisit the privately owned former Horkheimer house in 2016—Pollock's has been torn down and replaced—and sit for a video interview in the very room where I had interviewed Horkheimer in 1969.

15 "The fact that everywhere today there is a tendency to record extempore speech and then to disseminate it is a symptom of the methods of the administered world which pins down the ephemeral word in order to hold the speaker to it. A tape recording is a kind of fingerprint of the living spirit." Adorno, *Gesammelte Schriften*, ed. Rolf Tiedemann, vol. 20.1, 360, cited in Rolf Tiedemann, "Editor's Afterword" to Theodor W. Adorno, *Kant's Critique of Pure Reason*, ed. Tiedemann, trans. Rodney Livingstone, Stanford: Stanford University Press, 2001, 283.

16 Martin Jay, "Ill at Ease in Weimar," *Midstream* 15: 2, 1969. The review was also of Peter Gay's *Weimar Culture: The Outsider as Insider*.

17 Friedrich Pollock to the author, Montagnola, June 20, 1969, in the author's collection.

18 G. E. Kluth to the author, Montagnola, August 14, 1969, in the author's collection.

19 Horkheimer to the author, Montagnola, January 5, 1971, in the author's collection. The loss of Pollock followed by a year the death of Horkheimer's wife, Maidon, on October 17, 1969.

20 See Tim B. Müller, *Krieger und Gelehrte: Herbert Marcuse und die Denksystem im Kalten Krieg*, Hamburg: HIS Verlag, 2010.

21 Horkheimer to the author, Montagnola, May 2, 1971, in the author's collection.

22 They were given by Becker's friend, Ottmar Preuß, to the Archivzentrum of the University Library in Frankfurt. See http://www.ub.uni-frankfurt.de/archive/becker.html.

23 Horkheimer to the author, Montagnola, June 8, 1971, in the author's collection. The phrase "God dwells in the detail" is normally attributed to Aby

Warburg, but it is sometimes also said to have been the motto of Mies van der Rohe.

24 Matthias Becker to author, Magliasina, Switzerland, July 21, 1971, August 10, 1971, and December 12, 1971, in the author's collection.

25 Becker to the author, August 10, 1971.

26 For recent considerations of the issue, see Monika Boll and Raphael Gross, eds., *Die Frankfurter Schule und Frankfurt: Eine Rückkehr nach Deutschland*, Göttingen: Wallstein, 2009; and Jack Jacobs, *The Frankfurt School, Jewish Lives and Anti-Semitism*, New York: Cambridge University Press, 2014.

27 See chapter 11.

28 Boll and Gross, *Die Frankfurter Schule und Frankfurt*, 165.

29 Felix Weil to the author, Ramstein, Germany, June 27, 1971, in the author's collection.

30 Horkheimer to the author, Montagnola, July 25, 1971, in the author's collection.

31 Leo Löwenthal, *An Unmastered Past: The Autobiographical Reflections of Leo Löwenthal*, ed. Martin Jay, Berkeley: University of California Press, 1987, 112.

32 Horkheimer to the author, January 31, 1972, in the author's collection.

33 Horkheimer to the author, March 5, 1972, in the author's collection.

34 Felix Weil to author, March 19, 1972, in the author's collection.

35 For an account, see Richard Wolin, *The Frankfurt School Revisited*, New York: Routledge, 2006.

36 Allan Bloom, *The Closing of the American Mind*, New York: Simon and Schuster, 1987.

37 Norman O. Brown, *Life against Death: The Psychoanalytic Meaning of History*, New York: Vintage, 1959, 318.

38 Jay, *Permanent Exiles*.

39 Horkheimer to the author, Montagnola, August 31, 1971, in the author's collection.

40 Matthias Becker to the author, Lilienthal, Switzerland, December 12, 1971.

41 Horkheimer to the author, Montagnola, March 5, 1972.

42 Horkheimer to the author, March 10, 1972.

3. Max Horkheimer and *The Family of Man*

1 This chapter was written for a talk given at Clervaux Castle in Luxemburg, where *The Family of Man* is permanently displayed, and was first published in *The Family of Man Revisited: Photography in a Global Age*, eds. Gerd Hurm, Anke Reitz and Shamoon Zamir, London: I.B. Taurus and Co., 2018.

2 Max Horkheimer, "Humanity," *Dawn and Decline: Notes, 1926–1931 and 1950–1969*, trans. Michael Shaw, New York: Seabury Press, 1978, 153.

3 Hal Foster, Rosalind Krauss, Yve-Alain Bois, Benjamin H. D. Buchloh, *Art Since 1900: Modernism, Antimodernism, Postmodernism*, New York: Thames and Hudson, 2004, 426.

4 For a general survey of the exhibition's reception with most of the relevant references, see Monique Berlier, "*The Family of Man*: Readings of an Exhibition," in *Picturing the Past: Media, History and Photography*, eds. Bonnie Brennan and Hanno Hardt, Champaign, University of Illinois Press, 1999.

5 Eric J. Sandeen, *Picturing an Exhibition: The "Family of Man" and 1950s America*, Albuquerque: University of New Mexico Press, 1995; Blake Stimson, *The Pivot of the World: Photography and Its Nation*, Cambridge: MIT Press, 2006; Fred Turner, "*The Family of Man* and the Politics of Attention in Cold War America," *Public Culture* 24: 1, 2012, 55–84; Sarah E. James, "A Post-Fascist *Family of Man*? Cold War Humanism, Democracy and Photography in Germany," *Oxford Art Journal* 35: 3, 2012, 315–36; Gerd Hurm, "Die Rhetorik des Details: Barthes, Brecht und die epochale Fotoausstellung *The Family of Man*," *Grenzen und Gestaltung: Figuren der Unterscheidung und Überschreitung in Literatur und Sprache*, eds. Nikolas Immer, Stefani Kugler and Nikolaus Ruge, Trier: WVT, 2015.

6 Max Horkheimer, "Eröffnung der Photo-Austellung *The Family of Man—Wir alle*" (1958) in *Gesammelte Schriften*, ed. Alfred Schmidt, vol. 13, Frankfurt, 1989. In English as "*The Family of Man—All of Us*," in *The Family of Man Revisited: Photography in a Global Age*, eds. Gerd Hurm, Anke Reitz and Shamoon Zamir, London: I.B. Taurus 2018, the source of the following citations.

7 Max Horkheimer, "The Concept of Man," *Critique of Instrumental Reason*, trans. Matthew J. O'Connell et al., New York: Seabury Press, 1974. For a consideration of this essay in the context of ecological issues and the humanist domination of nature, see Timothy W. Luke, "Toward a Critique of Post-Human Reason: Revisiting 'Nature' and 'Humanity' in Horkheimer's 'The Concept of Man,'" in *Critical Ecologies: The Frankfurt School and Contemporary Environmental Crises*, ed. Andrew Biro, Toronto: University of Toronto Press, 2011.

8 Clemens Albrecht, "'Das Allerwichtigste ist, daß man die Jugend für sich gewinnte': Die kultur-und bildungspolitischen Pläne des Horkheimer-Kreises bei der Remigration," in *Die intellektuelle Gründung der Bundesrepublik*, eds. Albrecht et al., Frankfurt: Campus, 1999.

9 Horkheimer acknowledged the limitations of his prewar Marxism but remained loyal to its critique of bourgeois society and capitalist economics, as demonstrated by his 1956 conversations with Adorno, which have been published as *Towards a New Manifesto*, trans. Rodney Livingstone, London: Verso, 2011.

10 "I believe," Horkheimer said in conversation with Adorno, "that Europe and America are probably the best civilizations that history has produced up to now as far as prosperity and justice are concerned. The key point now is to ensure the preservation of these gains." But then he added, "that can be achieved only if we remain ruthlessly critical of this civilization . . . We have nothing in common with the Russian bureaucrats. But they stand for a greater right as opposed to Western culture. It is the fault of the West that the Russian Revolution went the way it did." Ibid., 35–6.

11 Horkheimer, "*The Family of Man—All of Us*," 49.

12 Ibid. Lieber (1798?–1872), who was called Franz before emigrating to America in 1827, is best remembered as the author of a code of honorable military conduct during the Civil War, which has been deemed the forerunner of the Geneva Convention.

13 Ibid.

14 For the original text and a selection of insightful discussions of its significance, see Amélie Oksenberg Rorty and James Schmidt, eds., *Kant's Idea for a*

Universal History with a Cosmopolitan Aim, Cambridge: Cambridge University Press, 2009. It should be noted that Kant's "Absicht" is variously translated as "purpose," "aim" and "point of view."

15 Horkheimer, "The Family of Man—All of Us," 50.

16 Ibid.

17 Ibid., 51.

18 Ibid., 52.

19 For Kant's discussion of this term, see *Religion with the Limits of Reason Alone* (1793), where he claimed it was innate in human nature, not something historically variable. For a recent discussion of its implications, see Richard Bernstein, *Radical Evil: A Philosophical Investigation*, New York: Polity Press, 2002.

20 Horkheimer, "The Family of Man—All of Us," 52–3.

21 For a discussion, see Jay, "The Frankfurt School's Critique of Marxist Humanism," *Permanent Exiles*.

22 Michel Foucault, *The Order of Things: An Archaeology of the Human Sciences*, London: Vintage, 1994, 322. For a discussion, see Béatrice Han, *Foucault's Critical Project: Between the Transcendental and the Historical*, trans. Edward Pile, Stanford: Stanford University Press, 2002.

23 Max Horkheimer, "Schopenhauer Today," in *Critique of Instrumental Reason*, trans. Matthew J. O'Connell et al., New York: Seabury Press, 1974, 83.

24 Max Horkheimer and Theodor W. Adorno, *Dialectic of Enlightenment*, trans. Edmund Jephcott, Stanford: Stanford University Press, 2002, 200.

25 Max Horkheimer, *Eclipse of Reason*, New York: Oxford University Press, 1947, 156.

26 It might be thought that Horkheimer's enthusiasm for photographs shows that he was in conversation with another émigré, Siegfried Kracauer, who also positively invoked the exhibition and the authenticating power of photographs in *The Theory of Film: The Redemption of Physical Reality*, New York: Oxford University Press, 1960, 310. In fact, they remained personally at odds from the Weimar years, despite their common friendship with Adorno. Kracauer, moreover, remained in New York, while Horkheimer returned to Frankfurt. For a discussion of their fundamental theoretical differences, see Martin Jay, "Mass Culture and Aesthetic Redemption: The Debate between Max Horkheimer and Siegfried Kracauer," *Fin-de-siècle Socialism and Other Essays*, New York: Routledge, 1988.

27 Perhaps the first mention of it comes in 1947 in *Dialectic of Enlightenment*, 17–18. The Jewish taboo on images was also extended to a refusal to utter God's name, which is more prominent in this early passage.

28 For discussions, see Elizabeth A. Pritchard, "*Bilderverbot* Meets Body in Theodor W. Adorno's Inverse Theology," *Harvard Theological Review* 95: 3, 2002; and "Art and Politics in the Desert; German Exiles in California and the Biblical *Bilderverbot*," *New German Critique* 118, 2013.

29 Adorno's celebrated injunction against writing poetry after Auschwitz expresses this reluctance in linguistic terms, but it was evident as well in their ascetic attitude toward aesthetic realism in general.

30 For discussion of the importance of mimesis in Critical Theory, beginning with Walter Benjamin's early essays "On the Mimetic Faculty" and "Doctrine of the Similar" and becoming increasingly important for Adorno, see Karla A. Schultz, *Mimesis on the Move: Theodor W. Adorno's Concept of Imitation*, Berne: Peter Lang, 1990; Martin Jay, "Mimesis and Mimetology: Adorno and Lacoue-Labarthe," in *Cultural Semantics: Keywords of our Time*, Amherst: University of

Massachusetts Press, 1998, and Artemy Magun, "Negativity (Dis)embodied: Philippe Lacoue-Labarthe and Theodor W. Adorno on Mimesis," *New German Critique* 118, 2013.

31 Max Horkheimer, "The Concept of Man," in *The Critique of Instrumental Reason*, London: Verso, 2012.

32 Mark Greif, *The Age of the Crisis of Man: Thought and Fiction in America, 1933–1973*, Princeton: Princeton University Press, 2015. He includes a discussion of *The Family of Man* in his analysis.

33 Horkheimer, "The Concept of Man," 4.

34 Ibid.

35 Ibid., 6. The critique of authenticity was a staple of the Frankfurt School's attack on existentialism. See Martin Jay, "Taking on the Stigma of Inauthenticity: Adorno's Critique of Genuineness," in *Essays from the Edge*, 2011.

36 *Studien über Autorität und Familie: Forschungsberichte aus dem Institut für Sozialforschung*, Paris, 1936.

37 For a critique of Horkheimer's view of maternal warmth, see Mechtheld Rumpf, "'Mystical Aura': Imagination and Reality of the 'Maternal' in Horkheimer's Writings," in *On Max Horkheimer: New Perspectives*, eds. Seyla Benhabib, Wolfgang Bonß and John McCole, Cambridge: MIT Press, 1993. The phrase "haven in a heartless world," which Horkheimer did not directly use, is sometimes attributed to Marx, but it was not until Christopher Lasch's *Haven in a Heartless World: The Family Besieged*, New York: Basic Books, 1977, that it gained widespread currency.

38 Horkheimer, "The Concept of Man," 24.

39 T. W. Adorno, Else Frenkel-Brunswick, Daniel J. Levinson and R. Nevitt Sanford, *The Authoritarian Personality*, 2 vols., New York: Harper, 1950. For its relevance to the exhibition, see Turner, "*The Family of Man* and the Politics of Attention in Cold War America," 72.

40 Adorno et al., *The Authoritarian Personality*, vol. 1, 370.

41 Ibid., 357–8.

42 Roland Barthes, "The Great Family of Man," in *Mythologies*, trans. Annette Lavers, New York: Hill and Wang, 1972, 101. The title of the exhibition in France was "The Great Family of Man."

43 Horkheimer, "*The Family of Man*—All of Us," 52.

44 Gerd Hurm, "Reassessing Roland Barthes's Myth of *The Family of Man*," in Hurm, Reitz and Zamir, *The Family of Man Revisited*, 30–1.

45 Ryan Gunderson, "The First-Generation Frankfurt School on the Animal Question: Foundation for a Normative Sociological Animal Studies," *Sociological Studies* 57: 3, 2014.

46 Richard Bessell, *Violence: A Modern Obsession*, London: Simon and Schuster, 2015, chapter 6.

47 Immanuel Kant, "On Perpetual Peace," *The Philosophy of Kant: Immanuel Kant's Moral and Political Writings*, ed., Carl J. Friedrich, New York: Modern Library, 1993, 492.

48 Hannah Arendt, *The Human Condition*, Garden City: Doubleday, 1959, 218.

49 In the Frankfurt School's history, the most explicit defense of the critical potential of the concept came in Herbert Marcuse, "The Concept of Essence," (1936) in *Negations: Essays in Critical Theory*, trans. Jeremy J. Shapiro, Boston: Beacon Press, 1968.

50 Stefanos Geroulanos, *An Atheism That Is Not Humanist Emerges in French Thought*, Stanford: Stanford University Press, 2010.

51 Barthes, "The Great Family of Man," 100.

52 Karl Marx, "Contribution to the Critique of *Hegel's Philosophy of Right*," *Early Writings*, ed. and trans. T. B. Bottomore, New York: McGraw-Hill, 1964, 43–4.

53 For a consideration of the role that religion played in the postwar discussion of human rights, see Samuel Moyn, *Christian Human Rights*, Philadelphia: University of Pennsylvania Press, 2015.

4. "In Psychoanalysis Nothing Is True but the Exaggerations": Freud and the Frankfurt School

1   Erik H. Erikson, "The Legend of Hitler's Childhood," *Childhood and Society*, New York: Norton, 1963, 353–4. The last sentence in this quotation obliquely opens up the delicate question of the role the Jews themselves may have played in stimulating anti-Semitism, which Erikson answers by speculating on the jealousy aroused by their "responsible sense of relativity." At times of social anxiety, he argues, such relativity offends the groups that are struggling with the loss of their self-esteem and status, who become rigid defenders of absolute values and paranoid about those who threaten them. This is not the place to analyze the validity of this claim, but it is worth noting that in *Dialectic of Enlightenment*, Horkheimer and Adorno were also willing to consider the role Jews might have played in triggering anti-Semitism as the "pioneers of capitalism." Freud himself had entered this dangerous territory in *Moses and Monotheism*. For a recent consideration of its implications, see Gilad Sharvit and Karen S. Feldman, eds., *Freud and Monotheism: Moses and the Violent Origins of Religion*, New York: Fordham University Press, 2018.

2   Erik Erikson, "Hitler's Imagery and Germany Youth," *Psychiatry* 5: 4, 1942, which prefigured the argument in "The Legend of Hitler's Childhood." For an account of the relationship between them, see Lawrence J. Friedman, *Identity's Architect: A Biography of Erik H. Erikson*, New York: Scribner, 1999, 166–76. It is cited in T.W. Adorno, Else Frenkel-Brunswick, Daniel J. Levinson and R. Nevitt Sanford, *The Authoritarian Personality*, New York: Harper, 1964, on 231, 370, 376 and 762. Erikson repaid the compliment in *Childhood and Society*, 417. It should be noted that Erikson was teaching in the 1940s at the University of California, Berkeley, where the book was prepared with the collaboration of the Berkeley Public Opinion Study Group. His contribution to the *Freud in der Gegenwart* lecture series is mentioned in Stefan Müller-Doohm, *Adorno: A Biography*, trans. Rodney Livingstone, Cambridge: Polity, 2005, 388.

3   Max Horkheimer, "Miscellaneous Notes" in *Gesammelte Schriften*, eds. Alfred Schmidt and Gunzelin Schmid Noerr, vol. 14, Frankfurt: Fischer, 1988, 306.

4   Herbert Marcuse in conversation with Bryan Magee, *Talking Philosophy: Dialogues with Fifteen Leading Philosophers*, Oxford: Oxford University Press, 2001, 66.

5   Leo Löwenthal, *An Unmastered Past: The Autobiographical Reflections of Leo Löwenthal*, ed. Martin Jay, Berkeley: University of California Press, 1987, 50–1.

6 See, for example, Joel Whitebook, "The Marriage of Marx and Freud: Critical Theory and Psychoanalysis," *The Cambridge Companion to Critical Theory*, ed. Fred Rush, Cambridge: Cambridge University Press, 2004. I used it myself in *The Dialectical Imagination: A History of the Frankfurt School and the Institute for Social Research, 1923–1950*, Berkeley: University of California Press, 1996, where I wrote; "In the 1970s, it is difficult to appreciate the audacity of the first theorists who proposed the unnatural marriage of Freud and Marx" (86).

7 Walter Benjamin, "Capitalism as Religion," *Selected Writings*, vol. 1, 1913–1916, eds. Marcus Bullock and Michael W. Jennings, Cambridge: MIT Press, 1996, 289. See also Gershom Scholem, *Walter Benjamin: The Story of a Friendship*, trans. Harry Zohn, New York: Schocken, 1981, 57, 61; and Sarah Ley Roff, "Benjamin and Psychoanalysis," *The Cambridge Companion to Walter Benjamin*, ed. David S. Ferris, Cambridge: Cambridge University Press, 2004.

8 Fredric Jameson, *Late Marxism: Adorno, Or, The Persistence of the Dialectic*, London: Verso, 1990, 254.

9 Jameson, *Late Marxism*, 26. The Marxist philosopher Richard Lichtman went even further, proclaiming the marriage stillborn, as Freud's biologism, metapsychological instinct theory and clinical practice were too inherently conservative ever to be compatible with Marx's revolutionary program. Richard Lichtman, *The Production of Desire: The Integration of Psychoanalysis into Marxist Theory*, New York: Free Press, 1982.

10 See, for example, Rainer Funk, *Erich Fromm: The Courage to Be Human*, trans. Michael Shaw, New York: Seabury, 1982, chapter 1.

11 See, for example, Peter Homans, *Disillusionment and the Social Origins of Psychoanalysis*, Chicago: University of Chicago Press, 1989. After writing that "Marx had no psychology in his theory of historical materialism," he adds, "Marx did so because there was no psychology in Marx the man. As a person Marx was devoid of any capacity to reflect empathetically upon his own or others' unconscious inner worlds in a psychological way" (230).

12 Philip Rieff, *Freud: The Mind of a Moralist*, Garden City: Doubleday, 1961, 234.

13 Eli Zaretsky, *Secrets of the Soul: A Social and Cultural History of Psychoanalysis*, New York: Knopf, 2004, 320. There was, to be sure, a brief moment in France, in the mid-1960s, when Marxist Louis Althusser believed that Lacan's Freud could be a strong ally in the battle against phenomenological Marxism and wrote an influential essay in 1964: "Freud and Lacan," *Lenin and Philosophy and Other Essays*, trans. Ben Brewster, New York: Monthly Review Press, 1971. But by the end of the decade, the romance was over, and Althusser was heard to call Lacan a "magnificent, pathetic Harlequin." Cited in Catherine Clément, *The Lives and Legends of Jacques Lacan*, trans. Arthur Goldhammer, New York: Columbia University Press, 1983, 21.

14 For a concise account, see Elisabeth Roudinesco, *Jacques Lacan and Co.: A History of Psychoanalysis in France, 1925–1985*, trans. Jeffrey Mehlman, Chicago: University of Chicago Press, 1990, chapter 2.

15 Paul A. Robinson, *The Freudian Left: Wilhelm Reich, Geza Roheim, Herbert Marcuse*, New York: Harper, 1969; Russell Jacoby, *The Repression of Psychoanalysis: Otto Fenichel and the Political Freudians*, Chicago: University of Chicago Press, 1983.

16 Habermas's use of Freud, developed most clearly in *Knowledge and Human Interests*, trans. Jeremy J. Shapiro, Boston: Beacon Press, 1971, was limited to an extrapolation from the model of individual therapy—involving both external, theoretically informed observation with hermeneutic intersubjectivity—to that of emancipatory social practice. For an overview of his argument, see Thomas McCarthy, *The Critical Theory of Jürgen Habermas*, Cambridge: MIT Press, 1978, chapter 3, section 4. For a critique by a debunker of both Freud and hermeneutics, see Adolf Grünbaum, *The Foundations of Psychoanalysis: A Philosophical Critique*, Berkeley: University of California Press, 1984. For a critique by a defender of Freud, see Joel Whitebook, "Reason and Happiness: Some Psychoanalytic Themes in Critical Theory," in *Habermas and Modernity*, ed. Richard J. Bernstein, Cambridge: MIT Press, 1985. For Axel Honneth's thoughts on the continuing relevance of Freud, understood largely in terms of object relations and an intersubjective theory of recognition, see "Postmodern Identity and Object-Relations Theory: On the Seeming Obsolescence of Psychoanalysis," *Philosophical Explorations* 2: 3, 1999; and *Pathologies of Reason: On the Legacy of Critical Theory*, trans. James Ingram, New York: Columbia University Press, 2009. The latter includes a discussion of another figure in the history of the Institute of Social Research, Franz Neumann, who came to Freud near the end of his life in an essay written in 1954 on "Anxiety and Politics."

17 For an account, see Lawrence J. Friedman, *The Lives of Erich Fromm: Love's Prophet*, New York: Columbia University Press, 2013, 18–27. For Löwenthal's recollection of this episode, see *An Unmastered Past*, 50–1.

18 For a thorough account of Landauer, Horkheimer and the personal origins of the Frankfurt School's interest in Freud, see John Abromeit, *Max Horkheimer and the Foundations of the Frankfurt School*, Cambridge: Cambridge University Press, 2011, chapter 5.

19 Löwenthal, *An Unmastered Past*, 51. A similar effort to encourage the Nobel Prize for Freud in 1936 was unsuccessful. See Horkheimer's letter to Karl Landauer, December 31, 1936, in Max Horkheimer, *A Life in Letters: Selected Correspondence*, eds. and trans. Manfred R. Jacobson and Evelyn M. Jacobson, Lincoln: University of Nebraska Press, 2007, 99–101.

20 Freud's letter has not survived, but is mentioned by Horkheimer in a letter to Sidney Lipshires on January 11, 1971. See Horkheimer, *A Life in Letters*, 366.

21 Max Horkheimer to Sigmund Freud, March 18, 1932, first published in 2011 by Davide Ruggieri as "Ein unveröffentliche Brief von Max Horkheimer an Sigmund Freud," publikationen.soziologie.de.

22 Wilhelm Reich, *Sex-Pol: Essays, 1929–1934*, ed. Lee Baxandall, trans. Anna Bostock, Tom Dubose and Lee Baxandall, New York: Random House, 1972.

23 Max Horkheimer, "Difficulties with a Psychoanalytic Concept," *Dawn and Decline: Notes 1926–1931 and 1950–1969*, trans. Michael Shaw, New York: Seabury, 1978, 108. It was originally published under the pseudonym Heinrich Regius in 1934.

24 Initially, the Institute intended to conduct interdisciplinary research in the framework set by Critical Theory, combining psychology with sociology, cultural studies, economics and political science. See Helmut Dubiel, *Theory and Politics: Studies in the Development of Critical Theory*, trans. Benjamin Gregg, Cambridge: MIT Press, 1985; and Jay, "Positive and Negative Totalities: Implicit Tensions in Critical Theory's Vision of

Interdisciplinary Research," in *Permanent Exiles: Essays on the Intellectual Migration from Germany to America*, New York: Columbia University Press, 1985.

25 Traces of these theological ideas could sometimes appear directly—for example, in the invocation of the Jewish taboo on graven images—and sometimes indirectly, as in Horkheimer's appeal to Protestant theologian Rudolf Otto's term "das ganz Andere" ("the entirely other") as a telos of Critical Theory. Löwenthal and Fromm had gone through periods of orthodox religious involvement but left them behind when they joined the Institute. Perhaps the most glaring example of the split can be seen in the Institute's most eminent collaborator, Walter Benjamin, who drew on theological motifs from Judaism, often developed in dialogue with his friend Gershom Scholem, but was never an observant Jew.

26 The classic (1937) statement is Max Horkheimer, "Traditional and Critical Theory," in *Critical Theory: Selected Essays*, trans. Matthew J. O'Connell et al., New York: Seabury, 1972.

27 See, for example, Theodor W. Adorno's remarks in *Minima Moralia: Reflections from Damaged Life*, trans. E .F. N. Jephcott, London: New Left Books, 1974: "The therapeutically much-lauded transference, the breaking of which is not for nothing the crux of analytic treatment, the artificially contrived situation where the subject performs, voluntarily and calamitously, the annulment of the self which was once brought about involuntarily and beneficially by erotic self-abandonment, is already the pattern of the reflex-dominated, follow-my-leader behavior which liquidates, together with all intellect, the analysts who have betrayed it" (61).

28 There have been subsequent efforts to explore some of these questions—for example, the Horkheimer/Pollock friendship in Nicola Emery, *Per il Non Conformismo: Max Horkheimer e Friedrich Pollock: l'altra Scuola di Francoforte*, Rome: Castelvecchi, 2014. With the continuing publication of new materials revealing hitherto unavailable personal details of their lives—ranging from their voluminous correspondences to Horkheimer's journals and Adorno's dream protocols—would-be psychohistorians of the School have ample fodder.

29 Max Horkheimer, "History and Psychology" (1932), in *Between Philosophy and Social Science: Selected Early Writings*, trans. G. Frederick Hunter, Matthew S. Kramer and John Torpey, Cambridge: MIT Press, 1993, 119.

30 Horkheimer, "History and Psychology," 120.

31 Ibid., 124.

32 Erich Fromm, "The Method and Function of an Analytic Social Psychology: Notes on Psychoanalysis and Historical Materialism" (1932), in *The Essential Frankfurt School Reader*, eds. Andrew Arato and Eike Gebhardt, New York: Urizen, 1978.

33 Ibid., 490.

34 Ibid., 491.

35 For accounts of Fromm's role in the Institute and his ultimate estrangement from his former colleagues, see, in addition to Friedman, *The Lives of Erich Fromm*, chapter 3; *Erich Fromm und die Kritische Theorie, Yearbook of the International Erich Fromm Society* 2, 1991; Michael Kessler and Rainer Funk, eds., *Erich Fromm und die Frankfurter Schule*, Tübingen: Francke, 1992; Neil McLaughlin, "Origin Myths in the Social Sciences: Fromm, the

Frankfurt School and the Emergence of Critical Theory," *Canadian Journal of Sociology* 24: 1, 1999; Joan Braune, *Erich Fromm's Revolutionary Hope: Prophetic Messianism as a Political Theory of the Future*, Rotterdam: Sense, 2014. By and large, these discussions defend Fromm's version of his split with the Institute against earlier ones, which adopted the perspective of Horkheimer and his other colleagues, e.g., Rolf Wiggershaus. *The Frankfurt School: Its History, Theories and Political Significance*, trans. Michael Robertson, Cambridge: MIT Press, 1994; and Jay, *The Dialectical Imagination.*

36 Erich Fromm, *The Working Class in Weimar Germany: A Psychological and Sociological Study*, ed. Wolfgang Bonss, trans. Barbara Weinberger, Leamington Spa: Berg, 1984.

37 *Studien über Autorität und Familie: Forschungsberichte aus dem Institut für Sozialforschung*, Paris: Alcan, 1936; Adorno et al., *The Authoritarian Personality*; Bruno Bettelheim and Morris Janowitz, *Dynamics of Prejudice: A Psychological and Sociological Study of Veterans*, New York: Harper, 1950; Nathan W. Ackerman and Marie Jahoda, *Anti-Semitism and Emotional Disorder: A Psychoanalytic Interpretation*, New York: Harper, 1950; Paul W. Massing, *Rehearsal for Destruction: A Study of Political Anti-Semitism in Imperial Germany*, New York: Harper, 1949; Leo Löwenthal and Norbert Guterman, *Prophets of Deceit: A Study of the Techniques of the American Agitator*, New York: Harper, 1949.

38 Fromm, *The Working Class in Weimar Germany*, 228.

39 For a general account, see William David Jones, *The Lost Debate: German Socialist Intellectuals and Totalitarianism*, Urbana: University of Illinois Press, 1999. It should be acknowledged that the Frankfurt School was far more concerned with the Nazi than the Italian fascist or Soviet cases. Marcuse's *Soviet Marxism* (1958), written after he was directly associated with the Institute, eschewed entirely a psychoanalytic interpretation of the appeal of Communism.

40 For an extensive account of Fromm's debts and personal entanglements with Horney and Sullivan, see Friedman, *The Lives of Erich Fromm*, chapter 3.

41 Erich Fromm, *The Fear of Freedom*, London: Routledge/Kegan Paul, 1942, 9. This edition is the British version, which had a different title, but the same text as the American.

42 Ibid., 18.

43 Horkheimer wrote a short piece on "Ernst Simmel and Freudian Psychoanalysis," *International Journal of Psychoanalysis* 29, 1949, and Adorno an essay called "Die revidierte Psychoanalyse," *Psyche* 6, 1952, each of which expressed some of these sentiments.

44 Adorno to Fromm, November 16, 1937, in *Logos*, 2003, with an introduction by Eva-Maria Zeige.

45 Adorno to Fromm, November 16, 1937, 5.

46 Adorno to Benjamin, June 5, 1935, in Theodor Adorno and Walter Benjamin, *The Complete Correspondence 1928–1940*, ed. Henri Lonitz, trans. Nicholas Walker, Cambridge: Harvard University Press, 1999, 93. Benjamin replied on June 10, 1935, "Amongst all the things in your letter, none struck me more forcibly than the position you seem to take up with regard to the question of the 'mediation' between society and psychology. Here we are both pulling at the *same* rope, although I was unaware of the fact in this particular

form—although it is hardly an ideal situation to find Fromm and Reich are both pulling hard at the other end" (99).

47 Else Frenkel-Brunswik, "Parents and Children as Seen through Interviews," *The Authoritarian Personality*, 337–89. The class background of families was no longer central in the distinction made between, on the one hand, prejudiced subjects whose relations with their parents were characterized by idealized glorification mixed with actual lack of love, and unprejudiced ones, on the other, who grew up in families providing security and genuine love.

48 See Max Horkheimer and Theodor W. Adorno, *Dialectic of Enlightenment: Philosophical Fragments*, ed. Gunzelin Schmid Noerr, trans. Edmund Jephcott, Stanford: Stanford University Press, 2002.

49 Theodor W. Adorno, "The Fetish Character of Music and the Regression of Listening," in *The Essential Frankfurt School Reader*.

50 Adorno, "The Fetish Character of Music and the Regression of Listening," 278.

51 Theodor W. Adorno, *The Psychological Technique of Martin Luther Thomas' Radio Addresses*, Stanford: Stanford University Press, 2000. In this essay, published only posthumously, Adorno analyzes the appeal of Hitler as a rebellious "son"-figure rather than a patriarchal one, paralleling the argument made around the same time by Erikson in his influential essay on "The Legend of Hitler's Childhood."

52 Adorno, "Freudian Theory and the Pattern of Fascist Propaganda," *The Essential Frankfurt School Reader*, 120. For a critique of his adoption of Freud's group psychological analysis, see Espen Hammer, *Adorno and the Political*, London: Routledge, 2006, 56–64. For an account of the more general reception of Freud's argument, see Stefan Jonsson, "After Individuality: Freud's Mass Psychology and Weimar Politics," *New German Critique* 119, 2013. He notes the slippage from Freud's more general analysis of group behavior, including in traditional institutions like the army and church, to Adorno's focus on fascist mass psychology.

53 For a defense of a certain version of narcissism against Adorno's critique of it, see C. Fred Alford, *Narcissism: Socrates, The Frankfurt School and Psychoanalytic Theory*, New Haven: Yale University Press, 1988.

54 Ibid., 135.

55 Ibid., 136. Marcuse would flesh out this analysis in "The Obsolescence of the Freudian Concept of Man," *Five Lectures: Psychoanalysis, Politics and Utopia*, trans. Jeremy J. Shapiro and Shierry Weber, Boston: Beacon Press, 1970. Adorno, however, could never entirely relinquish the notion of at least some individuals capable of resisting the lure of the culture industry. See Deborah Cook, *The Culture Industry Revisited: Theodor W. Adorno on Mass Culture*, Lanham: Rowman and Littlefield, 1996.

56 Theodor W. Adorno, "How to Look at Television," *The Culture Industry: Selected Essays on Mass Culture*, ed. J.M. Bernstein, London: Routledge, 1991, 143.

57 Adorno, *Minima Moralia*, 60. Adorno's suspicion of Fromm's therapeutic practice, which he likened to the sympathetic, supportive treatment of Georg Groddeck and Sandor Ferenczi, was evident as early as the mid-1930s. See Friedman, *The Lives of Erich Fromm*, 60. Later he would mock Fromm's faith that an "art of loving" might counteract the harshness of the modern world, preferring the ascetic coldness of those who understood the need to change the world radically. Similar reservations were independently voiced by

Fenichel. See Jacoby, *The Repression of Psychoanalysis*, 107–10. For a discussion of the ways in which Freud's therapeutic coldness could serve as a screen for different projections, including the idealization of psychoanalysis as a science and the analyst as a role model for intellectuals, see Ulrich Koch, "'Cruel to be Kind?' Professionalization, Politics and the Image of the Abstinent Psychoanalyst," *History of the Human Sciences* 30: 2, 2017.

58 Adorno, *Minima Moralia*, 61.

59 Ibid., 49.

60 Ibid., 61.

61 Ibid., 62.

62 Ibid., 213. For a defense of a modified version of sublimation, see Joel Whitebook, "Weighty Objects: On Adorno's Kant-Freud Interpretation," *The Cambridge Companion to Adorno*, ed. Tom Huhn, Cambridge: Cambridge University Press, 1974. Adorno's critique of sublimation did not, however, mean he was not in accord with other Freudian insights into art, especially concerning its relationship to magic and mimesis. See the discussion in Peter Uwe Hohendahl, *The Fleeting Promise of Art: Adorno's Aesthetic Theory Revisited*, Ithaca: Cornell University Press, 2013, 94–7.

63 Adorno, *Minima Moralia*, 78.

64 Herbert Marcuse, "A Study on Authority," in *Studies in Critical Philosophy*, trans. Joris de Bres, Boston: Beacon, 1973.

65 For examples, see Robinson, *The Freudian Left*, 188–91.

66 For an account of the role of biology in his thinking, which argues it was thoroughly historicized, see Andrew Feenberg, *Heidegger and Marcuse: The Catastrophe and Redemption of History*, New York: Routledge, 2005, 119–22.

67 Herbert Marcuse, "The Social Implications of Freudian Revisionism," *Dissent* 2: 3, 1955; reprinted as the epilogue to *Eros and Civilization*. Erich Fromm, "The Humanist Implications of Distinctive 'Radicalism,'" *Dissent* 2: 3, 1955; Marcuse, "A Reply to Erich Fromm," *Dissent* 3: 1, 1966; Erich Fromm, "A Counter-rebuttal," *Dissent* 3: 1, 1966. For an overview that defends Fromm's perspective and claims he is wrongly grouped with the neo-Freudian revisionists, see John Rickert, "The Fromm-Marcuse Debate Revisited," *Theory and Society* 15, 1986. See also, Friedman, *The Lives of Erich Fromm*, 191–8. Adorno had already given a paper in 1946 in Los Angeles in which he heavily criticized the neo-Freudian revisionists, but it was not published until later. "Social Science and Sociological Tendencies in Psychoanalysis," *Sociologica II: Reden und Vorträge*, eds. Max Horkheimer and Theodor W. Adorno, Frankfurt: EVA, 1962. For a summary, see Jay, *The Dialectical Imagination*, 103–5.

68 He was to edit a volume titled *Socialist Humanism: An International Symposium* (Garden City: Anchor, 1965), to which Marcuse also contributed. Horkheimer and Adorno, however, were far less persuaded by the importance of the early Marx. See Jay, "The Frankfurt School's Critique of Marxist Humanism," *Permanent Exile*.

69 Marcuse, *Eros and Civilization: A Philosophical Inquiry into Freud*, Boston: Beacon Press, 1955, 239. The phrase had been employed by Norman Vincent Peale, an inspirational clergyman of the time, and was contrasted invidiously with what Marcuse called the dialectical "power of negative thinking" in the preface to *Reason and Revolution: Hegel and the Rise of Social Theory*, Boston, Beacon Press, 1960, viii.

70 Aside from some passing remarks on Adorno's musical writings and one citation from *Dialectic of Enlightenment*, Marcuse did not credit his former colleagues. Adorno expressed his chagrin to Horkheimer about the omission in a letter of August 1955, cited in Wiggershaus, *The Frankfurt School*, 497.

71 Marcuse, *Eros and Civilization*, 246–7.

72 Marcuse's argument about the possibility of ending scarcity is criticized by Joel Whitebook, drawing on Paul Ricoeur, for failing to appreciate its source in temporal rather than material terms. That is, Marcuse underestimates the inevitable loss produced by the inexorable aging process, which prevents the restoration of pre-Oedipal narcissistic omnipotence. See Whitebook, *Perversion and Utopia: A Study in Psychoanalysis and Critical Theory*, Cambridge: MIT Press, 1995, 24–41. C. Fred Alford makes a similar point, citing Norman O. Brown on scarcity as "not a material lack but an emotional and relational one, a scarcity of undivided mother-love," "Marx, Marcuse, and Psychoanalysis: Do They Still Fit after All These Years?" in *Marcuse: From the New Left to the Next Left*, eds. John Bokina and Timothy J. Lukes, Lawrence: University of Kansas Press, 1994, 135.

73 Marcuse, *Eros and Civilization*, 199. He attacks Fourier, however, for confusing de-alienated work with genuine, libidinally charged free play. Another inspiration seems to have been Nietzsche's yea-saying "philosophy of life." See Christopher Holman, "Marcuse's Affirmation: Nietzsche and the Logos of Gratification," *New German Critique* 115, 2012.

74 Marcuse, *Eros and Civilization*, 248.

75 Ibid., 215.

76 Herbert Marcuse, *One-Dimensional Man: Studies in the Ideology of Advanced Industrial Society*, Boston: Beacon Press, 1964, 72.

77 Marcuse, however, was not willing to go as far in the direction of mystical union as his friend Norman O. Brown in *Love's Body*. See their exchange, "Love Mystified: A Critique of Norman O. Brown" and "A Reply to Herbert Marcuse," in *Negations: Essays in Critical Theory*, Boston: Beacon Press, 1968. In an earlier work, *Life against Death: The Psychoanalytic Meaning of History*, New York: Vintage, 1959, Brown had coined the term "the dialectical imagination," in which he included "psychoanalysis, mysticism, poetry, the philosophy of organism, Feuerbach and Marx" (318) because all circumvented the limits of formal logic.

78 Any sustained attempt to explain the eclipse of Marcuse's reading of Freud would also have to account for the influential critique of Freudo-Marxism by Michel Foucault, as well as the alternative view of Freud generated by Lacan and his followers.

79 Only published posthumously in the first volume of his *Gesammelte Schriften*, ed. Rolf Tiedemann, Frankfurt: Suhrkamp, 1973, it was not accepted by Cornelius. See the account in Susan Buck-Morss, *The Origin of Negative Dialectics: Theodor W. Adorno, Walter Benjamin, and the Frankfurt Institute*, New York, Free Press, 1977, 17–20. See also Helmut Dahmer, "Adorno's View of Psychoanalysis," *Thesis Eleven* 111, 2012.

80 Theodor W. Adorno, *Negative Dialectic*, trans. E. B. Ashton, New York: Seabury Press, 1973, 221–2.

81 For all of his vaunted pessimism, Adorno never entirely lost his belief that somatic pleasure was a necessary aspect of any meaningful notion of

emancipation. Thus, Alford goes too far in arguing that "in abandoning the quest for the whole, Adorno abandons eros itself." *Narcissism,* 118.

82 Adorno never reduced moral imperatives to nothing but expressions of psychological needs or sociological interests. As Gerhard Schweppenhäuser has noted, "Adorno also, conversely, uses Kant to take Freud to task. Adorno thoroughly approved of Kant's refusal to subject human conscience to genetic-psychological critique," "Adorno's Negative Moral Philosophy," *The Cambridge Companion to Adorno,* 342.

83 Theodor W. Adorno, "Sociology and Psychology," *New Left Review,* November–December 1967, 74.

84 For an account of the events and their impact, see Müller-Doohm, *Adorno: A Biography,* 387–91. For a discussion of Mitscherlich's role in Germany in the sixties, see Tobias Freimüller, ed., *Psychoanalyse und Protest: Alexander Mitscherlich und die "Achtundsechziger,"* Göttingen: Wallstein, 2008.

85 Max Horkheimer, "Sigmund Freud—Zum 110. Geburtstag," *Gesammelte Schriften,* 8, ed. Günzelin Schmid Noerr, Frankfurt: S. Fischer, 1985.

86 Horkheimer to Löwenthal, January 20, 1956, in Horkheimer, *A Life in Letters,* 301.

87 See Abromeit, *Max Horkheimer and the Foundations of the Frankfurt School,* 196–7, for an insightful discussion of this attitude.

5. Leo Löwenthal and the Jewish Renaissance

1 Jack Jacobs, *The Frankfurt School, Jewish Lives, and Anti-Semitism,* Cambridge: Cambridge University Press, 2015. A review symposium, to which I contributed, appeared in *German Quarterly* 89: 1, 2016, 80–100.

2 This chapter was written for a conference on "Jews and the Ends of Theory" at Duke University in 2015, which resulted in the publication of Shai Ginzburg, Martin Land and Jonathan Boyarin, eds., *Jews and the Ends of Theory,* New York: Fordham University Press, 2018.

3 Löwenthal dropped the umlaut from his name when he emigrated to America in 1934, but it is retained in his German-language publications. We will use the original spelling.

4 His name was sometimes alternatively spelled Nehemias.

5 Rachel Heuberger, "Die Entdeckung der jüdischen Wurzeln," in Peter-Erwin Jansen, ed., *Das Utopische soll Funken schlagen ... zum hundertsten Geburtstag von Leo Löwenthal,* Frankfurt: Vittorio Klostermann, 2000, 67. See also her informative essay, "Leo Löwenthal und Erich Fromm. Die 'jüdischen' Juden der Frankfurter Schule," in Monika Boll and Raphael Gross, eds., *Die Frankfurter Schule und Frankfurt: Eine Rückkehr nach Deutschland,* Frankfurt: Wallstein, 2009. For a general account of Löwenthal's early period, see Alfons Söllner, "Der junge Leo Löwenthal: Vom neoorthodoxen Judentum zur aufgeklärten Geschichtsphilosophie," in Ulrich Beilefeld, Heinze Bude and Bernd Greiner, eds., *Gesellschaft—Gewalt—Vertrauen: Jan Philipp Reemtsma zum 60. Geburtstag,* Hamburg: Hamburger Edition, 2012. For a comparison of his Jewish experiences with those of his colleagues in the Frankfurt School, see Jacobs, *The Frankfurt School, Jewish Lives and Antisemitism.*

6 Siegfried Kracauer to Leo Löwenthal, January 24, 1922, Frankfurt, in *In Steter Freundschaft: Briefwechsel*, eds. Peter-Erwin Jansen and Christian Schmidt, Hamburg: Zu Klampen, 2003, 35. The *Zaddikim* is an allusion to the legend, based in Talmudic dicta, that in every generation thirty-six (rather than Kracauer's thirty, as here) righteous souls sustain the world. See Gershom Scholem, "The Tradition of the Thirty-Six Hidden Just Men," in *The Messianic Idea in Judaism and Other Essays on Jewish Spirituality*, trans. Michael A. Meyer, New York: Schocken, 1971.

7 Franz Rosenzweig to Martin Buber, January 25, 1922, Frankfurt, in *The Letters of Martin Buber*, eds. Nahum N. Glatzer and Paul Mendes-Flohr, trans. Richard and Clara Winston and Harry Zohn, New York: Schocken, 1991, 257. See also his memorial essay, "Der Denker: Nachruf auf N.A. Nobel," in *Der Mensch und sein Werk: Gesammelte Schriften, III: Zweistromland*, The Hague: Martinus Nijhoff, 1984.

8 See Rachel Heuberger, "Orthodox versus Reform: The Case of Rabbi Nehemiah Anton Nobel of Frankfurt a. Main," *Leo Baeck Yearbook*, 37, London: Secker and Warburg, 1992. She has expanded her discussion in *Rabbiner Nehemias Anton Nobel; Die jüdische Renaissance in Frankfurt am Main*, Frankfurt: Frankfurter Societäts-Druckerei, 2005.

9 Rosenzweig to Gertrud Oppenheim, October 5 and 21, in Nahum N. Glatzer, *Franz Rosenzweig: His Life and Thought*, New York: Schocken, 1961, 104.

10 The depth of their attachment is evident in two postcards Nobel sent to Löwenthal in 1921 in which the rabbi worries about his health, gives Löwenthal permission not to fast on Yom Kippur, says he is praying for him and mentions the sending of money to his doctor. See Nobel to Löwenthal, October 10, 1921, and October 17, 1921, in Peter-Erwin Jansen, ed., *Das Utopische soll Funken schlagen . . . Zum hundertsten Geburtstag von Leo Löwenthal* (Frankfurt: Vittorio Klostermann, 2000). Speaking of his own father, Löwenthal remembered that "it was a terrible disappointment for him that his son, whom he, the father, the true scion of the enlightenment, had raised so 'progressively,' was now being pulled into the 'nonsensical,' 'obscure' and "deceitful' clutches of a positive religion." Leo Löwenthal, *An Unmastered Past: The Autobiographical Reflections of Leo Löwenthal,* ed. Martin Jay, Berkeley: University of California Press, 1987, 20. Significantly, his father, Victor, refused to go to his wedding in December 1923 to Golde Ginsburg because she came from Königsberg and was thus uncomfortably close to being an *Ostjude*. As he later told an interviewer, "My parents' home symbolized, so to speak, everything I didn't want—bad liberalism, bad enlightenment, and two-sided morality." " 'We Never Expected Such Fame': A Conversation with Matthias Greffrath, 1979," in *Communication in Society*, vol. 4, *Critical Theory and Frankfurt Theorists*, ed. Helmut Dubiel, trans. Don Reneau et al., New Brunswick, NJ, 1989, 240. He did, however, also come to appreciate the positive role his father had played in his development, telling Helmut Dubiel: "Even today I feel very indebted to my father. He was a typical representative of the educated German-Jewish middle class. I was encouraged to read Goethe, Schopenhauer, and Darwin. I was encouraged to go to concerts and to the theater, to prepare myself for operas and the like. Later my father was very dissatisfied with me because I pursued my university studies without a definite goal, changing from one faculty to another. Quite frankly, I studied everything but medicine. That certainly has to do with the

just-mentioned Oedipus complex." See Jay, ed., *An Unmastered Past*, 43.

11 Löwenthal, "Rabbiner Dr. N.A. Nobel, verschieden am 24.Januar 1922," *Der jüdische Student. Zeitschrift des Kartells jüdischer Verbindungen* 2, 1922, 87–8.

12 Löwenthal, *An Unmastered Past*, 21. The subdued erotic side of the "cult" can be read between the lines in the contribution Siegfried Kracauer was to make to the Festschrift for Nobel, which was the second half of his long essay *Über die Freundschaft*, ed. Karsten Witte, Frankfurt, 1974.

13 See David Ellenson, *Rabbi Ezriel Hildesheimer and the Creation of a Modern Jewish Orthodoxy*, Tuscaloosa: University of Alabama Press, 1990.

14 See the discussion in Albert H. Friedlander, *Leo Baeck: Teacher of Theresienstadt*, New York: Holt, Reinhart and Winston, 1968, 36–7.

15 For brief accounts of its role, see Walter Laqueur, *A History of Zionism*, New York: Holt, Reinhart and Winston, 1978, 481–4; Michael Stanislawski, *Zionism and the Fin de Siècle: Cosmopolitanism and Nationalism from Nordau to Jabotinsky*, Berkeley: University of California Press, 2001, 164–7.

16 See Michael Löwy, *Redemption and Utopia: Jewish Libertarian Thought in Central Europe*, trans. Hope Heaney, Stanford: Stanford University Press, 1992; Anson Rabinbach, *In the Shadow of Catastrophe: German Intellectuals between Apocalypse and Enlightenment*, Berkeley: University of California Press, 1997; and Benjamin Lazier, *God Interrupted: Heresy and the European Imagination between the World Wars*, Princeton: Princeton University Press, 2008.

17 For Buber's development during these years, see Paul Mendes-Flohr, *From Mysticism to Dialogue: Martin Buber's Transformation of German Social Thought*, Detroit: Wayne State University Press, 1981; for a discussion of Rosenzweig's attitude toward Cohen, see Peter Eli Gordon, *Rosenzweig and Heidegger: Between Judaism and German Philosophy*, Berkeley: University of California Press, 2003, chapter 1.

18 *Gabe Herrn Rabbiner Dr. Nobel zum 50. Geburtstag* by Martin Buber et al., Frankfurt, 1921.

19 The term had in fact been coined by Martin Buber as early as 1901—see his "Jüdische Renaissance," *Ost und West* (1901)—but was only realized after the war. For a general discussion, see Michael Brenner, *The Renaissance of Jewish Culture in Weimar Germany*, New Haven: Yale University Press, 1996. He writes of Nobel, "A new type of rabbi, like Nehemias Anton Nobel of Frankfurt and Joseph Carlebach of Hamburg, reached out to non-orthodox Jewish students and intellectuals. By their new approaches toward Jewish mysticism or by their modern pedagogical techniques, those leaders of Weimar Orthodox Jewry were indeed able to awaken new interest in Judaism—although not necessarily in Orthodoxy—on the fringes of Jewish society" (54).

20 For a discussion of Goethe's celebration of the daemonic, see Angus Nicholls, *Goethe's Concept of the Daemonic: After the Ancients*, Rochester: Camden House, 2006. In contrast, according to Wolfgang L. Zucker, Jaspers "relates genius and the demonic to the dialectic of the self; but true to his Kantian rejection of all theology, he does not see the problem in religious terms. For him both genius and the demonic are existentially experienced in the lonely dialogue of the self with itself. Both can be objectified and therefore mythologized as angels and devils, but precisely such otherness of genius and demon leads into untruth and inauthenticity where the self loses itself. They are the dialectical explications of the wholeness of the self, experienced as guides of the soul (the Greeks would have said *psychopompoi*), in the process of

self-illumination. They certainly are not the same in Jaspers's analysis; genius leads into the light of reality and permanence, it wants order and rationality, and raises its warning voice whenever the soul is in danger of getting lost. In contrast, the demonic leads to the depths, into the darkness that threatens, where the light ends; it beckons with the total catastrophe of existence not only as an always present possibility but as a luring temptation." "The Demonic: From Aeschylus to Tillich," *Theology Today* 26: 1, 1969, 47.

21 Löwenthal, *An Unmastered Past*, 49.

22 Ibid.

23 It can now be found in Leo Löwenthal, *Schriften*, vol. 5, *Philosophische Frühschriften*, ed. Helmut Dubiel, Frankfurt: Suhrkamp, 1987, and in English translation in Eduardo Mendieta, ed., *The Frankfurt School on Religion: Key Writings of the Major Thinkers*, New York: Routledge, 2005.

24 Löwenthal, "The Demonic," in Mendieta, ed., *The Frankfurt School on Religion*, 107. In *An Unmastered Past* (49), Löwenthal alludes to suicide notes he had composed in 1920, an indication of his fragile and vulnerable state of mind when he composed this essay.

25 For an account of the fascination of German Jews for *Bildung*, see David Sorkin, *The Transformation of German Jewry, 1780–1840*, New York: Oxford University Press, 1987; and George Mosse, *German Jews beyond Judaism*, Bloomington: Indiana University Press, 1985; for a discussion of their disillusionment, see Steven E. Aschheim, "German Jews beyond *Bildung* and Liberalism: The Radical Jewish Revival in the Weimar Republic," *Culture and Catastrophe: German and Jewish Confrontations with National Socialism and Other Crises*, New York: New York University Press, 1996.

26 Michael Löwy, *Redemption and Utopia: Jewish Libertarian Thought in Central Europe: A Study in Elective Affinity*, trans. Hope Heany, Stanford: Stanford University Press, 1992, 70. For more on this theme, see Micha Brumlik, "Messianic Thinking in the Jewish Intelligentsia of the Twenties," *Wissenschaft vom Menschen/Sciences of Man*, vol. 2, *Erich Fromm und die Kritische Theorie* (Münster: LIT-Verlag, 1991).

27 Löwenthal, "The Demonic," 112.

28 Löwenthal, "Recollections of Adorno," in *An Unmastered Past*, 204.

29 Kracauer's disdain for Bloch was made public in the review he wrote in the *Frankfurter Zeitung* on August 27, 1922, of *Thomas Müntzer als Theologe der Revolution*, which Bloch tried to rebut in *Durch die Wüste* (Berlin, 1923).

30 Kracauer to Löwenthal, December 4, 1921, in *In steter Freundschaft*, 31–2. Italics in original. For a discussion of Kracauer's more ambivalent attitude toward Nobel and the Frankfurt Lehrhaus, see Enzo Traverso, *Siegfried Kracauer; itinéraire d'un intellectual nomade*, Paris: La Découverte, 1994, chapter 2. For a consideration of his complicated relationship with Rosenzweig in particular, see Matthew Handelman, "The Forgotten Conversation: Five Letters from Franz Rosenzweig to Siegfried Kracauer," *Scientia Poetica* 15, 2011.

31 Leo Löwenthal, "Die Sozietätsphilosophie Franz von Baaders. Beispiel und Problem einer religösen Philosophie," PhD diss., University of Frankfurt, 1923. Sections were ultimately published in 1966 and 1967 in the *Internationales Jarhbuch für Religionsoziologie*. Löwenthal reports that Kracauer and Adorno mocked him for his interest in Baader and the expressionist style in which he wrote about him. See *An Unmastered Past*, 207. It is

worth recalling that Baader had been very interested in the work of the earlier Christian mystic Jakob Boehme, about whom, along with Nicholas Cusa, Martin Buber wrote his dissertation. Clearly, Jewish thinkers who were seeking to overturn conventional wisdom could find inspiration in heterodox Christian sources. For a discussion of Löwenthal's dissertation, see Söllner, "Der junge Leo Löwenthal," 311–17.

32 Kracauer to Löwenthal, August 31, 1922, in *In steter Freundschaft*, 46, where he calls the book "rubbish [ein Schmarren] . . . I despise this type of philosophy which makes a system out of a hymn, and for the sake of this system concocts the craziest constructions (for example Rosenzweig's distinction between Judaism and Christianity) and blathers in tones of wonder about Creation, Revelation and Salvation, which would arouse the pity of a dog. Rosenzweig is and remains an Idealist, if not an over-Idealist, from which even his [Jewish Star] won't save him—just as I don't believe that his book will have great success in the future, in spite of Scholem and his brother Benjamin." However, as late as 1924, it seems that Löwenthal was still considering a sequel to "The Demonic," in a project on "Religion and Magic," which was never realized. Kracauer wrote him a cautiously supportive response to the project statement, although commenting that it was too grandiose ever to be realized. See his letter of November 2, 1924, in *Im steter Freundschaft*, 63.

33 Kracauer, "The Bible in German," in *The Mass Ornament: Weimar Essays*, trans. and ed. Thomas Y. Levin, Cambridge: Harvard University Press, 1995. The dispute over the translation is discussed in Martin Jay, "Politics of Translation: Siegfried Kracauer and Walter Benjamin on the Buber-Rosenzweig Bible," *Permanent Exiles: Essays on the Intellectual Migration from German to America*, New York: Columbia University Press, 1985; Lawrence Rosenwald, "On the Reception of the Buber-Rosenzweig Bible," *Prooftexts* 14: 2, 1994; Klaus Reichert, "'It Is Time': The Buber-Rosenzweig Bible Translation in Context" in *The Translatability of Cultures*, eds. Sanford Budnick and Wolfgang Iser, Stanford: Stanford University Press, 1996; Leora Batnitzky, *Idolatry and Representation*, Princeton: Princeton University Press, 2000; Peter Eli Gordon, "Translation and Ontology: Rosenzweig, Heidegger, and the Anxiety of Affiliation," *New German Critique* 77, 1999; Brian Britt, "Romantic Roots of the Debate on the Buber-Rosenzweig Bible," *Prooftexts* 20: 3, 2000.

34 Affirming Adorno's dismissive appraisal of Kracauer's *Jacques Offenbach und das Paris seiner Zeit* (Amsterdam, 1937), Benjamin wrote that the latter's apologetic inclinations are "especially flagrant in those passages which touch upon Offenbach's Jewish origins. For Kracauer, the Jewish element remains rooted in origins. He doesn't even dream of recognizing it in the work itself." Benjamin to Adorno, May 9, 1937, in Theodor Adorno and Walter Benjamin, *The Complete Correspondence, 1928–1940*, ed. Henri Lonitz, trans. Nicholas Walter, Cambridge: Harvard University Press, 1999, 186.

35 The public break came in an essay, written under the pseudonym "Hereticus," called "Die Lehren von Chinas," *Jüdisches Wochenblatt* 2: 25 (June 26, 1925), in which he compared the events in the China of his day, in which Westerners were buying up lands from rich landowners, with those in Palestine; in both cases, he predicted a rebellion of dispossessed peasants.

36 Löwenthal to his parents, June 17, 1920, in Jansen, ed., *Das Utopische soll Funken schlagen*, 38. As Aschheim has noted, "The young Loewenthal's [sic]

Zionism had little to do with Palestine. It was rather, as he wrote to Ernst Simon, a mode of consciousness, the most appropriate way the Jews could realize Bloch's *Spirit of Utopia*." "German Jews beyond *Bildung* and Liberalism: The Radical Jewish Revival in the Weimar Republic," 37.

37 Löwenthal, *An Unmastered Past*, 26. In his memoir, *From Berlin to Jerusalem: Memories of My Youth*, trans. Harry Zohn, New York: Schocken, 1980, Gershom Scholem had a more sour recollection: "Some of my best students and acquaintances from Zionist youth groups, such as Simon, Fromm and Leo Löwenthal, visited the sanatorium on an outpatient basis. With the exception of one person they all had their Orthodox Judaism analyzed away" (156).

38 Löwenthal, *An Unmastered Past*, 112. The project was supported by Buber and Rosenzweig, but failed to get backing from the Moses Mendelssohn Foundation—possibly, Löwenthal conjectured, because of opposition from Leo Strauss.

39 Erich Fromm, Fritz Goethin, Leo Löwenthal, Ernst Simon and Erich Michaelis, "Ein prinzipielles Wort zur Erziehungsfrage," *Jüdische Rundschau* 27: 102–3, 1922.

40 Löwenthal, "German Jewish Intellectual Culture: Essays from the 20s," in *Communication in Society*, vol. 4. The 1925 essay on Maimonides, who, of course, was not German in origin, is not included in this selection, but can be found in Jansen, ed., *Das Utopische soll Funken schlagen . . .*

41 Löwenthal, "German Jewish Intellectual Culture," 18.

42 Ibid., 17.

43 Ibid., 34. The positive reference to "Jewish-universalist" values suggests the abiding importance of Hermann Cohen's neo-Kantianism for Löwenthal, which is emphasized in Söllner, "Der junge Leo Löwenthal."

44 Löwenthal, "German Jewish Intellectual Culture," 45.

45 Cited from interviews given to Ernst von Schenk in John Abromeit, *Max Horkheimer and the Foundations of the Frankfurt School*, Cambridge: Cambridge University Press, 2011, 64.

46 Susan Buck-Morss, *The Origin of Negative Dialectics: Theodor W. Adorno, Walter Benjamin, and the Frankfurt Institute*, New York: Free Press, 1977, 5–7.

47 Stefan Müller-Doohm, *Adorno: A Biography*, trans. Rodney Livingstone, Malden: Polity, 2005, 19.

48 See the remarkably intimate and affectionate correspondence in Theodor W. Adorno, *Letters to His Parents, 1939–1951*, ed. Christoph Gödde and Henri Lonitz, trans. Wieland Hoban, Malden: Polity, 2003.

49 Cited in Müller-Doohm, *Adorno*, 20.

50 See, for example, the essays in the section "Frankfurter Schule und Judentum," in Boll and Gross, eds., *Die Frankfurter Schule und Frankfurt*; and Margarete Kohlenbach and Raymond Geuss, eds., *The Early Frankfurt School and Religion*, New York: Palgrave Macmillan, 2005.

51 For a consideration of their work on anti-Semitism, see Lars Rensmann, *The Politics of Unreason: The Frankfurt School and the Origins of Modern Antisemitism*, Albany: SUNY Press, 2017.

52 Max Horkheimer, "Die Juden und Europa," *Zeitschrift für Sozialforschung* 8: 1/2, 1939. See Scholem to Benjamin, February [?] 1940, in *The Correspondence of Walter Benjamin and Gershom Scholem*, ed. Gershom Scholem, trans. Gary Smith and Andre Lefebvre, New York: Schocken, 1989. For a more sympathetic reading, see Dan Diner, "Reason and the 'Other': Horkheimer's

Reflections on Anti-Semitism and Mass Annihilation," in *On Max Horkheimer*, eds. Seyla Benhabib, Wolfgang Bonß, and John McCole, Cambridge: MIT Press, 1993.

53 Leo Löwenthal, "Heine's Religion: The Messianic Idea of the Poet," *Commentary* 4: 2, 1947. *Commentary*, under the later editorship of Norman Podhoretz, would become a forum for neoconservative ideas, but in the years the Institute was in New York, its outlook was more progressive.

54 Thomas Wheatland, *The Frankfurt School in Exile*, Minneapolis: University of Minnesota Press, 2009, 157.

55 Ibid., 158.

56 Theodor W. Adorno, "Heine the Wound," *Notes to Literature*, 2 vols., ed. Rolf Tiedemann, trans. Shierry Weber Nicholsen, vol. 1, New York: Columbia University Press, 1991.

57 In his infamous anti-Semitic polemic *Judaism in Music*, Richard Wagner had also decried what he saw as the failure of Heine's German—its being built on a lie—but for Adorno, it was precisely Heine's achievement to resist ideological wholeness and open a wound that had universal implications.

58 Adorno, "Heine the Wound," 85.

59 Jürgen Habermas, "Heinrich Heine and the Role of the Intellectual in Germany," in *The New Conservatism: Cultural Criticism and the Historians' Debate*, ed. and trans. Shierry Weber Nicholsen, Cambridge: MIT Press, 1989. Habermas, to be sure, also wrote an essay on "The German Idealism of the Jewish Philosophers" in 1981, where he detailed the vital role of Jewish thinkers in modern German culture. See Habermas, *Religion and Rationality: Essays on Reason, God, and Modernity*, ed. Eduardo Mendieta, Cambridge: MIT Press, 2002.

60 Habermas, "Heinrich Heine and the Role of the Jewish Intellectual in Germany," 82.

61 That his anxiety was by no means unwarranted is demonstrated by the anti-Semitic motifs in the recent allegations of right-wing conspiracy theorists who blame "cultural Marxism" and "political correctness" on the Institute. See chapter 11.

62 Löwenthal, "Walter Benjamin: The Integrity of the Intellectual," in *Communication in Society*, vol. 4, *Critical Theory and Frankfurt Theorists*, 83.

63 In his 1979 interview with Helmut Dubiel, Löwenthal admitted (much to my delight): "However much I once tried to convince Martin Jay that there were no Jewish motifs among us at the Institute, now, years later and after mature consideration, I must admit to a certain influence of Jewish tradition, which was codeterminative." *An Unmastered Past*, 112.

64 Löwenthal, "'We Never Expected Such Fame,'" 240–1.

65 According to Michael Brenner, "Like groups of non-Jewish intellectuals (the most famous being that of Stefan George), the Jewish groups were organized around one dominant figure. They included the study group of the charismatic Rabbi Nehemias Anton Nobel in Frankfurt, the Talmud study circle of Salman Baruch Rabinkow in Heidelberg, the private kosher psychoanalytic clinic in Heidelberg where Frieda Reichmann cultivated both Torah and Freudian analysis, the wartime Berlin Volksheim of Siegfried Lehmann, and the Berlin group centered around an obscure scholar of Jewish mysticism, Oskar Goldberg." *The Renaissance of Jewish Culture in Weimar Germany*, 71. The pattern was, of course, not only

followed by German Jews during a traumatic era in which patriarchal authority was challenged by the collapse of the Kaiserreich and the economic chaos of the postwar years. What Austrian psychoanalyst Paul Federn called a "fatherless society" was experienced by many in central Europe during that era. See Paul Federn, *Zur Psychologie der Revolution: die Vaterlose Gesellschaft*, Wein: Anzengruber-Verlag, 1919.

66 It is important to acknowledge that from his adolescence, Löwenthal had been actively involved in socialist and pacifist causes, often involving political activity of one sort or another. See his account in *An Unmastered Past*, 33–43.

67 Rosenzweig to Joseph Prager, end of January 1922, in *Franz Rosenzweig: His Life and Thought*, 106–7.

68 Ibid., 107.

69 David Biale, *Not in the Heavens: The Tradition of Secular Jewish Thought*, Princeton: Princeton University Press, 2011.

70 Brenner, *The Renaissance of Jewish Culture in Weimar Germany*, 208.

6. Adorno and Blumenberg: Nonconceptuality and the *Bilderverbot*

1 The literature on Adorno's warning is voluminous. For a particularly insightful example, see John Zilcosky, "Poetry after Auschwitz? Celan and Adorno Revisited," *Deutsche Vierteljahrsschrift für Literaturwissenschaft und Geistesgeschichte* 79: 4, 2005.

2 This chapter initially appeared in *A Companion to Adorno*, eds. Peter E. Gordon, Espen Hammer and Max Pensky, New York: John Wiley, 2020.

3 See Angus Nicholls, *Myth and the Human Sciences: Hans Blumenberg's Theory of Myth*, New York: Routledge, 2015, 7. Blumenberg had been alerted to the work by Jacob Taubes, who noted similarities in their philosophies. The first edition of *Die Legitimität der Neuzeit* was published by Suhrkamp, Adorno's publisher, in 1966. In English it appeared as Hans Blumenberg, *The Legitimacy of the Modern Age*, trans. Robert M. Wallace, Cambridge: MIT Press, 1983. This is a translation of the second edition, which appeared in 1973 and contains a passing, obliquely critical reference to Adorno's reliance in *Negative Dialectics* on the concept of a "societal delusional system." Blumenberg lumped it with other overly general explanations of contemporary problems, which included the secularization thesis his book sought to debunk. For an analysis of their undeveloped relationship, see Christian Voller, "Kommunikation verweigert. Schwierige Beziehungen zwischen Blumenberg und Adorno," *Zeitschrift für Kulturphilosophie* 2 (2013).

4 To be precise, although "*das Unbegriffliche*" or "*unbegrifflich*" does appear in *Negative Dialectics,* more often Adorno uses "*das Nichtbegriffliche*" or "*nichtbegrifflich*." It might be possible to discern the distinction addressed later in this chapter between his position and Blumenberg's in this terminological slippage, but it is not explicitly developed by either author. I am indebted to Sebastian Tränkle for alerting me to this ambiguity.

5 For discussions, see David Adams, "Metaphors for Mankind: The Development of Hans Blumenberg's Anthropological Metaphorology," *Journal of the History of Ideas* 52: 1, 1991; Robert Savage, "Laughter from the Lifeworld: Hans

Blumenberg's Theory of Nonconceptuality," *Thesis Eleven* 94, 2008; Anselm Haverkamp, "The Scandal of Metaphorology," *Telos* 158, 2012; and Pini Ifergan, "Hans Blumenberg's Philosophical Project: Metaphorology as Anthropology," *Continental Philosophy Review* 48, 2015.

6 Adorno to Blumenberg, September 25, 1967, in the Blumenberg archive, Schiller-Nationalmuseum, Marbach am Neckar. I am grateful to Ari Edmundson for drawing my attention to this letter, which read as follows:

Vielleicht wissen Sie, daß ich zu dem unter den Namen „Soziologie und Philosophie" bei Suhrkamp in der Reihe Theorie erscheinenden Band von Durkheim eine längere Einleitung geschrieben habe. Diese Vorrede enthält eine Theorie der Pedanterie. Als ich das Korrektur las, wurde ich von einer Mitarbeiterin darauf aufmerksam gemacht, daß Ihr Buch an einer Stelle etwas Verwandtes enthält.

Ich habe es mir deshalb gestattet, noch nachträglich eine Fußnote einzufügen, die auf die Beziehung hinweist, und habe Unseld gebeten, daß diese Fußnote, obwohl sie den heiligen Umbruch in Unordnung bringt, noch aufgenommen wird. Er hat mir das auch zugesagt. Einen Durchschlag der Fußnote füge ich Ihnen bei. Es ist wirklich eine höchst merkwürdige Koinzidenz.

Die Sache hatte ihr Gutes, insofern, als ich mich nun endlich daraufhin, mit Ihrem Buch ein wenig näher befaßt habe. Daß das nicht schon vorher geschah, hat lediglich den Grund, daß ich, im Bestreben, meine großen Entwürfe noch einigermaßen unter Dach und Fach zu bringen, solange ich mir die Kraft zutraue (die "Negative Dialektik" ist das erste Produkt dieser Anstrengungen), wirklich das Lesen über dem Schreiben verlerne, und ich möchte Sie um Verständnis dafür bitten und um Geduld. Aber nach dem Eindruck, den ich nun immerhin von Ihrem Buch gewonnen have, das ja fast gleichseitig mit meinem erschien, glaube ich doch mir gestatten zu dürfen, diesem Buch eine wahrhaft bedeutende Zukunft zu prophezien.

7 Hans Blumenberg, *Theorie der Unbegrifflichkeit*, ed. Anselm Haverkamp, Frankfurt: Suhrkamp, 2007.

8 Hans Blumenberg, *Shipwreck with Spectator: Paradigm for a Metaphor for Existence*, trans. Steven Rendall, Cambridge: MIT Press, 1997.

9 Hans Blumenberg, "Light as Metaphor for Truth: At the Preliminary Stage of Philosophical Concept Formation," trans. Joel Anderson in David Michael Levin, ed., *Modernity and the Hegemony of Vision*, Berkeley: University of California Press, 1993.

10 Ibid., 30 [translation emended].

11 See Hans Blumenberg, *Work on Myth*, trans. Robert M. Wallace, Cambridge: MIT Press, 1985. In addition to metaphor and myth, rhetoric in general and laughter were examples of nonconceptuality. For a discussion of the last of these, see Savage, "Laughter from the Lifeworld."

12 It is translated as *Paradigms for a Metaphorology*, trans. Robert Savage, Ithaca: Cornell University Press, 2010.

13 Friedrich Nietzsche, *Genealogy of Morals*, ed. Walter Kaufman, trans. Walter Kaufman and R. J. Hollingdale, New York: Vintage, 1989, 80.

14 Blumenberg, *Paradigms*, 3, emphasis in original.

15 Ibid., 5.

16 Theodor W. Adorno, "The Essay as Form," *Notes to Literature*, ed. Rolf Tiedemann, trans. Shierry Weber Nicholsen, vol. 1, New York: Columbia

University Press, 1991, 13, 14.

17 Theodor W. Adorno, *Hegel: Three Studies*, trans. Shierry Weber Nicholsen, Cambridge: MIT Press, 1993, 96–111.

18 Theodor W. Adorno, *The Jargon of Authenticity*, trans. Knut Tarnowski and Frederic Will, London: Routledge and Kegan Paul, 1973.

19 Theodor W. Adorno, *Negative Dialectics*, trans. E. B. Ashton: New York: Seabury, 1973, 136.

20 Anselm Haverkamp, "The Scandal of Metaphorology," 40.

21 Blumenberg's struggle to deal with this challenge is discussed in Adams, "Metaphors for Mankind."

22 Jacques Derrida, "White Mythology: Metaphor in the Text of Philosophy," *Margins of Philosophy*, trans. Alan Bass, Chicago, University of Chicago, 1982, where he writes: "Metaphor remains, in all its characteristics, a classical philosopheme, a metaphysical concept. It is therefore enveloped in the field that a general metaphorology of philosophy would seek to dominate" (2).

23 Blumenberg, "Prospect for a Theory of Nonconceptuality," *Shipwreck with Spectator*, 83.

24 Arnold Gehlen, *Der Mensch. Seine Natur und seine Stellung in der Welt* (Berlin, Junker und Dünnhaupt, 1940). For accounts of what is sometimes called Blumenberg's "negative anthropology," see, in addition to the essays cited in note 3, Franz Josef Wetz and Hermann Timm, eds. *Die Kunst des Überlebens: Nachdenken über Hans Blumenberg*, Frankfurt: Suhrkamp, 1999; Oliver Müller, *Sorge um die Vernunft: Hans Blumenbergs phänomenologische Anthropologie*, Paderborn: Mentis, 2005; Vida Pavesich, "Hans Blumenberg's Philosophical Anthropology: After Heidegger and Cassirer," *Journal of the History of Philosophy* 46: 3, 2008; Franz Josef Wetz, "The Phenomenological Anthropology of Hans Blumenberg," *Iris* 1: 2, 2009; Hannes Bajohr, "The Unity of the World: Arendt and Blumenberg on the Anthropology of Metaphor," *The Germanic Review: Literature, Culture, Theory* 90: 1, 2015. Blumenberg's debt to Gehlen seems, however, to have been tempered by his greater appreciation of the positive as well as compensatory character of cultural creation, as well as his wariness about the conservative implications of Gehlen's faith in institutions.

25 Another example would be the anecdote, which Blumenberg often used in his reconstructing of philosophical issues, a resource on which Adorno rarely drew.

26 In *Care Crosses the River*, trans. Paul Fleming, Stanford: Stanford University Press, 2010, Blumenberg defended the value of detours: "Culture consists in detours—finding and cultivating them, describing and recommending them, revaluing and bestowing them. Culture therefore seems inadequately rational, because strictly speaking only the shortest route receives reason's seal of approval. Everything right and left along the way is superfluous and can justify its existence only with difficulty. It is, however, the detours that give culture the function of humanizing life" (96). For a discussion of the importance of detour in his work, see Sebastian Tränkle, "Die Vernunft und ihre Umwege. Zur Rettung der Rhetorik bei Hans Blumenberg und Theodor W. Adorno," in *Permanentes Provosorium: Hans Blumenbergs Umwege*, eds. Michael Heidgen, Matthias Koch and Christian Köhler, Paderborn: Wilhelm Fink, 2015.

27 Blumenberg, "Prospect for a Theory of Nonconceptuality," 94.

28 Blumenberg, "An Anthropological Approach to the Contemporary Significance of Rhetoric," in *After Philosophy: End or Transformation?* eds. Kenneth Baynes, James Bohman and Thomas McCarthy, Cambridge: MIT Press, 1987, 440.

29 In *Dialectic of Enlightenment*, Horkheimer and Adorno had a less benign reading of sacrifice as a primitive version of the exchange principle, but they too acknowledged its importance as a human way to enable self-preservation in a hostile world.

30 Hans Blumenberg, *Die ontologische Distanz: Eine Untersuchung über die Krisis der Phänomenologie Husserls*, Habilitationsschrift: Kiel, 1950.

31 For accounts, see Nicholls, *Myth and the Human Sciences*, 93–103; and Peter E. Gordon, *Continental Divide: Heidegger, Cassirer, Davos*, Cambridge: Harvard University Press, 2010, 349–51. In *Legitimacy of the Modern Age*, he explicitly took exception to Heidegger's "negative idealization of the modern age in the 'history of Being'" (2).

32 Blumenberg, *Paradigms for a Metaphorology*, 17.

33 Blumenberg, "Prospect for a Theory of Nonconceptuality," 101. Derrida also noted Heidegger's hostility to metaphor, because he saw it as expressing a perniciously metaphysical separation of sensory and the nonsensory, the physical and the nonphysical. See Derrida, "White Mythology," 226.

     Blumenberg, it should be noted, analyzed the way meaning worked metaphorically, suggesting several major models: simultaneity in which meaning was derived from another event happening at the same time; meaning as the revelation of a latent identity; meaning as the temporal return of the same, and meaning as a spatial homecoming. See the discussion in Felix Heidenreich, "Porträtsammlung und Bilderverbot, Hans Blumenberg (20–96)," *Ideengeschichte der Bildwissenschaft*, eds. Jörg Probst and Jost Philipp Klenner, Frankfurt: Suhrkamp, 2009, 18.

34 Hans Blumenberg, "Being—A MacGuffin: How to Preserve the Desire to Think," *Salmagundi* 90–1, 1991; the original was a 1987 essay in the *Frankfurter Allgemeine Zeitung*.

35 Adorno, *Negative Dialectics*, 70–1.

36 Ibid., 76.

37 Ibid., 154.

38 Ibid., 172.

39 See the discussion in "Nonconceptual Mental Content," in the *Stanford Encyclopedia of Philosophy* (stanford.edu).

40 For a discussion of Adorno's critique of the sufficiency of propositional thought, see Gerhard Richter, "Aesthetic Theory and Non-Propositional Truth Content in Adorno," in Gerhard Richter, ed., *Language without Soil: Adorno and Late Philosophical Modernity*, New York: Fordham University Press, 2010.

41 For a recent overview, see Emmanuel Alloa, "The Most Sublime of All Laws: The Strange Resurgence of a Kantian Motif in Contemporary Image Politics," *Critical Inquiry* 41, 2015. See also Eckhard Nordhofen, ed. *Bilderverbot: die Sichtbarkeit des Unsichtbaren*, Paderborn: Schöningh, 2001. For a discussion of its importance for Blumenberg, see Felix Heidenreich, "Porträtsammlung und Bilderverbot. Hans Blumenberg (1920–1996)," in Jörg Probst and Jost Philipp Klenner, eds., *Ideengeschichte der Bildwissenschaft—Siebzehn Porträts*, Frankfurt: Suhrkamp, 2009. He ponders the importance of Blumenberg's own collection of portraits of various thinkers, concluding that it was consonant

with his skepticism about the use of images to illustrate concepts and metaphors.

42 For a discussion of its role in the larger context of the twentieth-century suspicion of the primacy of vision, see Martin Jay, *Downcast Eyes: The Denigration of Vision in Twentieth-Century French Thought*, Berkeley: University of California Press, 1993.

43 Blumenberg, "Prospect for a Theory of Nonconceptuality," 97.

44 All forms of positive revelation, Adorno argued, must be rejected. As he put it in the final sentence of "Reason and Revelation," "I see no other possibility than an extreme ascesis toward any type of revealed faith, an extreme loyalty to the prohibition of images far beyond what this once originally meant." *Critical Models: Interventions and Catchwords*, trans. Henry W. Pickford, New York: Columbia University Press, 1998, 142.

45 Adorno, "Something's Missing: A Discussion between Ernst Bloch and Theodor W. Adorno on the Contradictions of Utopian Longing," in Ernst Bloch, *The Utopian Function of Art and Literature: Selected Essays*, trans. Jack Zipes and Frank Mecklenburg, Cambridge: MIT Press, 1988, 10–11.

46 Adorno, *Negative Dialectics*, 362.

47 Gerhard Richter, *Afterness: Figures of Following in Modern Thought and Aesthetics*, New York: Columbia University Press, 2011, 64.

48 Adorno, *Negative Dialectics*, 207.

49 Ibid. The motif of the resurrection of the flesh is, of course, a powerful image in Christianity, but it is also present in Jewish lore as well. See in particular the "valley of dry bones" prophecy in Ezekiel 37.

50 Adorno, *Negative Dialectics*, 3.

51 For a comparison of Adorno and Levinas, see Hent de Vries, *Minimal Theologies: Critiques of Secular Reason in Adorno and Levinas*, Baltimore: Johns Hopkins University Press, 2005.

52 Adorno, *Negative Dialectics*, 137.

53 Ibid., 408.

54 Adorno/Scholem, *Briefwechsel, 39–69*, ed. Asaf Angermann, Frankfurt: Suhrkamp, 2015, 413.

55 Blumenberg, *Paradigms for a Metaphorology*, 132.

56 Adorno, *Negative Dialectics*, 153.

57 According to Adorno, it was Aristotle who first taught "the immanence of the concept in the object, by which he appears to dissolve the abstractness of the concept in relation to what it subsumes, for him this immanence of the concept is *ontological*; that is, the concept is *in itself* in the object, without reference to the abstracting subject." But then he added: "True, it is connected to the nonconceptual element within the object in a matter which Aristotle never clearly elaborated; and I would even say that it is inseparable from that element." Theodor W. Adorno, *Metaphysics: Concept and Problems*, ed. Rolf Tiedemann, trans. Edmund Jephcott, Stanford: Stanford University Press, 2000, 56.

58 Adorno's extended critique of reification as a fundamental category of Marxist humanism is developed in *Negative Dialectics*, 189–92.

59 Adorno, *Negative Dialectics*, 152.

60 Ibid., 149.

61 For a discussion of the role of mimesis in Adorno, see Martin Jay, "Mimesis and Mimetology: Adorno and Lacoue-Labarthe," in *Cultural Semantics:*

Keywords of our Time, Amherst: University of Massachusetts Press, 1998. It might also be noted that Adorno's attribution of the human emotion of "longing" [*Sehnsucht*] to a concept shows how persistent the metaphoric moment in conceptualization can be.

62 Adorno, *Negative Dialectics*, 162.

63 For a thorough analysis, see Brian O'Connor, *Adorno's Negative Dialectic: Philosophy and the Possibility of Critical Rationality*, Cambridge: MIT Press, 2004, chapter 2.

64 Adorno, to be sure, was not himself averse to drawing on its rhetorical power in his own writing. For insightful discussions of Adorno's views of language, see Peter Uwe Hohendahl, *Prismatic Thought*, Lincoln: University of Nebraska Press, 1995, chapter 9; and Steven Helmling, *Adorno's Poetics of Critique*, London: Continuum, 2009.

65 In *Negative Dialectics*, he acknowledges the impossibility of getting beyond the conceptual moment in language and chastises Benjamin's own concepts for "an authoritarian concealment of their conceptuality." But the only way to approach the name, he concedes, is indirectly, through a constellation of concepts: "The determinable flaw in every concept makes it necessary to cite others; this is the font of the only constellations which inherited some of the hope of the name. The language of philosophy approaches that name by denying it" (53). The Jewish prohibition on the name of God, a variation on the *Bilderverbot*, is the model for this idea. See David Kaufmann, "Adorno and the Name of God," *Flashpoint* I: 1, 1996.

66 Theodor W. Adorno, "On the Contemporary Relationship of Philosophy and Music," in *Essays on Music*, ed. Richard Leppert, trans. Susan H. Gillespie, Berkeley: University of California Press, 2002, 139-40. It should be noted, however, that the claim that music tends toward pure naming is itself very much a metaphor. It would be highly instructive to contrast Adorno's writings on music with Blumenberg's, most notably his *Matthäuspassion* (Frankfurt: Suhrkamp, 1988), but that is a task for another day.

67 Blumenberg, *Care Crosses the River*, 63.

68 See Martin Jay, "Adorno's Musical Nominalism," *New German Critique* 43: 3, 2016. For a discussion of the Jewish origins of this argument, see Agata Bielek-Robson, "The Promise of the Name: 'Jewish Nominalism' as the Critique of the Idealist Tradition," *Bamidbar* 2: 1, 2012.

69 Robert Hullot-Kentor, *Things beyond Resemblance: Collected Essays on Theodor W. Adorno*, New York: Columbia University Press, 2006.

70 Theodor W. Adorno, *Aesthetic Theory*, eds. Gretel Adorno and Rolf Tiedemann, trans. Robert Hullot-Kentor, Minneapolis: University of Minnesota Press, 1997, 112.

71 Ibid., 56.

72 Ibid., 203.

73 Ibid. See also his linkage of the non-scientific essay to rhetoric in "The Essay as Form," 20.

74 See Adorno, *Kant's Critique of Pure Reason*, ed. Rolf Tiedemann, trans. Rodney Livingstone, Stanford: Stanford University Press, 2001, lecture 18. For an analysis of Adorno's critique of Kant, see O'Connor, *Adorno's Negative Dialectic*, chapter 4.

75 Blumenberg, "An Anthropological Approach to the Contemporary Significance of Rhetoric," 456. He argues that "man comprehends himself only by way of

what he is not. It is not only his situation that is potentially metaphorical; his constitution already is."

76 Ibid., 124. The Frankfurt School was wary of Gehlen in part because of his prior Nazi sympathies. For a discussion of Adorno's attempt to block his appointment to a chair in Heidelberg in 1958 and their subsequent public debates on German television, see Müller-Doohm, *Adorno: A Biography*, 378–9. Apparently, they remained on personally cordial terms despite their political differences. Jürgen Habermas also criticized Gehlen's philosophical anthropology. See the discussion in Nicholls, *Myth and the Human Sciences*, 1–4. It should be noted that a primary source of the Critical Theorists' distance from Gehlen was his authoritarian institutionalism, which Blumenberg also rejected. The Frankfurt School, to be sure, also favored a negative over a positive philosophical anthropology. See Dennis Johannßen, "Toward a Negative Anthropology: Critical Theory's Altercations with Philosophical Anthropology," *Anthropology and Materialism* 1, 2013.

77 Birgit Recki, "Auch eine Rehabilitierung der instrumentellen Vernunft. Blumenberg über Technik und die kulturellen Natur des Menschen," in *Erinnerung an das Humane. Beiträge zur phänomenologische Anthropologie Hans Blumenbergs*, ed. Michael Moxter, Tübingen: Mohr-Siebeck, 2011.

78 Savage, "Laughter from the Lifeworld," 127. See Blumenberg, *The Laughter of the Thracian Woman: A Protohistory of Theory*, trans. Spencer Hawkins, London: Bloomsbury, 2015.

79 For a discussion, see Sebastian Tränkle, "Ideologiekritik und Metaphorologie. Elemente einer philosophischen Sprachkritik bei Adorno und Blumenberg," in *Sprache und Kritische Theorie*, eds. Philip Hogh and Stefan Deines, Frankfurt: Campus Verlag, 2016.

80 There are, to be sure, ways to mobilize metaphor for more critical, defamiliarizing purposes, as Richard Rorty has argued in distinguishing between hermeneutic and poetic uses. See the discussion in Anthony Reynolds, "Unfamiliar Methods: Blumenberg and Rorty on Metaphor," *Qui Parle* 12: 1, 2000. In fact, it could be argued that whereas metaphor may have familiarized, metaphorology, as a self-conscious reflection on that function, is inherently defamiliarizing, and thus potentially critical.

81 Savage, "Laughter from the Lifeworld," 130.

7. Chromophilia: *Der Blaue Reiter*, Walter Benjamin and the Emancipation of Color

1 Adorno, to be sure, did venture into film aesthetics in his critique of the culture industry, as Miriam Bratu Hansen shows in *Cinema and Experience: Siegfried Kracauer, Walter Benjamin and Theodor W. Adorno*, Berkeley: University of California Press, 2012. But the center of gravity of his work was always music and literature.

2 For an exploration of Benjamin's incomplete and often cryptic attempts to access the absolute and open the door to messianic redemption during this period in his career, see Peter Fenves, *The Messianic Reduction: Walter Benjamin and the Shape of Time* (Stanford: Stanford University Press, 2011). He includes a discussion of Benjamin's thoughts on color.

3 An earlier version of this chapter was presented at the 2011 Yale University Forum on Art, War and Science in the 20th Century, hosted by the Jeffrey Rubinoff Sculpture Park on Hornby Island, British Columbia, and appeared on the park's website: rubinoffsculpturepark.org. It was then translated into Spanish in *DEF-GHI; Comunicación y Arte* 5, 2014, and published in English in *Positions* 26: 1, 2018.

4 Adorno, *Negative Dialectics*, 404–5.

5 Richard W. Gassen, ed., *Der Blaue Reiter: Die Befreiung der Farbe*, Ludwigshafen am Rhein: Hatje Cantz, 2003.

6 The caveat "more or less common" has to be introduced because Marc in particular had a far less spiritual understanding of the meaning of color in his work. Some observers have gone so far as to deny that there was a common position at all—for example, Peter Selz, who claimed that "the Blaue Reiter was neither a school nor a movement." *German Expressionist Painting*, Berkeley: University of California Press, 1974, 206.

7 Wassily Kandinsky, *Concerning the Spiritual in Art*, Lexington: University of Kentucky Press, 2010, 60.

8 Howard Caygill, *Walter Benjamin: The Experience of Colour*, London: Routledge, 1998, Esther Leslie, *Hollywood Flatlands: Animation, Critical Theory and the Avant-Garde*, London: Verso, 2002, 263–78, and Heinz Brüggemann, *Walter Benjamin: Über Spiel, Farbe und Phantasie*, Würzburg: Königshausen and Neumann, 2007. Earlier studies of Benjamin did not foreground his debts to expressionists like Kandinsky. Eugene Lunn, in his still valuable *Marxism and Modernism: An Historical Study of Lukács, Brecht, Benjamin and Adorno*, Berkeley: University of California Press, 1982, acknowledges only the influence of Symbolism and later Surrealism.

9 According to a later reminiscence of Kandinsky, "We [he and Franz Marc] invented the name 'Der Blaue Reiter' while sitting at a coffee table in the garden in Sindelsdorf; we both loved blue, Marc liked horses. I riders. So the name came by itself." Kandinsky, "'Der Blaue Reiter' (Ruckblick), *Das Kunstblatt* 14, 1930, 59. It is sometimes noted Kandinsky had already named one of his 1903 paintings *The Blue Rider*, but Klaus Lankheit, in his introduction to the republication of *The Blaue Reiter Almanac*, trans. Henning Falkenstein (New York: Viking Press, 1974), 19, stated that it was originally called *Der Reiter* and renamed only when the Almanac appeared. Franz Marc also painted many horses and the color blue was identified by him with the male principle: creative, strong and *geistig*.

10 See Volker Adolph, "Von 'inneren Klängen' und der 'Bewegung des Lichtes': Das Problem der Farbe im Blauen Reiter," in Gassen, ed., *Der Blaue Reiter*.

11 For a helpful recent account, see Rein Undusk, "*Disegno e Colore*: Art Historical Reflections on Space," *KOHT ja PAIK / PLACE and LOCATION; Studies in Environmental Aesthetics and Semiotics* 5, eds. Eva Näripea, Virve Sarapik, Jaak Tomberg, Tallinn: Estonian Literary Museum, 2006. There is also an illuminating chapter on the theme in John Gage's indispensable *Color and Culture*, London: Thames and Hudson, 1993. See also his *Color in Art*, London: Thames and Hudson, 2006.

12 David Batchelor, *Chromophobia*, London: Reaktion, 2000.

13 On the links between rhetoric and color, see Jacqueline Lichtenstein, *The Eloquence of Color: Rhetoric and Painting in the French Classical Age*, trans.

Emily McVarish, Berkeley: University of California Press, 1993; and Wendy Steiner, *The Colors of Rhetoric*, Chicago: University of Chicago Press, 1982.

14 Batchelor, *Chromophobia*, 52.

15 Cited in Charles A. Riley II, *Color Codes: Modern Theories of Color in Philosophy, Painting and Architecture, Literature, Music, and Psychology*, Hanover: University Press of New England, 1995, 6. This remarkable book will inform much of what follows.

16 David Batchelor has used this term for a show of his own work, mounted, among other places, in Rio de Janeiro in 2009. See coolhunting.com/culture/chromophilia/.

17 Edwin A. Abbott, *Flatland: A Parable of Spiritual Dimensions*, Oxford: Oneworld Publications, 1994.

18 In John Russell's well-known *The Meanings of Modern Art* (New York: MoMA, 1974), the second volume was entitled "The Emancipation of Color." He sees it foreshadowed by Van Gogh and Maurice Denis, but argues that it was still a shock when exhibitions in Paris (1905), Dresden (1906), Munich (1911) and New York (1913) made clear how much of a breakthrough had occurred. Although he emphasizes the importance of the Fauves, most notably Matisse, he also stresses Picasso's contribution, especially during his "blue" and "rose" periods.

19 See Batchelor, *Chromophobia*, 98f. Picasso had already used house paint made by Ripolin as early as 1912. See Gage, *Color in Art*, 124.

20 Theodor W. Adorno, *In Search of Wagner*, trans. Rodney Livingstone, London: Verso, 1981, 71. See also his discussion of Wagner's orchestration and use of instrumental color in "Wagner's Relevance for Today," in *Essays on Music*, trans. Susan H. Gillespie, ed. Richard Leppert, Berkeley: University of California Press, 2002, 93–4. Significantly, he calls Wagner "the first case of uncompromising musical nominalism" (588), which alerts us to the link between the emancipation of color and the nominalist impulse in much of modern art. Adorno extolled the role of color in the compositions of Mahler as well. For a discussion, see John J. Scheinbaum, "Adorno's Mahler and the Timbral Outsider," *Journal of the Royal Musical Association* 131: 1, 2006.

21 Riley, *Color Codes*, 274.

22 For a discussion, see Ossian Ward, "The Man Who Heard His Paintbox Hiss," *Telegraph*, June 10, 2006.

23 The essay by Sabaneiev is particularly apposite to our theme, as it deals with a work by Scriabin called *Prometheus*, which was a "symphony of colors," based on a correspondence of notes and colors.

24 For a discussion of the French Academy's defense of design over color, see Lichtenstein, *The Eloquence of Color*, chapter 6. In "On the Question of Form" in *The Blaue Reiter Almanac*, Kandinsky wrote, "The academy is the surest way of destroying the power of the child. Even the greatest, strongest talent is more or less retarded in this respect by the academy. Lesser talents perish by the hundreds. An academically trained person of average talent excels in learning practical meanings and losing the ability to hear his inner sound. He produces a 'correct' drawing that is dead" (176).

25 For a discussion of the valorization of formlessness in certain modernist circles, see my essay "Modernism and the Retreat from Form," in *Force Fields: Between Intellectual History and Cultural Critique*, New York: Routledge, 1993.

26 The rhetoric of the "emancipation of form" is also sometimes used to characterize the first of these alternatives.

27 In his defense of Delacroix as a colorist, Charles Baudelaire wrote of his critics in 1861: "It would seem that when I contemplate the works of one of those men who are specifically called 'colorists,' I am giving myself up to a pleasure whose nature is far from a noble one; they would be delighted to call me 'materialistic,' reserving for themselves the aristocratic title of 'spiritual.'" "The Life and Work of Eugène Delacroix," *The Painter of Modern Life and other Essays*, trans. and ed., Jonathan Mayne, London: Phaidon, 1970, 51. This essay appeared in 1863, but the passage was cited from a review published two years before.

28 For an account that stresses the importance of scientific advances in understanding color, see Paul C. Vitz and Arnold B. Glimcher, *Modern Art and Modern Science: The Parallel Analysis of Vision*, New York: Praeger, 1984, chapter 4. They claim that Kandinsky's early ideas about the psychological response to colors was similar to that of Charles Henry, but acknowledge that any direct influence was unlikely. Later, during his Bauhaus years, he seems to have been influenced by Ewald Hering's more Goethean theories. Selz, however, emphatically questions the influence of science on Kandinsky's color theory: "Kandinsky's color symbolism is in no way based upon physical laws of color or upon the psychology of color vision: 'All these statements are the results of empirical feelings, and are not based on exact science.'" *German Expressionist Painting*, 230. The citation is from "The Language of Form and Color" in Kandinsky's *On the Spiritual in Art*.

29 Jonathan Crary, *Techniques of the Observer: On Vision and Modernity in the Nineteenth Century*, Cambridge: MIT Press, 1990, chapter 3.

30 George L. Mosse, *The Crisis of German Ideology: Intellectual Origins of the Third Reich*, New York: Grosset and Dunlap, 1964, 54.

31 August K. Wiedmann, *The German Quest for Primal Origins in Art, Culture and Politics, 1900–1933*, Lewiston: Edwin Mellen, 1995, 319.

32 Kandinsky, *Concerning the Spiritual in Art*, 36.

33 David Pan, *Primitive Renaissance: Rethinking German Expressionism*, Lincoln: University of Nebraska Press, 2001, 101.

34 See, for example, A. E. Carter, *The Idea of Decadence in French Literature: 1830–1900*, Toronto: University of Toronto Press, 1968, 151.

35 In *Concerning the Spiritual in Art*, he even chastised Matisse for laying too much stress on color (29).

36 Kandinsky had apparently learned to associate colors with shapes from Adolf Hoelzel, but came to somewhat different conclusions about their connections. See Gage, *Color in Art*, 85.

37 Kandinsky, "On the Question of Form," *The Blaue Reiter Almanac*, 149.

38 Kandinsky, *Concerning the Spiritual in Art*, 43.

39 Ibid., 52–3.

40 According to Gage, "Kandinsky was almost the only painter to use this repertory of 'primary' shapes in the 1920s, and since this was a visual language as flexible and ambiguous as any verbal language, it is not surprising that we find these precise color equivalents only occasionally in his work." *Color in Art*, 91.

41 There were, of course, other politically radical enthusiasts who were equally enamored of Kandinsky; for example, Dadaist Hugo Ball, who compared Kandinsky's spiritual quest and purity of color with Bakunin's anarchism. In

April 1917, he lectured on him in Galarie Dada in Zurich. See the discussion in Anson Rabinbach, *In the Shadow of Catastrophe: German Intellectuals between Apocalypse and Enlightenment*, Berkeley: University of California Press, 1997, chapter 2.

42 Benjamin to Scholem, January 13, 1920, *The Correspondence of Walter Benjamin 1910–1940*, eds. Gershom Scholem and Theodor W. Adorno, trans. Manfred R. Jacobsen and Evelyn M. Jacobson, Chicago: University of Chicago Press, 1994, 156. See also Gershom Scholem, *Walter Benjamin: The Story of a Friendship*, trans. Harry Zohn, Philadelphia: Jewish Publication Society of America, 1981, 65. He writes, "Evidently Benjamin was attracted to the mystical elements of the theory contained therein."

43 Benjamin to Scholem, January 13, 1920, 178.

44 He already owned Klee's *Vorführung des Wunders*, which his wife, Dora, gave him as a birthday present in 1920.

45 One exception is Marcus Bullock, "In a Blauer Reiter Frame: Walter Benjamin's Intentions of the Eye and Derrida's *Specters of Marx*," *Monatshefte* 93: 2, 2001. He does not comment, however, on Benjamin's prewar writings on color.

46 See Benjamin's letter to Scholem, October 22, 1917, in *The Correspondence of Walter Benjamin*, 100–1. For discussions, see Brüggemann, *Walter Benjamin*, 143–53, and Annie Bournef, "Radically Uncolorful Painting: Walter Benjamin and the Problem of Cubism, *Grey Room*, 39, Spring 2010. Scholem, it should be mentioned, many years later came to appreciate the color symbolism in the Jewish tradition, most notably the Kabbalah. See his "Farben und ihre Symbolik in der jüdischen Überlieferung," *Eranos* 41 (Leiden, 1974).

47 Brüggemann, *Walter Benjamin*, 134–43. For a longer discussion of that tradition in France, see Max Imdahl, *Farbe: Kunsthistorische Reflexionen in Frankreich*, Munich: Fink, 1988.

48 Walter Benjamin, "A Child's View of Color," *Selected Writings, 1913–1926*, vol. 1, eds. Marcus Paul Bullock, Michael Jennings, Howard Eiland and Gary Smith, Cambridge: Harvard University Press, 1996, 50.

49 Ibid., 51. This argument goes back at least as far as German romantic educator Friedrich Froebel (1782–1852). According to John Gage, "Late twentieth-century research into infant development supported Froebel's observation that color discrimination precedes form discrimination in the youngest children, and that babies are able to distinguish red, blue, green and yellow many years before they have words to name them." *Color in Art*, 64.

50 Benjamin, "A Child's View of Color," 51.

51 Benjamin, "Der Regenbogen: Gespräch über die Phantasie," *Gesammelte Schriften*, ed. Rolf Tiedemann and Hermann Schweppenhäuser, vol. 7.1, Frankfurt: Suhrkamp, 1989. The English-language version of the *Selected Writings* omits this essay.

52 Ibid., 19.

53 We sometimes think the rainbow has seven individual colors—red, orange, yellow, blue, indigo, violet—but apparently when Newton described the results of passing white light through a prism, he was influenced by his understanding of musical harmonies. According to Batchelor, "He divided the spectrum into seven colors in order to make it correspond to the seven distinct notes in the musical scale." *Chromophobia*, 93.

54 Benjamin, "Painting, or Signs and Marks," *Selected Writings*, vol. 1, 85.

55 Benjamin, "Painting and the Graphic Arts," *Selected Writings*, vol. 1, 82. In this

fragment, Benjamin mulls over the differences between painting as a vertical phenomenon and graphic arts as horizontal, with children's drawings in the latter category. He seems to be saying that Kandinsky somehow overcomes this opposition.

56 Immanuel Kant, *Critique of Judgment*, trans. James Creed Meredith, Oxford: Oxford University Press, 1978, 67.

57 Benjamin, "On Language as Such and the Language of Man," *Selected Writings*, vol. 1. Like the essays and fragments on color, this essay was only posthumously published.

58 Ibid., 70. "The Task of the Translator" from 1921 is included in the same volume.

59 A similar argument was later made by Umberto Eco, "How Culture Conditions the Colors We See," *On Signs*, ed. Marshall Blonsky, Baltimore: Johns Hopkins University Press, 1985.

60 Lichtenstein, *The Eloquence of Color*, 151.

61 Riley, *Color Codes*, 53.

62 Kandinsky, *Concerning the Spiritual in Art*, 47.

63 Mark A. Cheetham, *The Rhetoric of Purity: Essentialist Theory and the Advent of Abstract Painting*, Cambridge: Cambridge University Press, 1991, 68. He sees the quest for purity and essence, which is also evident in Mondrian, as politically very problematic.

64 The Theosophical Society, in fact, promoted the idea that there was a key to colored auras, which somehow hovered around human beings. Clairvoyants were able to discern the astral body. See, for example, C. W. Leadbeater, *Man Visible and Invisible*, London: Theophilosophical Publication Society, 1902. For his importance for Kandinsky, see Gage, *Color in Art*, 154–8.

65 Pan, *Primitive Renaissance*, 115.

66 For an attempt to flesh out this concept, see my essay "Magical Nominalism: Photography and the Re-enchantment of the World," *Culture, Theory and Critique* 50: 2–3, 2009; reprinted in Neal Curtis, ed., *The Pictorial Turn*, London: Routledge, 2010.

67 Caygill, *Walter Benjamin: The Color of Experience*, 3.

68 As early as his October 22, 1917 letter to Scholem on cubism, Benjamin noted, "As in these jottings I also allow the problem of painting to flow into the large domain of language whose dimensions I outline in my essay on language." *The Correspondence of Walter Benjamin 1910–1940*, 101.

69 As Rainer Nägele writes, the "dialectical image" is "not a picture or a painting, but instead a figure: it belongs to a graphic sphere in contrast to the sphere of painting." "Thinking Images," in *Benjamin's Ghosts: Interventions in Contemporary Literary and Cultural Theory*, ed. Gerhard Richter, Stanford: Stanford University Press, 2002, 23.

70 Bullock, "In a Blauer Reiter Frame," 194.

71 On Benjamin's messianic hopes in the postwar era, see Michael Löwy, *Redemption and Utopia: Jewish Libertarian Thought in Central Europe*, trans. Hope Heany, Stanford: Stanford University Press, 1992.

72 Benjamin, "Notes for a Study of the Beauty of Colored Illustrations in Children's Books," *Selected Writings*, vol. 1, 264.

8. Timbremelancholy: Walter Benjamin and the Fate of Philately

1 This chapter was first published in *Salmagundi* 194, 2017.

2 Louis Aragon, *Paris Peasant*, trans. Simon Watson Taylor, London: Cape, 1971, 72.

3 Michael Chabon, "Imaginary Homelands," *Maps and Legends: Reading and Writing along the Borderlands*, San Francisco: McSweeney's, 2008; the essay was originally published in 1997.

4 Walter Benjamin, *One-Way Street and Other Writings*, trans. J. A. Underwood, London: Penguin, 2009; *Radio Benjamin*, ed. Lecia Rosenthal, trans. Jonathan Lutes, London: Verso, 2014. You can listen to a reading of the script on http://clocktower.org/show/walter-benjamin-postage-stamp-swindles.

5 Pierre Missac, *Walter Benjamin's Passages*, trans. Shierry Weber Nicholsen, Cambridge: MIT Press, 1995, French original in 1987; and Jeffrey Mehlman, *Walter Benjamin for Children: An Essay on His Radio Years*, Chicago: Chicago University Press, 1993. Other commentators have discussed his comparable interest in collecting postcards—for example, Allan Wall in the *Fortnightly Review*: fortnightlyreview.co.uk/2015/03/reflections-benjamin-5/; and his general interest in collecting has been more widely acknowledged—for example, by Michael Steinberg, "The Collector as Allegorist," in *Walter Benjamin and the Demands of History*, ed. Michael Steinberg, Ithaca: Cornell University Press, 1996; and Ralph Shain, "Benjamin and Collecting," *Rethinking History* 20: 1, 2016.

6 Benjamin, *One-Way Street*, 101.

7 Ibid.

8 In America, according to David Henkin, "Throughout the state-banking era (before the Treasury Department began issuing currency in 1863), stamps were the only pieces of paper authorized by the federal government to circulate at a set value through the country. During the war, when specie was rare and banknotes depreciated, stamps became useful as money, and stores in cities would give them as change." *The Postal Age: The Emergence of Modern Communications in Nineteenth-Century America*, Chicago: University of Chicago Press, 2007, 37.

9 Ibid., 102.

10 More recently, deliberately fashioned "artistamps" (a *portmanteau* from "artist" and "stamp") have proliferated with the digital revolution, allowing anyone to become a designer of replicable miniature artworks, sometimes with political intent. Unlike genuine postage stamps, they have no utilitarian function or exchange value beyond their aesthetic merit, although if printed in limited editions and sold to art collectors, they too can be monetized. There is also a movement to create "mail art," which uses postcards to evade the gallery and museum system. See Mike Mosher, "Mail Art," *Bad Subjects* 74, 2005.

11 Missac, *Walter Benjamin's Passages*, 45.

12 Aragon, *Paris Peasant*, 72–3. For an analysis of the complicated debts Benjamin owed to Aragon's novel, see Vaclav Paris, "Uncreative Influence: Louis Aragon's *Paysan de Paris* and Walter Benjamin's *Passagen-Werk*," *Journal of Modern Literature* 31: 1, 2013.

13 Benjamin, *One-Way Street*, 103.

14 Ibid., 103. Benjamin, the editor of the text points out, was off in calling Stephan

a contemporary of romantic novelist Jean Paul, who died six years before his birth.

15 Benjamin's interest in the bourgeois letter as a serious form of literature manifested in the series of letters from 1783 to 1888 that he published pseudonymously, first in 1931 and 1932 in the *Frankfurter Zeitung* and then with some changes as *Deutsche Menschen* in 1936, while in exile. In the script for one of his (undelivered) radio talks, "On the Trail of Old Letters," (1931 or 1932), he spelled out his reasons for valuing letters as a way into the "living tradition" of a culture.

16 Benjamin, "The Work of Art in the Age of Mechanical Reproduction," *Illuminations*, ed. Hannah Arendt, New York: Harcourt, Brace and World, 1968.

17 Mehlman, *Walter Benjamin for Children*, 16.

18 See for example, Jasper Copping, "Philately Gets You Nowhere—Stamp Decline Sparks Fears for Collectors," *Telegraph*, October 16, 2011.

19 Girls, it has been argued, have many other outlets for their collecting inclinations: dolls, figurines, stuffed animals, spoons, beanie babies, quilts and so on, most of which reflect traditional domestic gender roles. Stamps, in contrast, supposedly connect boys with the larger, more public world they are expected to enter.

20 In an earlier essay, "Momentoes Post-Mori: Thoughts on the Collectors Mania," *Salmagundi* 180–1, 2013–14, I conjectured that collected objects often served as transitional objects leading us away from life into what follows. But insofar as stamp collections are so often begun at an early age and lose their magic for many as they grow older, it is likely that they are exceptions to this generalization.

21 Aragon, *Paris Peasant*, 72.

22 Benjamin, *One-Way Street*, 61.

23 Henkin, *The Postal Age*.

24 For those who want to follow the controversy, see Nick Allen, "Harry Potter and the Philatelists' Ire: Collectors Angry over Stamps," *Telegraph*, November 20, 2013. Other gimmicks have been more favorably received. In 2013 the US Postal Service commemorated its most famous mistake, reprinting the famous 1918 upside-down Jenny biplane stamp. In order to increase interest, it mischievously printed 100 with the plane right side up, which whetted investor appetites. According to one account, one lucky collector sold a plate of them for $45,000 to an anonymous buyer.

25 Benedict Anderson, *Imagined Communities: Reflections on the Origins and Spread of Nationalism*, London: Verso, 1991.

26 See Peter Butler, "It's like Magic: Removing Self-Adhesive Stamps from Paper," *American Philatelist*, October, 2010. Ironically, there has emerged a new variant of the stamp scams about which Benjamin wrote on the doctoring of gummed backings to restore a simulacrum of their original unlicked status.

27 See Max Pensky, *Melancholy Dialectics: Walter Benjamin and the Play of Mourning*, Amherst: University of Massachusetts, 1993; and Ilit Ferber, *Philosophy and Melancholy: Benjamin's Early Reflections on Theater and Language*, Stanford: Stanford University Press, 2013.

28 See my essay, "Against Consolation: Walter Benjamin and the Refusal to Mourn," *Refractions of Violence*, New York: Routledge, 2003.

9. The Little Shopgirls Enter the Public Sphere: Miriam Hansen on Kracauer

1 Max Horkheimer and Theodor W. Adorno, *Dialectic of Enlightenment: Philosophical Fragments*, ed. Gunzelin Schmid Noerr, trans. Edmund Jephcott, Stanford: Stanford University Press, 2002; for other essays on the same theme, see Theodor W. Adorno, *The Culture Industry: Selected Essays on Mass Culture*, ed. J. M. Bernstein, London: Routledge, 1996.

2 Miriam Bratu Hansen, *Cinema and Experience: Siegfried Kracauer, Walter Benjamin and Theodor W. Adorno*, Berkeley: University of California Press, 2012. The book appeared in the University of California's "Weimar and Now" series, which Anton Kaes, Edward Dimendberg and I edited.

3 "Miriam Hansen: Cinema, Experience and the Public Sphere," *New German Critique* 122, 2014.

4 Siegfried Kracauer, "The Little Shopgirls Go to the Movies," in *The Mass Ornament: Weimar Essays* , ed. and trans. Thomas Y. Levin, Harvard: Harvard University Press, 1995, 292.

5 Theodor W. Adorno, "The Curious Realist: On Siegfried Kracauer," in *Notes to Literature*, ed. Rolf Tiedemann, trans. Shierry Weber Nicholsen, New York: Columbia University Press, 1992, vol. 2, 66.

6 See note 2.

7 Hansen, *Cinema and Experience*, x. For a discussion of Kluge's friendship with Adorno, see Stefan Müller-Doohm, *Adorno: A Biography*, trans. Rodney Livingstone, Cambridge: Harvard University Press, 2005, 408–9.

8 Oskar Negt and Alexander Kluge, *Öffentlichkeit und Erfahrung. Zur Organisationsanalyse von bürgerlicher und proletarischer Öffentlichkeit*, Frankfurt a. Main: Suhrkamp 1972.

9 Miriam Hansen, "Cooperative Auteur Cinema and Oppositional Public Sphere: Alexander Kluge's Contribution to *Germany in Autumn*" and Alexander Kluge, "On Film and the Public Sphere," *New German Critique* 24–5, 1981–2.

10 Miriam Hansen, *Babel and Babylon: Spectatorship in American Silent Film*, Cambridge: Harvard University Press, 1991, introduction.

11 Oskar Negt and Alexander Kluge, *Public Sphere and Experience: Toward an Analysis of the Bourgeois and Proletarian Public Sphere*, trans. Peter Labanyi, Jamie Owen Daniel and Assenka Oksiloff, Minneapolis: University of Minnesota Press, 1993.

12 Hansen acknowledged that in his subsequent work, Kluge dropped the idea of a separate proletarian public sphere and in certain ways returned to a Habermasian position. See her foreword to *Public Sphere and Experience*, xxxv.

13 The *Bildungsbürgertum* meant a bourgeoisie defined in cultural terms, as opposed to the *Besitzbürgertum* defined in terms of the possession of property or capital.

14 Hansen, "Early Cinema, Late Cinema: Permutations of the Public Sphere," *Screen*, 34, 3 Autumn 1993, 203.

15 Ibid., 210.

16 Hansen, *Babel and Babylon*, 13.

17 Ibid., 111.

18 Ibid., 123.

19 Ibid., 112, where she wrote, "For Kracauer, who was both more familiar with and more skeptical vis-à-vis the cinema than Benjamin, this mode of reception [the projection of subjectivity onto the world of things] entails just as much a sense of de-realization, isolation and loss."

20 Hansen, *Cinema and Experience*, 54–5.

21 Ibid., 55.

22 Ibid., 56

23 Ibid., 265.

24 Ibid., 277.

25 Ibid., 98.

26 Ibid., 146.

27 Ibid., 174.

28 Ibid., 203.

29 As might be expected, however, Adorno's attitude was not unequivocally hostile, as shown by his participation in an ill-fated attempt to create a movie attacking anti-Semitism in the late 1940s. See the discussion in David Jenemann, *Adorno in America*, Minneapolis: University of Minnesota Press, 2007, chapter 3.

30 Theodor W. Adorno, *Minima Moralia: Reflections from Damaged Life*, trans. E.F.N. Jephcott, London: Verso, 1974, 25.

31 Hansen, *Cinema and Experience*, 249.

32 Ibid., 214.

33 See, for example, the essays in Craig Calhoun, ed., *Habermas and the Public Sphere*, Cambridge: MIT Press, 1992; and Harold Mah, "Phantasies of the Public Sphere: Rethinking the Habermas of Historians," *Journal of Modern History* 72, 2000. For a good summary of the early German response, see Peter Uwe Hohendahl, *The Institution of Criticism*, Ithaca: Cornell University Press, 1982, chapter 7. There continue to be attempts to find the public sphere in other times and places, even in the Middle Ages. See Alex J. Novikoff, "Toward a Cultural History of Scholastic Disputation," *American Historical Review* 117: 2, 2012.

34 Hansen, *Cinema and Experience*, 56.

35 See, for example, John Durham Peters, "Distrust of Representation: Habermas on the Public Sphere," *Media, Culture and Society* 15, 1993.

36 See, for example, Michael T. Gilmore, *Differences in the Dark*, New York: Columbia University Press, 1998.

37 Hansen, foreword to *Public Sphere and Experience*, xxvii.

38 Hansen, *Babel and Babylon*, 12–13.

39 Martin Jay, *Songs of Experience: Modern American and European Variations on a Universal Theme*, Berkeley: University of California Press, 2006.

40 See, for example, the discussion in Habermas, *Truth and Justification*, ed. and trans. Barbara Fultner, Cambridge: MIT Press, 2005, 60.

10. Irony and Dialectics: *One-Dimensional Man* and 1968

1 For another consideration of the role of irony in history, see Martin Jay, "Intention and Irony: The Missed Encounter between Hayden White and Quentin Skinner," *History and Theory* 52, 2013.

2 This chapter was first published in the *Revista Mexicana de Ciencias Politicas y Sociales* 63: 234, 2018.

3 Herbert Marcuse, *One-Dimensional Man: Studies in the Ideology of Advanced Industrial Society*, 2nd ed., Boston: Beacon, 1991, 257.

4 The earlier discussions are noted in Jeremy J. Shapiro's "One-Dimensionality: The Universal Semiotic of Technological Experience," *Critical Interruptions: New Left Perspectives on Herbert Marcuse*, ed. Paul Breines, New York: Herder and Herder, 1970, 184. He challenges the idea that somehow "two-dimensionality" is normal and "one-dimensionality" an aberration caused by technological domination.

5 Theodor W. Adorno, *Minima Moralia: Reflections from Damaged Life*, trans. E. F. N. Jephcott, London: Verso, 1978, 49.

6 The later dispute between Marcuse and his erstwhile Institute colleagues over when the bottle was to be uncorked is treated in Hanning Voigts, *Entkorkte Flaschenpost: Herbert Marcuse, Theodor W. Adorno und die Streit um die Neue Linke*, Berlin: LIT, 2010. He notes that the metaphor was first used by Horkheimer in a letter written to Adorno in 1940 (21). It reappeared in a number of places, none perhaps as well-known as in *Minima Moralia*, where Adorno wrote, "Even at the time the hope of leaving behind messages in bottles on the flood of barbarism bursting on Europe was an amiable illusion: the desperate letters stuck in the mud of the spring of rejuvenescence and were worked up by a band of Noble Human-Beings and other riff-raff into highly artistic but inexpensive wall ornaments" (209). Interestingly, the "even then" refers to the early twentieth-century reception of Nietzsche, not his own era, but the phrase seemed even more apt for his own predicament as an exile in America.

7 Douglas Kellner, "Herbert Marcuse's Reconstruction of Marxism," in Robert Pippen, Andrew Feenberg, Charles P. O. Webe, eds., *Marcuse: Critical Theory and the Promise of Utopia*, South Hadley: Bergin and Garvey, 1988, 180.

8 Ibid.

9 Adorno, *Minima Moralia*.

10 Ibid., 210. Whether Adorno himself honored this prohibition on irony is questionable. In *Minima Moralia*, after all, he employed a number of ironic inversions—e.g., "melancholy science" for Nietzsche's "gay science"; "the whole is the untrue" for Hegel's "the whole is the true"—which suggested he expected his readers to be able to read ironically. For a discussion, see Gillian Rose, *The Melancholy Science: An Introduction to the Thought of Theodor W. Adorno*, New York: Columbia University Press, 1978, 16.

11 Adorno, *Minima Moralia*, 211.

12 Marcuse, *One-Dimensional Man*, xli.

13 Ronald Aronson, "Dear Herbert," *The Revival of American Socialism*, ed. George Fischer, New York: Oxford University Press, 1971, 261.

14 Mitchell Franklin, "The Irony of the Beautiful Soul of Herbert Marcuse," *Telos* 6, 1970. Franklin taught at the University of New York, Buffalo, where he was a mentor of many of *Telos*'s founding figures during their graduate school days. When he died in 1986, the journal published a special section of essays in his honor (*Telos* 70, 1986–87).

15 G. W. F. Hegel, *The Philosophy of Fine Art*, London: G. Bell and Sons, 1920, vol. 1, 93–4.

16 Alex Delfini and Paul Piccone, "Our Mitchell Franklin," *Telos* 70, 1986-7, 54.
17 Helmut Lethen, *Cool Conduct: The Culture of Distance in Weimar Germany*, trans. Don Reneau, Berkeley: University of California Press, 2002.
18 Peter Sloterdijk, *Critique of Cynical Reason*, trans. Michael Eldred, Minneapolis: University of Minnesota Press, 1987, 441.
19 Ibid.
20 See the discussion in Timothy Bewes, *Cynicism and Postmodernity*, London: Verso, 1997, 37-41.
21 Friedrich Schlegel, *Philosophische Lehrjahre 1796-1806*. ed. Ernst Behler. Munich: Schöningh, 1963. *Kritische Ausgabe*. vol. 18, 85. De Man's use of this aphorism has been widely discussed, for example, in Ayon Roy, "Hegel contra Schlegel: Kierkegaard contra de Man," *PMLA* 124: 1, 2009.
22 Kevin Newmark, *Irony on Occasion: From Schlegel and Kierkegaard to Derrida and de Man*, New York: Fordham University Press, 2012, 38.
23 Michael Saler, "Modernity, Disenchantment, and the Ironic Imagination," *Philosophy and Literature* 28: 1, 2004, 140.
24 For a useful discussion of their differing attitudes toward irony, see Mark C. Taylor, *Journeys to Selfhood: Hegel and Kierkegaard*, Berkeley: University of California Press, 1980, 94-5.
25 Harvie Ferguson, *Melancholy and the Critique of Modernity: Søren Kierkegaard's Religious Psychology*, London: Routledge, 1995, 42.
26 Marcuse, *One-Dimensional Man*, 12.
27 Ibid., 68.
28 Ibid., 189.
29 Herbert Marcuse, *The Aesthetic Dimension: Toward a Critique of Marxist Aesthetics*, Boston: Beacon, 1978.
30 Marcuse, *One-Dimensional Man*, 239.
31 Ibid., 247.
32 J. M. Bernstein, *The Philosophy of the Novel: Lukács, Marxism and the Dialectics of Form*, Minneapolis: University of Minnesota Press, 1984, 161.
33 For an argument that the collapse of faith in "world history" as a legible narrative also undermines the premise of Georg Lukács's *History and Class Consciousness*, see Martin Jay, "Fidelity to the Event? Lukács' *History and Class Consciousness* and the Russian Revolution," *Studies in East European Thought* 3: 4, 2018.
34 Jürgen Habermas, *Die Neue Unübersichtlichkeit*, Frankfurt: Suhrkamp, 1985.
35 Richard Rorty, *Contingency, Irony and Solidarity*, Cambridge: Cambridge University Press, 1989, 73.
36 Christoph Menke, *Tragic Play: Irony and Theater from Sophocles to Beckett*, trans. James Phillips, New York: Columbia University Press, 2009.
37 Ibid., 50.
38 Jonathan Lear, *A Case for Irony*, with commentary by Cora Diamond, Christine M. Korsgaard, Richard Moran and Robert A. Paul, Cambridge: Harvard University Press, 2011.
39 Ibid., 22.
40 Ibid., 36.
41 Ibid., 67.

11. Dialectic of Counter-Enlightenment: The Frankfurt School as Scapegoat of the Lunatic Fringe

1 At this writing, there is a long thread discussing the competing Wikipedia entries on the WikiProjects Alternative Views "talk" section: https://en.wikipedia.org/wiki/Talk:Frankfurt_School_conspiracy_theory.

2 See Will Weissert, "Fidel Castro fascinated by Bilderberg Club conspiracy theory," *Christian Science Monitor*, August 20, 2010. Originally written in Spanish as *La Verdadera Historia del Club Bilderberg*, the book is translated as *The True Story of the Bilderberg Group*, Waterville: TrineDay, 2007. In the English translation, all references to the Frankfurt School, Walter Lippmann and the Beatles have been purged.

3 Daniel Estulin and Fidel Castro, "Humanity Must Preserve Itself in Order to Live for Thousands of Years," *Granma Internacional*, August 31, 2010.

4 Weissert, "Fidel Castro fascinated by Bilderberg Club conspiracy theory." Castro's paraphrase of Estulin reads as follows: "The responsibility of devising a social theory of rock and roll fell to the German sociologist, musicologist and composer Theodor Adorno, 'one of the leading philosophers at the Frankfurt School of Social Research . . .' Adorno was sent to the United States in 1939 to direct the Princeton Radio Research Project, a joint effort between Tavistock and the Frankfurt School with the aim of controlling the masses, which was financed by the Rockefeller Foundation and founded by one of David Rockefeller's trusted men, Hadley Cantril." One of Estulin's main players in the Bilderberg conspiracy, it should be noted, is the Tavistock Institute for Human Relations in London.

5 Patrick J. Buchanan, *The Death of the West: How Dying Populations and Immigrant Invasions Imperil our Country and Civilization*, New York: St. Martin's Griffin, 2002.

6 Michael Minnicino, "New Dark Age: Frankfurt School and Political Correctness," *Fidelio* 1, 1991–2; reprinted by the Schiller Institute: schillerinstitute.org.

7 See William S. Lind, "The Roots of Political Correctness," *American Conservative*, November 19, 2009.

8 Ralph de Toledano, *Cry Havoc! The Great American Bringdown and How it Happened*, Washington: Regnery, 2007.

9 In later incarnations of his narrative, Lind would elaborate this point, arguing in a chapter of the 2012 book edited by Pat Boone and Ted Baehr, *The Culture-Wise Family: Upholding Christian Values in a Media-Wise World* (Ada: BakerBooks): "The Frankfurt School was well on the way to creating political correctness. Then suddenly, fate intervened. In 1933, Adolf Hitler and the Nazi Party came to power in Germany, where the Frankfurt School was located. Since the Frankfurt School was Marxist, and the Nazis hated Marxism, and since almost all its members were Jewish, it decided to leave Germany. In 1934, the Frankfurt School, including its leading members from Germany, was re-established in New York City with help from Columbia University. Soon, its focus shifted from destroying traditional Western culture in Germany to doing so in the United States. It would prove all too successful."

10 www.stormfront.org/forum/t633959-3/. For similar anti-Semitic rants against the Frankfurt School, see www.thejewishquestion.com/.../jews-created-spread-political-correctness-to-destroy-western-civilization; and buchanan.org/.../kevin-macdonald-pat-buchanan-is-censored-by-human-events-3754.

Kevin Macdonald, a professor of psychology at California State, Long Beach, has written several unapologetically anti-Semitic books blaming Jews for the fall of Western civilization, in which the Frankfurt School figures prominently.

11 Timothy Matthews, "The Frankfurt School: Conspiracy to Corrupt," *Catholic Insight*, March 2009.

12 When the invasion took place, I was asked to support a commission that had been set up in Belgium by Lieven de Cauter based on the Vietnam Russell Tribunal. All the alleged perpetrators turned out to share certain ethnic traits. When I pointed this out to de Cauter, he publicly acknowledged my warning. See his blog of March 18, 2003: www.mail-archive.com/nettime-l@bbs.thing.net/msg00582.html.

13 Estulin, *La Verdadera Historia del Club Bilderberg*, 15n25.

14 See Savage's show on YouTube entitled "Liberalism and Frankfurt School Marxism," in which he blames Obama for the influence of the evil Herbert "Marcoosee."

15 See the incredulous response to one of the more prominent conservative voices, Andrew Breitbart, in the May 24, 2010, *New Yorker* by Rebecca Mead, as well as the blog post "Who Let Andrew Breitbart into the Critical Theory Section of the Book Store?" by John Knefel on May 18, 2010, searchable through https://johnknefel.wordpress.com. They focus on Breitbart's claim that Obama was a tool of the Frankfurt School but do not comment on the larger phenomenon. There is, however, an excellent piece by Bill Berkowitz called "Reframing the Enemy," buried in the *Intelligence Report* of the Southern Poverty Law Center, 110 (Summer 2003), which draws attention to the right's adoption of "cultural Marxism" as a term of indiscriminate opprobrium. Unfortunately, it has had very little resonance.

16 David Jenemann, *Adorno in America*, Minneapolis: University of Minnesota Press, 2007; and Thomas Wheatland, *The Frankfurt School in Exile*, Minneapolis: University of Minnesota Press, 2009.

17 Leo Löwenthal and Norbert Guterman, *Prophets of Deceit: A Study of the Techniques of the American Agitator*, New York: Harper and Brothers, 1949.

18 For example, see James Simpson, "Frankfurt School Reigns Supreme at Notre Dame," *American Thinker*, May 19, 2009.

19 Theodor W. Adorno, "Spengler after the Decline," *Prisms*, trans. Samuel and Sherry Weber, London: Neville Spearman, 1967, 65.

20 "Dialektik der Gegenaufklärung: Die Frankfurter Schule im Verschwörungsnarrativ extremistischer Randgruppen," *Westend: Neue Zeitschrift für Sozialforschung* 8: 1, 2011.

21 See Anders Behring Breivik, *2083: A European Declaration of Independence*, "Further Readings on the Frankfurt School," https://info.publicintelligence.net/AndersBehringBreivikManifesto.pdf. See also Peter Thompson, "The Frankfurt School Part 1: Why Did Anders Breivik Fear Them?," *Guardian*, March 25, 2013.

22 Cited in Chip Berlet, "Author Cited by Anders Behring Breivik Regrets Original Essay," July 26, 2011: http://www.talk2action.org/story/2011/7/26/161347/099.

23 There has been a growing public awareness of the spread of the conspiracy theory. Perhaps the most visible critique was made by Samuel Moyn, "The Alt Right's Favorite Meme is 100 Years Old," *New York Times*, November 13, 2019. William Lind attempted to reply in "The Marxism That Must Not Be

Named," *traditionalRIGHT*, December 23, 2019. Lind advises Moyn to see his video and read some books on the Frankfurt School, including *The Dialectical Imagination*. Moyn has the last laugh, noting in a tweet the same day: "William Lind discovers my @nytopinion piece on 'cultural Marxism,' and recommends I educate myself by reading the works of Martin Jay, not realizing Jay was my dissertation adviser," https://twitter.com/samuelmoyn/status/1077004111193755649.

24 Ben Davis, "How a Right-Wing Obsession with Art Theory Became a Racist 'Star Wars' Boycott," *Art News*, October 27, 2015; "Is 'Political Correctness' to Blame for Orlando Massacre?," *Econospeak*, June 15, 2016, econospeak.blogspot.com.

25 For an insightful analysis of the role of the Frankfurt School conspiracy in Breitbart's worldview, see Andreas Huyssen, "Breitbart, Bannon, Trump, and the Frankfurt School: A Strange Meeting of Minds," *Public Seminar*, September 28, 2017, publicseminar.org. The influence of the conspiracy theory, or at least the denunciation of "cultural Marxism" as the source of political correctness, has appeared as well in more mainstream journalism, as evidenced by its casual invocation by *New York Times* columnist and public television pundit David Brooks in "Liberal Parents, Radial Students," *New York Times*, November 26, 2019. See also his tweet of November 29, 2018: https://twitter.com/nytdavidbrooks/status/1068299229997801479?lang=en, where he promotes an essay by Alexander Zubatov, "Just Because Anti-Semites Talk about 'Cultural Marxism' Doesn't Mean It Isn't Real," *Tablet*, November 29, 2018.

26 Andrew Breitbart, *Righteous Indignation: Excuse Me While I Save the World*, New York: Grand Central Publishing, 2012.

27 "Andrew Breitbart on the Frankfurt School of Cultural Marxism," June 14, 2011, YouTube.com.

28 "Ben Shapiro: Frankfurt School," February 22, 2016, YouTube.com.

29 Austin Ruse, "Cultural Marxism Is the Enemy: Review of Michael Walsh, *The Devil's Pleasure Palace*," *Breitbart*, November 19, 2015, breitbart.com.

30 Josh Harkinson, "Meet the White Nationalist Trying to Ride the Trump Train to Lasting Power," *Mother Jones*, October 27, 2016; see also Talya Zax, "Richard Spencer's Master's Thesis Was an Anti-Semitic Critique—of a Jewish Philosopher," *Forward*, January 17, 2017; see also his 2012 podcast interview with radical right-wing British author Jonathan Bowden, "Frankfurt School Revisionism"—the transcript can be found at counter-currents.com.

31 Bill Berkowitz, " 'Cultural Marxism,' a conspiracy theory with an anti-Semitic twist, is being pushed by much of the American right," *Intelligence Report*, August 15, 2003, splcenter.org.

32 Cited as "Eyes on the Right," "Meet William S. Lind: The Extremist Author Who May Have Influenced Donald Trump," *Angry White Men (Tracking White Supremacy)*, November 25, 2016, angrywhitemen.org; *The Barnes Review* was named for twentieth-century anti-Semite and Holocaust denier Harry Elmer Barnes, who had once been a respected historian involved in debates about the origins of World War I. It was founded by Willis Carto, who also launched the radical right-wing Liberty Lobby and the Institute for Historical Review (IHR), which denies the Holocaust.

33 Jack Jacobs, *The Frankfurt School, Jewish Lives and Anti-Semitism*, Cambridge: Cambridge University Press, 2015. For a review symposium, including my own response, see *German Quarterly* 89: 1, 2016.

34 Kevin MacDonald, "Breivik's 'The Great Satan, His Cult and the Jews,'" *Occidental Observer*, July 29, 2011, theoccidentalobserver.net.

35 For a history of its development in the context of the American reception of Critical Theory, see Robert Zwarg, *Die Kritische Theorie in Amerika: Das Nachleben einer Tradition*, Göttingen: Vandenhoeck and Ruprecht, 2017, 396–7. Symptomatic of the journal's evolution is the participation of their current and past editors, David Tse-Chien Pan and Russell Berman, in Mike Pompeo's Commission on Inalienable Rights, which was designed to mobilize the discourse of human rights largely to defend "religious liberty," while the administration it serves cynically ignores other violations.

36 Jacob Siegel, "The Alt-right's Jewish Godfather," *Tablet*, November 29, 2016.

37 Gottfried on Spencer: "When I criticize him, I am not making moral judgments, except when I note his futile attempt to keep up with leftist Millennials by siding with gay rights and abortion. What I object to in Richard is his, well, strategic stupidity, not the fact that he has committed the 'sin' of being a white nationalist. Since 'educated' whites are taught to hate their own race, I can't see how one can appeal to Millennials and leftist college students by calling for white nationalism. Nor does one win their sympathy by mimicking their positions on feminism and homosexuality while trying to convert them to a racialist ideology. What seems to me the only chance left to the Right to be effective is by mobilizing the 'Deplorables' and then turning them against the social-cultural Left." Quoted in Ilana Mercer "Paul Gottfried Ponders Richard Spencer's Strategy (and My Paleolibertarian Take)," bareleyablog.com, n/d. Can one take seriously someone who can't feel any moral outrage against an avowed neo-Nazi like Spencer?

38 Paul Gottfried, "Misadventuring on Wikipedia: The anonymized wiki editors misconstrue conservative scholarship on the Frankfurt School," *American Conservative*, December 11, 2014; the reference in the title is to a battle that took place in the pages of Wikipedia between competing versions of the Frankfurt School conspiracy, which involved two articles and several interventions in each. Gottfried also wrote a glowing review of Lind's novel *Victoria: A Novel of 4th Generation War*, a fantasy of violent retribution against all the exponents of "political correctness," which appeared on an anti-immigrant blog *Dvare*, May 26, 2015. Oddly, in light of his critique of the claim of anti-Semitism, Gottfried admits that "Lind sees them mostly as the product of the Institute for Social Research, a think-tank that was founded in interwar Frankfurt by mostly Jewish, self-described Marxists. In contrast, I stress the acquired American identity of the 'Cultural Marxists.'"

39 Joel B. Pollack, "Ha'aretz Calls Andrew Brietbart an Anti-Semite," *Brietbart*, August 19, 2016.

40 See Jeff Greenfield, "The Ugly History of Stephen Miller's 'Cosmopolitanism' Epithet," *Politico Magazine*, August 3, 2017. For a lame attempt to defend Miller as "good for the Jews" by an allegedly Jewish supporter of anti-Semite Kevin MacDonald, see Marcus Alethia, "What's Good for the Jews? Stephen Miller," *Occidental Observer*, February 8, 2018.

41 See Jana Winter and Elias Groll, "Here's the Memo That Blew up the NSC," *Foreign Policy*, August 10, 2017; and Jeet Heer, "Trump's Racism and the Myth of 'Cultural Marxism,'" *New Republic*, August 15, 2017.

42 Winter and Groll, np.

43 William S. Lind, "The Next Conservatism," *Traditional Right*, April 16, 2016.

44 In an interview with a conservative Fox News host, Trump explained his reading habits: "Well, you know, I love to read. Actually, I'm looking at a book, I'm reading a book, I'm trying to get started. Every time I do about a half a page, I get a phone call that there's some emergency, this or that. But we're going to see the home of Andrew Jackson today in Tennessee and I'm reading a book on Andrew Jackson. I love to read. I don't get to read very much, Tucker, because I'm working very hard on lots of different things, including getting costs down. The costs of our country are out of control. But we have a lot of great things happening, we have a lot of tremendous things happening." Cited in Donald Rowles, "Donald Trump on His Reading Habits: 'I Love Book!,'" *Pajiba*, March 17, 2017.

45 Roniel Aledo, "Trump, Cultural Marxism and the Counter-Revolution," thedailyjournalist.com, n/d.

46 For suggestive ways to proceed, see Wendy Brown, Peter E. Gordon and Max Pensky, *Authoritarianism: Three Inquiries into Critical Theory*, Chicago: University of Chicago Press, 2018.

47 T. W. Adorno, Else Frenkel-Brunswick, Daniel J. Levinson and R. Nevitt Sanford, *The Authoritarian Personality*, 2 vols., New York: Harper and Brothers, 1950, republished with Peter Gordon's new introduction by Verso Books in August 2019. The other most relevant study for understanding the alt-right's appeal was Leo Löwenthal and Norbert Guterman, *Prophets of Deceit: A Study of the Techniques of the American Agitator*, New York: Harper and Brothers, 1950, also forthcoming in a new edition from Verso Books with an introduction by Corey Robin. Adorno conducted a similar analysis of one agitator in particular in the 1940s, which was only published after his death as *The Psychological Technique of Martin Luther Thomas' Radio Addresses*, Stanford: Stanford University Press, 2000.

48 The earliest attempt of the Institute to conduct a theoretically informed empirical analysis of psychological attitudes was Erich Fromm's initially unpublished study, conducted in the waning years of Weimar; it showed that the alleged antiauthoritarian radicalism of many workers was undercut by their underlying psychological traits. It was only published in 1980 and translated into English as *The Working Class in Weimar Germany: A Psychological and Sociological Study*, ed. Wolfgang Bonss, trans. Barbara Weinberger, Leamington Spa: Berg, 1984. The Institute also conducted an ill-starred, lengthy survey of American labor and anti-Semitism that was never completed to its satisfaction. For an analysis, see Catherine Collomp, "Anti-Semitism among American Labor: A Study by the Refugee Scholars of the Frankfurt School of Sociology at the End of World War II," *Labor History* 52: 4, 2011.

49 Minnicino, "New Dark Age."

50 Ibid.

51 Kevin MacDonald, "The Frankfurt School of Social Research and the Pathologization of Gentile Group Allegiances," *The Culture of Critique*, kevinmacdonald.net.

52 Ibid., 192.

53 European Defence League, "The Authoritarian Personality: The Frankfurt School's Attack on White Identity," April 3, 2018, europeandefenceleague.com.

54 Alex Ross, "The Frankfurt School Knew Trump Was Coming," *New Yorker*, December 5, 2016.

55 Access the papers through Public Seminar's archives, publicseminar.org.

56 The October 25, 2017, discussion, is on YouTube under the title "The Frankfurt School Knew Trump Was Coming." See also Jonathon Catlin, "The Authoritarian Personality and its Discontents," *Journal of the History of Ideas* Blog, January 10, 2018, jhiblog.org.

57 For an example of the skepticism, see Jeffrey Friedman, "Are Trump Supporters Authoritarian?" *Niskinen Center*, August 23, 2017.

58 Grabien.com, "Sanders: Trump Has 'Strong Authoritarian Personality' and 'Disrespect for Democracy' in US," March 20, 2018.

59 Peter E. Gordon, "The Authoritarian Personality Revisited: Reading Adorno in the Age of Trump," in Brown, Gordon and Pensky, *Authoritarianism.*

60 Ibid., 57.

61 Sander Gilman and James M. Thomas, *Are Racists Crazy? How Prejudice, Racism and Anti-Semitism Became Markers of Insanity*, New York: New York University Press, 2016.

62 The role of social pathology in recent Critical Theory is perhaps most explicit in the work of Axel Honneth. See, for example, his "A Social Pathology of Reason," *The Cambridge Companion to Critical Theory,* ed. Fred Rush, Cambridge: Cambridge University Press, 2004. For a response, see Fabian Freyenhagen, "Honneth on Social Pathologies: A Critique," *Critical Horizons* 16: 2, 2015.

63 For an account of the different roles psychoanalysis played in the history of the Frankfurt School, see chapter 4 of this volume.

64 Theodor W. Adorno, *Minima Moralia: Reflections from Damaged Life*, trans. E. F. N. Jephcott, London: Verso, 1974, 39, where the translation of "*Es gibt kein richtiges Leben im falschen*" is rendered as "Wrong life cannot be lived rightly."

65 Ibid., 61.

66 See Sidney Bloch and Peter Reddaway, *Russia's Political Hospitals: The Abuse of Psychiatry in the Soviet Union*, London: Victor Gollancz, 1977, and Sidney Bloch and Peter Reddaway, *Soviet Psychiatric Abuse: The Shadow over World Psychiatry*, London: Victor Gollancz, 1984; Robin Munro, "Judicial Psychiatry in China and Its Political Abuses," *Columbia Journal of Asian Law* 14, 2000 and "Political Psychiatry in Post-Mao China and its Origins in the Cultural Resolution," *Journal of the American Academy of Psychiatry and the Law* 30, 2002.

67 Erich Fromm, "What Shall We Do with Germany?," *Saturday Review*, May 29, 1943, 10. Cited in Gilman and Thomas, *Are Racists Crazy?*, 122.

68 Jürgen Habermas, *Knowledge and Human Interests*, trans. Jeremy J. Shapiro, Boston: Beacon, 1971.

69 For an example of this approach, see Arlie Russell Hochschild, *Strangers in Their Own Land: Anger and Mourning on the American Right*, New York: New Press, 2016.

Index

A
Abbot, Edwin 100, 101
Abgrund 2, 11, 17, 18
Abromeit, John 8
Acosta, Jim 165
Adorno, Gretel 23
Adorno, Theodor ix, 20, 28, 35, 81,
    114, 124, 136, 152
Aesthetic Theory 16, 90, 94, 191, 204
Africa 105, 111
Ages of the World 12–13, 16, 176–8
Agnon, Shmuel Yosef 78
Albers, Joseph 100
Alaska, Sitka 113–14
Alexander, Eduard 8
Alinsky, Saul 163
alt-right 151, 160–1, 163–8, 171,
    221–2
American Revolution 17
anthropology 40, 45, 86–7, 95, 125,
    167, 201–2, 206
Anderson, Benedict 121
Antigone, 43
anti-elitism 129
anti-Semitism 22, 27–8, 48, 74–5, 158,
    160, 164–7, 181, 185, 189, 193–4,
    199, 215, 221–3
apriorism 11
Aragon, Louis 115, 116, 118
Arendt, Hannah 17, 44, 48, 72
archaeology 183

architecture 98, 186, 208
Aronson, Ronald 140
art 108, 109, 129, 131, 145–6, 184, 191
    Modern Art 96, 99, 207–11
    Impressionism 99
    Art criticism 103–5, 109, 204
    Folk art 105, 107
    Mechanically reproduced art 113,
        117, 128, 182, 213
    Concerning the Spiritual in Art
        104–6, 207, 209–11
    Artists 37, 60, 76, 99–106, 111, 145

atheism 45, 185
Auschwitz 80, 90, 184, 200
The Authoritarian Personality 41, 49,
    55–8, 64, 160, 167, 167–71,
    184–6, 189–90, 205–6
avant-garde 34, 99, 207
Avenarius, Richard 90

B
Babel and Babylon 126, 128, 131, 178,
    215–16
Bachofen, Johann Jakob 57
Baeck, Leo 69, 169
Ballestín, Lucas 169
Baltic 120
Bannon, Steve 163
baroque 15
Barthes, Roland 33, 34, 42, 44, 45

Barzun, Jacques 33
Batchelor, David 100
Bauhaus 209
The Beatles 153, 218
Becker, Matthias 25, 26, 30
Beckett, Samuel 147
Benjamin, Walter xii, 24, 50, 66, 98, 99, 103, 106, 113, 114, 122, 124
Berger, John 34
Berkowitz, Bill 164
Bernfeld, Siegfried 51
Berlin 69, 174, 177, 197–200, 202, 216
Berlioz, Hector 101
Bernhard, Prince 152
Bernstein, J. M. 146, 169
Biale, David 78
Bilderverbot 27–8, 33, 80, 89–90, 98, 132, 184, 200, 203, 204–5
Bin Laden, Osama 152
Der Blaue Reiter 98–9, 101, 105–7, 109, 111–12
    The Blue Rider (painting) 208
    The Blaue Reiter Almanac 102, 104
Bloch, Ernst 12, 70, 71, 77, 90
Blumenberg, Hans 81
Bloom, Allan 29
Boston 175–6, 185, 187, 191–3, 216–17, 224
Bottici, Chiara 169
Bowie, Andrew 15
Boyd Dale, Louise 118
Brecht, Bertolt 7, 10, 24, 96, 141
Breitbart, Andrew 163
    Breitbart News 163–4, 219–20, 222
Breivik, Anders Behring 161, 162, 164, 172
Brenner, Michael 78
Brickner, Richard 170
Briffault, Robert 57
Brown, Norman O. 30
Die Brücke 99, 101
Brüggemann, Heinz 99
Brunner, Otto 82, 83
Buber, Martin 67, 69, 71, 72, 75
Buchanan, Pat 154, 158
Buck-Morss, Susan 14
Budapest 24
Bullock, Marcus 111
Bundesrepublik 182
Bush, George W. 156, 158, 165

Butler, Nicholas Murray 22, 29

C
Cain 43
capitalism 7, 19, 34, 50–1, 57–8, 60–1, 74–5, 133, 136–8, 143, 153, 160, 169, 183, 185
    crisis of capitalism 3, 137, 138
    overthrow of capitalism 51
    gender and capitalism 57, 60
Care Crosses the River 94, 174, 203, 206
Cartesianism 82–3
Cassirer, Ernst 87
Castro, Fidel 151–4, 158, 159, 161, 162
Catholicism 71, 74, 219
Cato 97
Caygill, Howard 99, 109, 111
Chabon, Michael 113, 114, 122
Chagall, Marc 107
Chaplin, Charlie 141
Charlottesville 163, 165, 175, 184
Cheetham, Mark 110
Chevreul, Michel Eugène 103
Chicago, University of, 163
China 170, 198, 223–4
CIA 152
cinema 37, 124–34, 207, 214–15
    Cinema and Experience 124–5, 128, 131, 207, 214
    New German Cinema 126
Claussen, Detlev xiii
Clinton, Hilary 170
CNN 165
Cohen, Elliot 75
Cohen, Hermann 68, 69, 73
Cold War 34–5, 44, 46, 49
color 89, 98–111, 115, 207–12
    colorists 100
Columbia University 22–3, 124
Columbian Exposition of 1893, 121
commodification 40, 169
commodity 57–8, 92, 116
Communism 156, 189
    Communists 2, 8, 18, 152, 156, 162–3
Comte, Auguste 11
conformism 49, 170
    Conformismo 180, 188
Conservatism 155, 166, 199, 222
    conservative 11, 29, 41, 74, 154–5,

186, 203, 219, 221
conservatives 29
conspiracies 150–3, 159–60, 162–8, 199, 218–21
Constantinople 116
constructivism 81, 93
constructivist 81
consumerism 40, 57, 116
consumer 34, 58–9, 128
consumption 127, 130
Coors, Joseph 154
Cornelius, Hans 9, 63
counter-public sphere 129, 131
counter-revolution 166, 222
counterfactual 36, 46, 133–4
Crary, Jonathan 104
Critique of Judgement 85, 109, 211
Cuba 152
cubism 103, 107
cult 11, 38, 50, 60, 72, 154, 159, 162–3, 221

D
de Benoist, Alain 164
de Toledano, Ralph 156, 164
deconstruction 114, 117
Delacroix, Eugène 100
Delaunay, Robert 99
Democracy 29, 33–5, 41–3, 120, 130, 132, 134, 136, 145, 182, 223
Antidemocratic 43
democratization 134
Social Democrat 7
demonology 71
demon 196
demonic 70–1, 77, 90, 196–7
Derrida, Jacques 85, 89, 142
Descartes, René 12, 13, 83
The Destruction of Reason, 2, 14
Detroit 195
Dewey, John 36
Dialectic of Enlightenment 15, 23, 31, 35, 38, 40, 61, 65, 80, 83, 124, 136
The Dialectical Imagination 19, 20, 31, 32, 144, 155, 162, 179, 193
Diederichs, Eugen 104
Dresden 208
dualism 12, 59
Dubiel, Helmut xi, 28, 68

E
Eclipse of Reason 6, 16, 38, 40, 174, 183
economics 6, 39–40, 54, 58, 143, 152, 166, 175, 183, 188, 200
economist 7, 20
economy 54, 152
education 10, 65, 72, 129, 156, 224
Edward VII, 119
election 163, 168, 170
Emancipation 73, 110–11, 124, 193
of women 41
social emancipation 53
Jewish emancipation
Emancipation of color 98–9, 101–5, 110–11, 207–8
Emerson, Ralph Waldo 36
emigration 28–9, 36, 49, 53, 194
émigré 17, 29, 32, 48–9, 156, 158, 183
empiricism 9, 13, 40, 55–6, 58, 60, 91, 95, 142, 167, 174, 209
England 6, 208
Engels, Friedrich 7
English translation 2, 24, 31, 126, 176, 182, 196, 201, 207, 211, 218, 223
English-speaking world 136
Enlightenment 15, 18, 23, 65, 76, 80–1, 83, 124, 126, 136, 159, 166, 172, 183–5, 190, 192, 195, 203, 210, 214
Counter-Enlightenment 151, 153, 155, 157, 159–61, 163, 165–7, 169, 171–2, 218
environmentalism 156, 182, 208
epistemology 4, 14, 92, 95–6, 170, 174–5
Erfurt 7
Erikson, Erik 48, 49, 65
eros 37, 55, 57, 59–62, 64–5, 191–3
Eros and Civilization 57, 60–1, 65, 191–3
eroticization 62
escape 24, 56, 73, 102–3, 143, 146
escapism 150
Escher, M.C. 89
essentialism 44, 110, 211
Estulin, Daniel 152–4, 158, 161
ethnic 26, 29, 44, 76, 156, 168, 219
ethnonationalist 166
Europa 199
Europe 21, 31, 35–6, 51, 57, 70, 73, 75,

100, 161–2, 177, 183, 195–6, 200, 212, 216

evil 38, 98, 161, 171–2, 183, 219

exile 3, 11, 19, 28–30, 32–3, 35, 39, 56, 65, 67, 75, 78, 174, 180, 183–4, 188, 192, 197 199, 213, 216, 219

Existentialism 184, 44, 140, 173
   proto-existentialism 14

Exodus 39, 89

Expressionism 106
   Expressionists 70, 74, 77, 98, 104, 197, 207, 209

F

Farbe 99, 207–8, 210

Farbenlehre 104

fascism 41, 48–9, 51, 56, 58–9, 75, 130, 170
   fascist 11, 29, 33, 58–9, 129, 168–9, 189–90
   neofascist 161

fatalism 127

fate v, 40, 113, 119, 145, 147–8, 150, 152, 176–7, 212, 219

Fauvism 99, 101, 208

Feenberg, Andrew 135

Fenichel, Otto 51

Feuerbach, Ludwig 53, 136

Fichte, Johann Gottlieb 11, 12

film 98, 113, 117, 124–31, 133, 164, 183, 215

Filmer, Robert, 43,

fin-de-siècle ii, 174, 184

Flaschenpost 137, 179, 216

Florence 100

Flynn, Michael 165

Fotoausstellung 182

Fogarasi, Bela 8

Forst, Rainer, xiii

Foucault, Michel 38, 128

Fourier, Charles 62

France 45, 51, 99, 118, 185, 187, 210

Frankfurt Lehrhaus 9, 14, 27, 72

Frankfurter Zeitung 71, 125, 197, 213

Franklin, Benjamin, 118

Franklin, Mitchell, 140, 143, 145

The Free Congress Foundation 154, 158, 162

Freud, Anna 49

Freud, Sigmund 73, 74

Freudian 51, 54, 95, 167, 170, 187, 191, 200
   Freudo-Marxism 193
   neo-Freudian 48, 61, 192
   proto-Freudian 177

Freundschaft 178, 194–5, 197

Friedrich, Carl Joachim 48

Friedeburg, Ludwig von 178

Fromm-Reichmann, Frieda 52, 53, 72

Fromm, Erich xii, 9, 38, 49, 50, 52, 54, 66, 72, 170

G

Garden of Eden 80, 94

Gehlen, Arnold 86

Geist 76, 91, 104–5, 200, 208

Gelb, Adhémar 9

George V, 118

Geroulanos, Stefanos 45

Gestalt psychology 9, 53

Geneva 52, 183

Gilman, Sander L. 170

global 36, 116, 130, 137, 182
   globalization 160, 168

Goethe, Johann Wolfgang von 52, 67, 70, 74, 104, 106

Goethin, Fritz 72

Gordon, Peter E. 169

Gottfried, Paul 164

Gramsci, Antonio 156, 163

Grand Hotel Abgrund 2

Greif, Mark 40

Gross, Bill 118

Grossmann, Henryk xiii

Grosz, Georg 8

Grünberg, Carl 8, 9

Grünewald, Matthias 108

Gumperz, Hede 8

H

Habermas, Jürgen xi, 12, 21, 51, 76, 126, 129, 147, 171

Habermasian 134, 215

The Hague 194

Hallo, Rudolf 69

Hamburg 173, 175, 179, 181, 194, 196

Hansen, Miriam 124–34

Hardt, Michael 132

Harper 184, 186–7, 189, 220, 222

Harvard 20, 148, 169, 173, 175–6, 178,

184, 190, 197–8, 203, 210,
214–15, 218
Havana 152
Haverkamp, Anselm 85
Hegelianism 1, 4, 11, 13, 14, 16, 63,
92–4, 138, 145–6, 178
anti-Hegelianism 1, 6, 14, 173, 177
hegemony 10, 50, 82, 84, 100, 103, 120,
166, 202
Heidegger, Martin 44
Heine, Heinrich 52, 73, 75, 76, 116
Henkin, David 120
Henne, Friedrich 18
hermeneutics 171, 187, 206
Herpin, Georges 118
Higgins, Rich 165
Hildesheimer, Ezriel 69
Hiller, Kurt 104, 105
Himmelfarb, Gertrude 165
historicism 15, 45, 50, 110, 135, 141,
191
Hitchcock, Alfred 87
Hitler, Adolf 48, 49, 120
Hollywood 127, 130, 207
Holocaust 39–40, 75–6, 80, 90, 164,
221
Honneth, Axel xiii
homophobic 155
homosexual 68
homosexuality 157, 221
humanism 33–4, 43, 45, 50, 182–3,
192, 205
humanist 34, 38–9, 44, 46, 61, 77, 92,
182, 185, 191
the human condition 46, 76, 86, 95,
143, 150
The Human Condition 185
Hungary 156
Horkheimer, Maidon 31
Horkheimer, Max xi, xiii, 1, 3, 4, 6,
8–12, 14–16, 19–46, 51–4, 57, 58,
61, 64, 65, 74–7, 80, 83, 98, 124,
126, 136, 145, 152, 157, 160, 166
Horney, Karen 56
Horowitz, David 155, 164
Hughes, H. Stuart 25
Hullot-Kentor, Robert 4, 15, 94
Humboldt, Wilhelm von 134
Hurm, Gerd 34
Husserl, Edmund 9, 10, 83, 85, 110

I
Idealism 11–13, 52, 90–1, 95, 104, 107,
140, 176, 199
identitarian 14–15, 93, 95
Identitätsphilosophie 176
immanent critique, 4–6, 138–9
immigrants 128, 158, 218
immigration 36, 154, 161, 165
Ingres, Jean-Auguste-Dominique, 100
institutionalism 206
Institute for Social Research 1, 20, 74,
152, 156
Institut für Sozialforschung 3, 17,
35, 52
interwar 51, 69, 119, 140, 222
Iraq 158
Islam 161–2
Israel 114, 158, 165
Italy 22, 163–4, 189

J
Jacobs, Jack 66, 164, 169
Jacoby, Russell 135, 138
James, Sarah E. 34
Jameson, Fredric 50
Jaspers, Karl 70, 71
Jawlensky, Alexander 99
Jay, Martin, xi, 19, 28, 155, 169
Jenneman, David 158
Jephcott, E.F.N. ix
Jerusalem 198
Judaism 68–9, 72–4, 76, 78, 188, 194–9
Jews 28, 39, 48, 66, 70, 73, 75, 77–8,
114, 156–7, 164, 166, 185, 194,
196, 198, 200, 219, 221–2
Jewishness 27, 72
Weimar Orthodox Jewry 31, 196
Juvenal 138, 139

K
Kandinsky, Wassily 98, 99, 102
Kansas 192
Kant, Immanuel 36
Kantian 38, 46, 93, 196, 204
neo-Kantianism 63, 198
Kellner, Douglas 135, 137
Kierkegaard, Søren 70, 71, 142, 144,
146, 148
Kimball, Roger 155

Kirchheimer, Otto, xii
Kissinger, Henry 152, 154
Klages, Ludwig 105, 160
Klee, Paul 99, 107
Kluge, Alexander 124, 126
Kluth, G. E. 25
Koch, Richard 69
Korsch, Karl 2, 8
Koselleck, Reinhart 82, 83
Kracauer, Siegfried, xii, xiii, 67, 69–71,
    74, 77, 124, 125, 128, 129, 131,
    133
Kraushaar, Wolfgang 20
Krauthammer, Charles 165
Kristol, Irving and William 165
Kritische Theorie 21, 141, 180, 189,
    197, 199, 206, 217, 221
Krull, Germaine 9
Kulbin, Nikolai 102
Kuzuo, Fukumoto 8

L
Lacan, Jacques 50
labor 7, 9, 41, 130, 223
Landauer, Karl 52, 53
LaRouche, Lyndon 154, 158, 159, 162
Lassalle, Ferdinand 73
Lazarsfeld, Paul 22, 153
Le Bon, Gustave 58
Lear, Jonathan 148–50
left-wing 8, 56, 162, 167
leftist 2, 23, 56, 104, 151, 157, 160, 172,
    221
legalism 73
Leiden 176, 210
Lennon, John 118, 153
Leslie, Esther 99
Lethen, Helmut 141
Levin, Thomas 126
Levinas, Emmanuel 91
Lichtenstein, Jacqueline 110
liberal 9, 30, 33, 35, 44, 54, 66, 68–9,
    74–5, 77, 135, 147, 149, 157, 165,
    168
liberal-capitalist 132
liberalism 134, 160, 195–6, 198
liberals 180
libertarian 70, 195–6, 212
Lieber, Francis 36
Lilliputians 116

Limbaugh, Rush 153
Lincoln, Abraham 42
Lind, William 154–6, 157, 162, 164,
    166
Lippmann, Walter 153
Locke, John 43, 100
London iii–iv, 120, 173–5, 177–8, 180,
    182–6, 188, 190–1, 193–4, 202,
    205–9, 211–12, 214–18, 220, 223
Löwenthal, Leo, xi, 7, 9, 22, 28, 49, 52,
    66–79, 152
Löwy, Michael 70
Lukács, Georg, xi, 1, 24
Luxemburg, Rosa 136, 182
Lyotard, Jean-François 89
Lyser, Johann Peter 111

M
MacDonald Kevin 164, 168
Mach, Ernst 90
Macke, August 99, 106, 107, 111
Maimon, Solomon 12, 73
Maimonides, 73
Mann, Thomas 2
Mannheim, Karl 3
Maoist China 170
Marc, Franz, xii, 9, 13, 25, 29, 67, 71,
    99, 111, 160
Marcuse, Herbert, x, 5, 20, 28, 49, 57,
    60, 135-150, 152, 154
Marx, Karl 73
Marxism 1, 7, 10–11, 14, 24, 38, 51, 50,
    53, 61, 92, 151, 175, 178, 183,
    186–7, 189, 207, 216–17
Cultural Marxism 151, 154, 156–158,
    162–7, 200, 219–22
Massachusetts 184, 205, 214
materialism 2, 9, 12, 14, 46, 50–1, 54,
    63, 90–2, 129, 135, 140, 145, 173,
    186, 206
    protomaterialist 12
    materiality 103
mathematical 100–2, 104, 107
Mayer, Eugen 70
The Mayflower Compact 17
McCloy, John H. 35
McMaster, H. R. 165
Mehlman, Jeffrey 114, 117
Mendelssohn, Moses 73
Meng, Heinrich 52

Menke, Christoph 147–50
Mercury, Freddy 118
metacritique 4, 174
metaphorics 82, 92
metaphorology, 81–2, 85, 87, 92, 96,
    201–2, 207
metaphysics 11–14, 16, 31, 32, 71, 82,
    85, 89, 92, 99, 104, 106, 110–11,
    142, 176–7, 202–3, 205
metapsychology 59, 62, 186
metasubject 4
metasubjectivity 91, 143
Mexico 173, 182
Michael, Max 70
Michaelis, Erich 72
Michelangelo, 100
Migration ii, 30, 55, 77, 174, 183, 188,
    192, 197
Millennials 221
Miller, Stephen 165
Mills, C. Wright 30
mimesis 17, 39, 90, 93, 103, 131, 184,
    191, 205
    mimetic 37–9, 102, 105, 126, 131,
    184
    mimetology 184, 205
Minima Moralia 3, 5, 11, 48, 59–63, 97,
    130, 137–8, 141, 144, 160, 170
Minnicino, Michael 154, 158, 162, 167
mobilization 124, 127, 131 145, 147,
    221
modernism 99, 182, 207
    modernists 98, 103, 209
modernity 70, 107, 129, 131, 141, 187,
    199, 202, 204, 209
    modernization 129
MoMA 208
Monaco 121
Montagnola, 20–3, 30
moralism 63
    moralist 187
    morality 195
    Morals 82, 202
Morgan, Michael 13
Morris, William 123
Mosse, George 104
multiculturalism 163, 168
Munich 9, 208, 210, 217
Münzenberg, Willi 156
Müntzer, Thomas 197

Mussolini, Benito 22
mysticism 68–9, 193, 195–6, 200
mythology 85, 176, 185, 202–3
    mythological 95
    Myths 86, 91, 189

N
narcissism 58, 60, 191, 193
nationalism 29, 36, 76, 195, 214, 221
nativist 160
nature 1, 6, 11–12, 15–16, 27, 33, 38,
    44, 49–50, 54–5, 58, 62–3, 74, 86,
    131, 174, 182–3, 209
Naturphilosophie 176
Nazi 4, 23, 35, 39, 43–4, 47, 49, 65120,
    156, 164, 167, 170, 189, 206, 219
    Nazism 35, 82
    neo-Nazi 156, 162, 164, 221
Negative Dialectics 16, 63, 80, 81, 83–4,
    88, 90, 92, 94–5, 177–8, 193, 199,
    201–2, 205, 207
Negri, Antonio, 132
Negt, Oskar, 124, 126–34
neoconservative 158, 165, 199
neoliberalism 160
Neumann, Franz, xii, 25, 29, 168
New Left 51, 61, 135, 154, 164, 166
Newmark, Kevin 142
Newton, Isaac 104
Nietzsche, Friedrich 82, 83
nihilation 140, 177
Nixon, Richard 154, 164
Nobel, Rabbi Nehemiah Anton 67, 69,
    74, 77
Noerr, Gunzelin Schmid 2
nominalism 206, 211
    nominalist 4, 85, 87–8, 94, 208
nonconceptuality v, 80–5, 87–97,
    200–3, 205
nondialectical 84
nonidentity 14, 16, 64, 84, 93, 178

O
Obama, Barack 157, 163
Oedipus 43, 143, 148, 195
    Oedipus Rex 150
    Oedipus Complex 55–6, 61
objective 3–4, 62, 92, 144–5, 169
    new objectivity 140
Offenbach, Jacques 71

Öffentlichkeit 127, 129, 131, 214
One-Dimensional Man 62, 135–9, 141,
    145–7, 150, 216–17
ontology 70, 84, 86, 88, 92, 96, 198,
    205
optics 104, 112
    optical 101, 119, 130
Ornament 197, 214
    ornamentation 100–1
orthodoxy 27, 51, 56, 59, 66, 69, 75, 77,
    90, 140, 143, 188, 195–6, 198
Orwell, George 139
Ostjude 72, 75, 195

P
painter 101–2, 108–9, 209
painting 98, 100–3, 106–10, 112,
    207–9, 211–12
paleoconservative 154, 164–6
Palestine 67, 72, 77, 122, 198
Pan, David 105, 110
pansexuality 56
parabasis 142
Paradigms for a Metaphorology 203
Paris 38, 115, 184, 189, 197–8, 208,
    213
pathologization 168–9, 223
    pathologies 35, 159, 160, 170–2,
        187, 223
    pathology 58, 170, 172, 223
patriarchal 41, 43, 55, 57–8, 60, 168,
    190, 200
Pasztor, Laszlo 156
Pavlovian 51
perception 80, 88–9, 91, 109, 131, 133
perspectival 101, 107
    perspectivalism 143
Phenomenology 202, 203, 206
phantasm 159
phantasmagoria 129, 143
phantasy 108, 207, 211
phenomenological 12, 173, 187, 202
phenomenology 4, 10, 70, 110, 176
philately 113, 118, 122–3, 212
    philatelist 113, 114, 214
    Philatelic Agency 121
photography 33–4, 47, 37–9, 98, 113,
    127, 182–3, 211
Piscator, Erwin 8
Platonic 111, 144

Plutarch 97
Podhoretz, Norman and John 165
poetry 76, 80, 90, 94, 141–2, 184, 193,
    206
    poet 42, 70, 73, 77, 138, 149
    Poetics 205
Poland 120
Polanski, Roman 157
politics, 6, 10–11, 43–4, 48, 56, 96,
    136, 154, 159, 163, 166–7, 170–2,
    182, 184–5, 187–8, 190–1, 204,
    209
polity 44, 172, 179, 183, 186, 193, 199,
    206
Pollock, Carlota 25
Pollock, Friedrich, xiii, 8, 19, 20, 25,
    28, 34, 54, 136
populism 160, 166, 168, 170
portraiture 8, 10, 73, 114, 204
    Porträts 204
positivism 70, 87–8, 107
postclassical 127, 131
postmodernism 135, 141, 146–7, 168,
    182, 217
    postmodernists 89
poststructuralism 14, 142
postwar 29, 33–5, 40, 47, 55, 111, 119,
    129, 167–8, 185, 200, 212
Poussin, 100
Prager, Joseph 70, 77
praxis 3, 6, 176
Presley, Elvis 121
proletarian 1–3, 126–7, 130–2, 174,
    214, 215
Promethean 145, 209
propaganda 34, 58, 159, 169, 190
Protestant 132, 188
proto-deconstructionist 117
proto-Derridean 14
psycho-historians 189
Psychoanalysis v, 9, 30, 48–53, 55–60,
    63–5, 70, 72, 74, 125, 137, 149,
    160, 167, 170–1, 185–7, 189–93
psychology 50, 53–8, 63–4, 70, 95, 167,
    169, 186, 188–90, 193, 200,
    208–9, 217, 219
    psychologism 59, 63
    psychologists 9, 48, 70, 164
    anti-psychological 50
psychopathologies 56

psychosomatic 130
psychotherapy 170
purity 78, 100, 103, 110, 210–11

R
Rabinbach, Anson 169
race 36, 42, 44, 221
racism 27, 161, 163, 220, 222–3
radicalism 35, 70, 223
radio 114, 117, 153, 158, 164, 180, 190,
    212–13, 218, 222
Ramstein 26, 181
rationalism 11, 14, 16, 69, 105
    rationalist 12–13, 16, 62–3, 104
re-enchantment 211
Readymades 115, 168
realism 86–7, 92–3, 184
Reason and Revolution 11, 16, 62, 176,
    192,
Reich, Wilhelm 35, 51, 53, 56, 57, 119,
    120
Reinhold, Karl Leonhard 12
relativism 3, 135, 147, 149
Religionsoziologie 197
Religionsphilosophie 177
religiosity 68
religion 9, 27, 45–6, 52–3, 66–7, 69,
    71–3, 76, 78–9, 83, 89, 104, 155,
    188, 196, 217
reparations 118
Republican 22, 166
revisionism 34, 48, 59, 61, 192
revolt 100, 137–8
revolution 11, 16–17, 62–3, 73, 103,
    120, 152–3, 173, 176, 179, 183,
    192, 197, 200, 213, 218
Richter, Gerhard 90
Rieff, Philip 50
right-wing 151, 155–6, 158, 160,
    163–165, 167, 170, 199, 220–1
Riley II, Charles A. 101, 110
Ringer, Fritz 9
Rockefeller 152, 153
Róheim, Geza 51
Romanticism 69, 76, 85, 100, 104, 107,
    140–5, 146, 178, 211, 213
    neo-romantic 104
Roosevelt, Franklin, D. 118, 121
Rome 180, 188
Rorty, Richard 147, 149

Rosenzweig, Franz 9, 13, 67
Ross, Andrew 168, 169
Rothacker, Erich 82, 83
Rothschilds 152
Rubens, Peter Paul 100
Ruskin, John 107

S
Sabaneiev, Leonid 102
Sacco, Nicola and Vanzetti,
    Bartolomeo 8
Safatle, Vladamir Pinheiro 169
Salmagundi 151, 161–2, 166, 203,
    212–13
Sandburg, Carl 42
Sandeen, Eric 34
Sanders, Bernie 169
Sartre, Jean-Paul 14
Savage, Michael 158, 164
Savage, Robert 96, 97
Scheler, Max 71
Schlegel, Friedrich 141–3
Schmidt, Alfred 21, 23
Schmitt, Carl 4, 160, 164
Schnädelbach, Herbert 16
Schoenberg, Arnold x, 89, 101, 102
Scholem, Gershom 14, 27, 72, 74, 75,
    92, 106, 107, 109
Schopenhauer, Arthur 2, 14, 38, 43, 67,
    68, 104
science 1, 10, 15, 19, 45, 50, 52–4, 83,
    95, 98, 103, 167, 175, 183, 188–9,
    191–2, 207, 209
    scientistic 38
secular 68, 73, 78, 89, 122, 128, 200,
    204
    secularization 45, 201
Sekula, Alan 34
Sellers, Wilfred 134
semantics ii, 184, 205
semiotics 110–11, 216, 208
sensationalism 107
sensory 88, 129, 131, 203
sex 53–5, 60, 156–7
    sexuality 56, 62
Sex-Pol 53, 188
Shakespeare, William 119, 120
Shapiro, Ben 163, 164
Shklovsky, Viktor 96
Simon, Ernst 69, 72

Sinclair, Upton 2, 8
simulacrum 132, 214
Sinzheimer, Hugo 7
skepticism 50, 59, 67–8, 71, 90, 130, 204
Sloterdijk, Peter 141
Snapchat 122
socialism 7–8, 53, 157, 174, 184, 196, 217
socialization 7, 170
sociology 55, 64, 174, 188–9, 223
sociologists 124, 168, 218
Socrates, 144
solipsism 12, 90
Solomon-Godeau, Abigail 34
somatic 52, 60, 63, 91, 125, 193
Sontag, Susan 33, 34
Sophocles, 147
Sorge, Richard 8
Soviet 51, 56, 168, 170, 189, 223
Sozialforschung 3, 17, 21, 35, 52, 54, 174–5, 179, 184, 189, 199, 220
Spencer, Richard 163, 164
Spengler, Oswald 160
Spinoza, Baruch 12, 13
Stahl, Friedrich Joseph 11
Stalin, Joseph 51
    Stalinism 35
    Stalinization 56
Steichen, Edward 33, 34, 36, 38, 41, 42, 44, 45, 47
Steiner, Rudolf 110
stereoscopes 119, 161
Stimson, Blake 34
Strauss, Bruno 70
Strauss, Eduard 70
Strauss, Leo 158
structural 103, 126, 129, 131
structuralism 14
    neostructuralism 177
subjectivity 91, 128, 131, 215
    subjectivism 12
    subjectivities 169
    subjectivization 104
sublimation 15, 60–2, 191
sublime 89, 204
Sullivan, Harry Stack 56
superstructure 57, 59
supremacist 11, 163, 165, 221
Surrealism 116, 207

surrealists 51, 113, 115
Switzerland 20, 23–4, 31, 121, 181–2
symbolism 76, 207, 209–10

T
Talmud 77, 94, 200
terrorism 161
Thales, 96, 97
theology 14, 27–8, 53–4, 66, 70–1, 84, 90–1, 98, 176, 184, 188, 196
theoretician 3, 56, 130, 160, 163
Thirlwall, Connop 147
Thomas, James, M. 170
Thracian 96, 206
Tiedemann, Rolf 24
Till, Emmett 42
Tillich, Paul 30
Titian, 100
Torah 200
totalitarianism 48, 136–7, 189
transcendentalism 6, 12, 63, 83, 95, 109, 142–3, 176, 183
Trilling, Lionel 30
Trotsky, Leon 51
Trump, Donald 159, 163, 165, 166, 168–70, 172
Trump Jr., Donald 165
tuberculosis 52, 66
Tübingen 7–8, 174, 189, 206
Turner, Fred 34
tyranny 62, 83, 94, 100, 102, 108, 111
    tyrannical 41, 103

U
Unabomber161
universalism 33, 44–5
    universalist 34, 66, 77, 166
Urgrund 13–14, 177
utilitarianism 54, 213
utopia, 3, 51, 130, 194, 198

V
van Reijin, Willem 2
Vasari, Giorgio 100
Vico, Giambattista 3
Vienna 24
Vietnam 49, 219
vitalist 60, 104
von Baader, Franz 71, 160
von Ferrary, Philipp 118

von Hartmann, Thomas 102

W
Wagner, Richard 101, 163
Walsh, Michael 163
Watergate 154
Weber, Adolph 7
Webster, Jamieson 169
Weil, Felix 7, 19, 22, 26, 31, 74, 160
Weil, Hermann 6, 7, 9
Weimar Republic 4, 6.13, 28, 31, 66–7,
    69, 70, 74–5, 77–8, 119, 125–6,
    154, 167
Weiss, Hilde 55
Weiss, Robert 70
Weissberg, Liliane 169
Weissert, Will 152
Wellmer, Albrecht, xiii, 23
Weyrich, Paul 154–6, 159, 166
Wheatland, Thomas 75, 76, 158
White, Reggie 155
Wiedmann, August 104
Wikipedia 151, 164, 218, 221
Wilbrandt, Robert 7

William of Ockham 4
Wittfogel, Karl August 8, 22
Wittgenstein, Ludwig, xi
Wolfowitz, Paul 165
Wood, Ron 118
World War I 6, 51, 69, 77, 118
World War II 75, 76, 113, 119, 136,
    139, 163, 167

X
xenophobia 29

Y
Yiddish Policemen's Union 113–14, 122,
YouTube 156, 163,

Z
Zetkin, Clara 8
Zetkin, Konstantin 8
Žižek, Slavoj 13, 14
Zionism 68, 72, 77, 195, 198
    Zionists 69, 72, 166, 198
    anti-Zionism 165